MARGINS IN THE CLASSROOM

PEDAGOGY AND CULTURAL PRACTICE

Edited by Henry Giroux and Roger Simon

Recognizing that pedagogy begins with the affirmation of differences as a precondition for extending the possibilities of democratic life, the series analyzes the diverse democratic and ideological struggles of people across a wide range of economic, social, and political spheres.

2. *Margins in the Classroom: Teaching Literature*, Kostas Myrsiades and Linda S. Myrsiades, editors

1. *The End of Education: Toward Posthumanism*, William V. Spanos

MARGINS IN THE CLASSROOM

TEACHING LITERATURE

KOSTAS MYRSIADES AND
LINDA S. MYRSIADES, EDITORS

PEDAGOGY AND CULTURAL PRACTICE
VOLUME 2

University of Minnesota Press
Minneapolis
London

Earlier versions of these chapters appeared in *College Literature* 17.2/3 (June-October 1990) and 18.2 (June 1991).

Published by the University of Minnesota Press
2037 University Avenue Southeast, Minneapolis, MN 55455-3092
Printed in the United States of America on acid-free paper

Library of Congress Cataloging-in-Publication Data

Margins in the classroom : teaching literature / Kostas Myrsiades and
Linda S. Myrsiades, editors.
p. cm.—(Pedagogy and cultural practice ; v. 2)
"Earlier versions of these chapters appeared in College
literature"—T.p. verso.
Includes bibliographical references and index.
ISBN 0-8166-2319-8 (hard : alk. paper).—ISBN 0-8166-2320-1
(pbk. : alk. paper)
1. Literature—Study and teaching (Higher)—United States.
2. Literature—Philosophy. 3. Criticism. I. Myrsiades, Kostas.
II. Myrsiades, Linda S. III. Series.
PN70.M35 1994 93-8692
807'.1'173—dc20 CIP

Contents

Introduction
Kostas Myrsiades and Linda S. Myrsiades vii

1 Rethinking the Boundaries of Educational Discourse: Modernism, Postmodernism, and Feminism
Henry A. Giroux 1

2 Chances of Being Kind: Rorty, Irony, and Teaching Modern Literature
Paul F. Griffin 52

3 The Political Responsibility of the Teaching of Literatures
Paul Smith 64

4 Literacy and Literature: Making or Consuming Culture?
Linda Shaw Finlay and Nathaniel Smith 74

5 (Post)modern Critical Theory and the Articulations of Critical Pedagogies
Mas'ud Zavarzadeh and Donald Morton 89

6 The Politics of Teaching ~~Literature~~: The "Paedagogical Effect"
Robert Miklitsch 102

7 Discipline and Resistance: The Subjects of Writing and the Discourses of Instruction
Suzanne Clark 121

8 Subversion and Oppositionality in the Academy
Barbara Foley 137

9 Entitlement and Empowerment: Claims on Canonicity
Jerry McGuire 153

10 Canon: New Testament to Derrida
Michael Payne 172

11 Freud, Lacan, and the Subject of Cultural Studies
Robert Con Davis 188

Contributors 203

Index 205

Anticipating the needs of the 1990s in the literature classroom, *Margins in the Classroom: Teaching Literature* acts as a catalyst for discussion and blends the work of established scholars and emerging voices not only to reexamine and question existing practices but to suggest fresh approaches to the expanding canon. Contributors present the points of view of teachers from small colleges as well as larger universities, from Ithaca College and Franklin and Marshall to Pennsylvania State, Oklahoma, Carnegie Mellon, Syracuse, and Johns Hopkins Universities. They address the issues of theory and politics from a range of areas of study, including educational pedagogy, cultural studies, literary criticism, political economy, sociology, philosophy, and psychoanalytic, poststructuralist, Marxist, and feminist theory.

The essays in this collection were selected from two special issues of *College Literature* (17.2/3 June-October 1990 and 18.2 June 1991) that treat the politics of teaching and theory in the classroom. These essays explore present practice and future implications of changing textual analysis, literary theory, and pedagogy. They are intended to speak to teachers of college literature who must negotiate the shifting sands of their disciplines and translate the nature and effects of new movements to classroom use. The volume takes a broad-spectrum approach to address issues that will have an impact on the delivery of instruction in the classroom itself, molding theory to the variety of classroom populations and materials the teacher encounters and addressing the politics of literature as they affect the classroom, the design of courses, and the creation of new courses. This volume not only applies new theoretical approaches to the traditional canon, but examines what new bodies of literature need to be addressed and shows how theory can be used to address those new literatures.

The dilemma of the contemporary classroom can be traced to critiques of classroom practice that have arisen through a series of what legal scholar Peter Fitzpatrick has called "dangerous supplements" (feminism and Marxism, for example) that challenge the institutional innocence of education. That education is implicated in social reproduction is clear; how it embraces its role, the degree of self-reflexivity it allows itself, and the kind of political responsibility it assumes in performing that role are not, however, at all clear. The relations at issue here are those between education and democracy, between positive freedom and power, between emancipation and totalization. It is not enough in the light thrown on present practice by marginalized discourses, Third World politics, and even First World reformist examinations to teach by avoiding engagement of these issues, for such inaction itself represents a choice that conditions our position in the larger debate.

Education, it appears, has become the prime site of struggle for the recovery of the political in the present age, the move from the descriptive to the evaluative and prescriptive having hit education with greater force than it has other social institutions. The debate, engaged over social norms, consensus, and heterogeneity, has implications for the possibility of agency, the nature of subjectivity, and interventions for social change—a burden that positions the educational institution at the heart of the complex pattern of social relations. The legitimation or delegitimation of social relations offered by education is the prize fought for. The strategic positioning of the academic—wriggling in and out of preferred spaces—evidences the fact that the modern educational institution has not become an ossified bureaucratic order, that its continuing affirmation of established values cannot be taken for granted, and that it is very much engaged in the larger world of which it is a part. The recognition that change takes place in practice, not merely in thought, and through the routine life of the institution is what drives the present collection of essays. It takes its point of departure from theory's recognition that it cannot by itself convey the "thick" texture of practice and that it must link with the classroom to discover that texture.

Henry A. Giroux's opening piece, "Rethinking the Boundaries of Educational Discourse: Modernism, Postmodernism, and Feminism," raises the central issues of the collection by asking not only how modernism, postmodernism, and feminism, viewed in terms of their interconnections, can "offer critical educators a rich theoretical and political opportunity for rethinking the relationship between schooling and democracy . . . as part of a broader radical democratic project," but how educators "might combine with other cultural workers in various movements to develop and advance a broader discourse of political and collective strength." He poses this task in the context of the postmodern view that civilization—after Auschwitz and Hiroshima—has in some sense failed us, and we now face the prospect of having to abandon justice, freedom, and equality. Negotiating the alternative forms of social discourse—consensus, binary opposition, and heterogeneous discourse—Giroux's project is one in which "a politics of difference can emerge within a shared discourse of democratic public life."

Pedagogy is thus not just something that happens in the classroom. It becomes a question of "how knowledge is produced, and how subject positions are constructed" in historical and political ways. It speaks to technologies of production and legitimation of modes of construction that can no longer be regarded as innocent; that is, it speaks to "how educators (in the broad sense of the term) construct the ideological and political positions from which they speak." Pedagogy is about the linkage of teaching to social empowerment, leading to a politics of social strength, but in the context of shared social conceptions of justice and rights—that is to say, the radical pedagogy of engaged intellectuals is connected to the politics of everyday life.

In taking this position, Giroux attempts to rescue aspects of modernism to counter the postmodern dismantling of the great narratives of totalization and emancipation ascribed to modernism. His critical exercise results in a ten-point program for political pedagogy that ranges from the production of political subjects as well as knowledge, a transformative focus on the issue of difference, resistance to master narratives, and destruction of disciplinary boundaries, to the development of teachers as transformative intellectuals. Held against present schooling and setting the context for the remaining essays in the volume, Giroux's program provides a provocative template for a postmodern examination of institutional learning.

The challenge to institutional learning presented by the postmodern cultural shift emanates from the fragmentary, even chaotic, interpretive spin postmodernism has introduced to the debate on the universality of human thought. The loss of the absolute has evoked a radical reaction from modernists threatened by what they perceive as cultural anarchy. The clash between liberal humanists and neoconservative pragmatists has had, as a result, to be played out on the contested sites of cultural institutions in a search for the space in which individuals can make a difference, where agency still counts, and the self as a subject has a place.

Paul F. Griffin's contribution, "Chances of Being Kind: Rorty, Irony, and Teaching Modern Literature," directs us to one such space, a space provided by modern literature, whereas Robert Miklitsch's piece, "The Politics of Teaching Literature: The 'Paedagogical Effect' " directs us to a counterlogic that insists, "Literature will no longer constitute the central medium for the cultural reproduction of society." Griffin puts it that in literature "ironic self-consciousness can have a positive social dimension" wherein individual existences assert themselves apart from the coercive "generalizations invoked by cultural and political institutions." Once again, "thick" description calls into play the human term in the historical moment, absent the ability to ensure an Auschwitz never happens again. We survive the unsurvivable, as Lyotard makes clear, in spite of having been "disauthorized" by it.

Once we admit that teaching, and teaching literature in particular, constitutes a political act, we are driven—as Paul Smith's piece, "The Political Responsibility of the Teaching of Literatures," drives us—to a consideration of the character of that act in the production of knowledge: "If we agree that as teachers we are agents in the circulation and accumulation of particular forms of cultural capital, we move immediately toward a definition of teaching that begins to grasp teaching in its inescapably political aspects." Thus the value of literature is no longer conceived of as an abstraction, but as a commodity that functions as a form of capital with use value. The presumption that literature is a privileged artifact capable of suppressing with its norms and canons historical contradictions is no longer viable. Such a re-formed perspective leads us to engage literature through what Spivak would call "interruptions" from different subject positions, the dialectics of which produce resistance both to the text and its codes and to subject positions themselves, thereby disrupting all privilege.

If teaching is a political act, literacy must represent the power to give meaning to action, meaning that does not represent an instantiation of deep structural knowledge or a reflection of reality as perceived by the mind but an intersubjective construction on the model of a conversation rather than mimesis or a vision. In the work of the Brazilian educator Paolo Freire, as explicated by Linda Shaw Finlay and Nathaniel Smith in "Literacy and Literature: Making or Consuming Culture?" the student is brought to literacy, rewrites texts to unmask cultural interests, and exposes power relations, transforming naive into critical thinking as a means of creating knowledge both of the self and of the world. It is a literacy that goes in more than one direction, for it requires dominant cultures to develop cultural literacy in dealings with minority cultures and their literatures in order to stimulate multicultural literacy.

The dilemma of teaching literacy is questioned by Mas'ud Zavarzadeh and Donald Morton in "(Post)modern Critical Theory and the Articulations of Critical Pedagogies"; they ask whether students are "produced by liberal education to think of themselves as free subjects [only to] 'freely' subject themselves to the economic needs of the capitalist system." Teachers would then themselves have been co-opted by the established system to produce a student commodity. Here curricula structured to transform a retrograde practice seek to raise new questions about the student as the subject, act, and material of study, only to find trivialized "the radical reconstitution of the student as a 'subject of study,' " or, as Suzanne Clark, in "Discipline and Resistance: The Subjects of Writing and the Discourses of Instruction," puts it, the "theorizing of the people who participate as classroom subjects." Robert Miklitsch raises the same cry in his call for students "to read themselves as carefully as they read the text that is their teachers' politics." Clark, attacking the colonization of the classroom and its production of partial knowledges that further mystify, asks the new pedagogy "to address this complication by examining the enigmas of classroom subjectivities."

In response to such calls, the reform curriculum and the pedagogy it implies have taken on commercial attributes responsive to entrepreneurial or consumer clients in a free market context. By contrast, a radical pedagogy teaches that an individual's understanding of a cultural text is the "result of her or his situatedness in a complex network of gender, class, and race relations" and that a new transdisciplinary learning is necessary to read the dominant social system against itself by finding spaces of resistance in the "fault lines of its ideologies" (Zavarzadeh and Morton). Like the therapist mining the unconscious, radical pedagogy surfaces resistance even if the subject positions of students and teachers are in conflict and students resist resistance. Falling into the story that Clark repeats (of students reading a fish until they discover in its text what they had already learned in the teacher's own writing), teachers create a discourse whereby they are fishing for themselves. If students are the fish, Clark holds, they regard their teachers as eating them alive. Striking back against the teacher who practices both therapy and imperialism, student resistances—even through mimicry—undermine discourse and reform the "master's" teaching narrative. The colonial subject thus reappears in the Western classroom in teacher-student relationships and the differences that arise in classroom exchanges.

Margins in the Classroom's treatment of teaching as a political act leads to its central preoccupation with the ability of canon busting to act subversively and oppositionally. Barbara Foley, in "Subversion and Oppositionality in the Academy," warns us that, for all the emancipatory rhetoric (that canon challenges both open up study of marginalized writers and rescue canonical writers from the grips of New Criticism), canon busting "frequently ends up reconfirming those very structures of authority to which it purports to be opposed." Silent voices do not always represent a threat to hegemony, nor do they always empathize with oppressed groups—even when we search their gaps and fissures. Foley warns that forays into literature under the fallacious notion that power "lurks everywhere" lead us to valorize the "act of rupture" for itself, what Jerry McGuire, in "Entitlement and Empowerment: Claims on Canonicity," would call, in another context, "ideological special pleading" for works "politically suppressed *because of their meanings*." McGuire's solution—recognizing the power of the canon to allow expression to some voices and suppress others—is to take into account both aspects of the canon: "its manifest passivity, as a museum of all literature that has proven value in the culture it represents, and its latent activity, as a set of criteria and economic influences applied whenever a [piece of literature] is conceived." The dilemma he poses is that of balancing entitlement and empowerment to ensure "multicultural interpenetration" without facing the dissolution of minority literature in a "macrocultural monopoetics."

As Michael Payne sees it, in his piece "Canon: New Testament to Derrida," the larger danger may be that the gatekeeping that offers access to the canon is controlled by like-minded aesthetes who clone themselves in granting access, even to the point of turning to marginalized literatures as an answer to "what I desire—and therefore lack." "What gets read?" and "Who says so?" are thus foregrounded as crucial canon questions in the ongoing debate in which the canon itself is considered a structure that, aspiring to closure, yet refuses to remain self-contained.

The broadest, most inclusive form of resistance to the canon is found in the cultural studies project that, as Robert Con Davis, in "Freud, Lacan, and the Subject of Cultural Studies," makes clear, aims at reconstituting the act of knowing through "the formulation of a strategy for critique—that is, a major reformulation of how to know and study culture." The focus here is on what it means to know something "based on a critique of the investigating subject of inquiry and knowledge." In this effort, we are brought back again to the therapeutic model, in this instance to Freudian—by way of Lacanian—psychoanalysis as a foundational elaboration of a subject. By means of this analysis, Con Davis draws three propositions: that "cultural studies will be subjective"—that is, the subject is historically situated and constructed—that it "will be undertaken by interested participants," and that it "will be ideologically oriented." Bringing the political act of teaching full circle, cultural studies thus positions us as committed "to a valued social situation and the responsibility defined by that commitment," quite a different stance from the disinterested assistance of members of power classes to the oppressed. Rather, through the critique of the subject, readers of culture "maneuver themselves into strategic conflicts with oppressive cultural practices in the oppositional style of one working from within an institution—as theorists and teachers in the academy—to enfranchise modes of intervention."

From Giroux to Con Davis, *Margins in the Classroom* thus brings us forcibly up against the dilemma of the modern practice of teaching literature. In the terms posed in this collection, we are faced with displacing the emphasis from an institutional structure legitimating an established order to subjectivizing the teacher-student relationship as a means of focusing on interventions that interrogate that order. Indeed, we are faced with "dangerous supplements" and political responsibilities that remove education from the comfortable role of passive onlooker in the greater cultural debate and place the academic squarely within the space of the contested site of struggle.

Acknowledgments

The editors would like to express their appreciation to West Chester University's Provost Stanley Yarosewich and Dean Richard Wells of the College of Arts and Sciences for their continued support of *College Literature*. We are also indebted to managing editors Claudia Nelson and Jerry McGuire for their careful copyediting of these essays and to our graduate assistant William H. Mendelsohn for his help in readying the manuscript for publication.

Works Cited

Fitzpatrick, Peter, ed. *Dangerous Supplements: Resistance and Renewal in Jurisprudence*. Durham, NC: Duke UP, 1991.

Lyotard, Jean-François. *The Differend: Phrases in Dispute*. Trans. Georges Van Den Abbeele. Minneapolis: U of Minnesota P, 1989.

Spivak, Gayatri Chakravorty. *The Post-Colonial Critic: Interviews, Strategies, Dialogues*. Ed. Sarah Harasym. New York: Routledge, 1990.

Rethinking the Boundaries of Educational Discourse: Modernism, Postmodernism, and Feminism

> Modern citizenship was formulated in a way that played a crucial role in the emergence of modern democracy, but it has become an obstacle to making it wider and more pluralistic. Many of the new rights that are being claimed by women or ethnic minorities are no longer rights that can be universalized. They are the expression of specific needs and should be granted to particular communities. Only a pluralistic conception of citizenship can accommodate the specificity and multiplicity of democratic demands and provide a pole of identification for a wide range of democratic forces. The political community has to be viewed, then, as a diverse collection of communities, as a forum for creating unity without denying specificity. (Mouffe, "Citizenship" 7)

Chantal Mouffe's comments suggest we have entered a new age, one that is marked by a crisis of power, patriarchy, authority, identity, and ethics.[1] This new age has been described, for better or worse, by many theorists in a variety of disciplines as the age of postmodernism.[2] It is a period torn between the ravages and benefits of modernism; it is an age in which the notions of science, technology, and reason are associated not only with social progress but also with the organization of Auschwitz and the scientific creativity that made Hiroshima possible (Poster 12-33). It is a time in which the humanist subject seems no longer to be in control of his or her fate. It is an age in which the grand narratives of emancipation, whether from the political right or left, appear to share an affinity for terror and oppression. It is also a historical moment in which culture is no longer seen as a preserve of white men whose contributions to the arts, literature, and science constitute its domain. We live at a time when a strong challenge is being waged against a modernist discourse in which knowledge is legitimated almost exclusively from a European model of culture and civilization. In part, the struggle for democracy can be seen in the context of a broader struggle against certain features of modernism that represent the worst legacies of the Enlightenment tradition. And it is against these features that a variety of oppositional movements have emerged in an attempt to rewrite the relationship between modernism and democracy. Two of the most important challenges to modernism have come from divergent theoretical discourses associated with postmodernism and feminism.

Postmodernism and feminism have challenged modernism on a variety of theoretical and political fronts, and I will take these up shortly, but there is another side to modernism that has expressed itself more recently in the ongoing struggles in Eastern Europe. Modernism is not merely about patriarchy parading as universal reason, the increasing intensification of human domination over nature in the name of historical development, or the imperiousness of grand narratives that stress control and mastery (Lyotard). Nor is modernism simply synonymous with forms of modernization characterized by the ideologies and practices of the dominating relations of capitalist production. It exceeds this fundamental but limiting rationality by offering the ideological excesses of democratic possibility. By this I mean, as Ernesto Laclau and Mouffe have pointed out, that modernism becomes a decisive point of reference for advancing certain and crucial elements of the democratic revolution.

Beyond its claims to certainty, foundationalism, and epistemological essentialism, modernism provides theoretical elements both for analyzing the limits of its own historical tradition and for developing a political standpoint from which the breadth and specificity of democratic struggles can be expanded through the modernist ideals of freedom, justice, and equality. As Mark Hannam observes, modernism does have a legacy of progressive ambitions that have contributed to substantive social change, and these ambitions need to be remembered in order to be reinserted into any developing discourses on democracy. For Hannam these include "economic redistribution towards equality, the emancipation of women, the eradication of superstition and despotism, wider educational opportunities, the improvement of the sciences and the arts, and so forth. Democratization was one of these ambitions and frequently was perceived to be a suitable means towards the realization of other, distinct ambitions" (113). What is important to note is that the more progressive legacies of modernism have been unleashed not in the West, where they have been undermined by modernism's undemocratic tendencies, but in Eastern Europe, where the full force of political modernism has erupted to redraw the political and cultural map of the region. What this suggests is neither the death of modernism nor the facile dismissal of the new oppositional discourses that have arisen within postmodernism and feminism, but a rethinking of how the most critical aspects of these discourses can be brought to bear to deepen the democratic possibilities within the modernist project itself. What is at stake here is not simply the emergence of a new language with which to rethink the modernist tradition, but also the reconstruction of the political, cultural, and social preconditions for developing a radical conception of citizenship and pedagogy.

That we live in an age in which a new political subject is being constructed can be seen most vividly in the events that have recently taken place in Eastern Europe. Within a matter of months, the Berlin Wall has fallen; the Stalinist Communist parties of the Eastern bloc are, for all intents and purposes, in disarray; the former Soviet

Union is radically modifying an identity forged in the legacy of Leninism and Bolshevism; the master narratives of Marxism are being refigured within the shifting identities, cultural practices, and imaginary possibilities unleashed in the nascent discourse of a radical democracy. In Eastern Europe, the theoretical and political preconditions for a postmodern citizen are being constructed, even if at present they exist only as a faint glimmer. This is a political subject that rejects the authoritarianism of master narratives, that refuses traditions that allow only for a reverence of what already is, that denies those instrumental and universalized forms of rationality that eliminate the historical and the contingent, that opposes science as a universal foundation for truth and knowledge, and that discredits the Western notion of subjectivity as a stable, coherent self. What these shifting perspectives and emergent social relations have done is to radicalize the possibilities of freedom, and to affirm the capacity of human beings to shape their own destinies as part of a larger struggle for democracy.

In the Western industrial countries, the revolutions in Eastern Europe for freedom, equality, and justice appear in the dominant media as the valiant struggle of the Other against enslavement through communism. But in the United States these are events that take place on the margins of civilization, related but not central to the political and cultural identity of the West except as mimesis. In the mass media, the struggles for equality and freedom in Eastern Europe have been analyzed through the lens of a modernist discourse that reproduces highly problematic notions of the Enlightenment tradition. For example, many Western theorists view the redrawing of the political and social borders of Eastern Europe in reductionist modernist terms as the "end of history," a metaphor for the already unquestionable triumph of capitalist liberal democracy. In this scenario, the ideological characteristics that define the center of civilization through the discourse of the Western democracies have now been extended to the culturally and politically "deprived" margins of civilization.

This is a curious position, because it fails to recognize that what the revolutions in Eastern Europe may be pointing to is not the "end of history" but the exhaustion of those hierarchical and undemocratic features of modernism that produce state oppression, managerial domination, and social alienation in various countries in both the East and the West. It is curious because the "end of history" ideology, when applied to the Western democracies, is quite revealing; that is, it points to a political smugness that presupposes that democracy in the West has reached its culmination. Of course, beneath this smugness lies the indifference of Western-style democracy toward substantive political life; in effect, what has become increasingly visible in this argument is the failure of democracy itself. Hannam captures this point: "Formal democracy has failed because it has generated indifference towards many of the substantive goals of political activity. Western democracy believes itself to be at its own endpoint; it has given up the ambition of social change, of which it was once a central, but never an exclusive part" (113).

While Western ruling groups and their apologists may choose to see only the triumph of liberal ideology beneath the changes in Eastern Europe, there is more being called into question than they suspect. In fact, the revolutions in Eastern Europe question not only the master narrative of Marxism, but all master narratives that make a totalizing claim to emancipation and freedom. In this case, the events taking place in Eastern Europe and in other places, such as South Africa, represent part of a broader struggle of oppressed peoples against all totalizing forms of legitimation and cultural practice that deny human freedom and collective justice. What the West may be witnessing in Eastern Europe is the emergence of a new discourse, one that pits not socialism against capitalism, but democracy against all forms of totalitarianism. In opposition to a limited modernist version of democracy, the struggles in Eastern Europe implicitly suggest the conditions for creating a radical democracy, one in which people control the social and economic forces that determine their existence. In this case, the struggle for democracy exceeds its modernist framework by extending the benefits of freedom and justice beyond the strictly formal mechanisms of democracy. What appears at work in these revolutions is a discourse that has the potential to deepen the radical implications of modernism through consideration of a rather profound set of questions: What set of conditions is necessary to create social relations enabling human liberation within historically specific formations? How might individual and social identities be reconstructed in the service of human imagination and democratic citizenship? How can the assertion of history and politics serve to deconstruct all essentialisms and totalizing rationalities? How can political and social identities be constructed within a politics of difference that is capable of struggling over and deepening the project of radical democracy while constantly asserting its historical and contingent character? Put another way, what can be done to strengthen and extend the oppositional tendencies of modernism?

I want to argue that modernism, postmodernism, and feminism represent three of the most important discourses for developing a cultural politics and pedagogical practice capable of extending and theoretically advancing a radical politics of democracy. While acknowledging that all three of these discourses are internally contradictory, ideologically diverse, and theoretically inadequate, I believe that when posited in terms of the interconnections between *both* their differences and the common ground they share for being mutually correcting, they offer critical educators a rich theoretical and political opportunity for rethinking the relationship between schooling and democracy. Each of these positions has much to learn from the theoretical strengths and weaknesses of the other two. Not only does a dialogical encounter among these discourses offer them the opportunity to reexamine the partiality of their respective views; such an encounter also points to new possibilities for sharing and integrating their best insights as part of a broader radical democratic project. Together these diverse discourses offer the possibility for illuminating how critical educators might combine with other cultural workers in various movements to develop and advance a broader discourse of political and collective struggle. At stake here is an attempt to provide a political and theoretical discourse that can move beyond a postmodern aesthetic and a feminist separatism in order to develop a project in which a politics of difference can emerge within a shared discourse of democratic public life. Similarly, at issue is also the important question of how the discourses of modernism, postmodernism, and feminism might be pursued as part of a broader political effort to rethink the boundaries and most basic assumptions of a critical pedagogy consistent with a radical cultural politics.

I want to develop these issues through the following approach. First, I will analyze in schematic terms some of the central assumptions that characterize various modernist traditions, including Jürgen Habermas's spirited defense of social and political modernism. Second, I will analyze some of the central issues that postmodernism has made problematic in its encounter with modernism. Third, I will highlight the most progressive aspects of what can be loosely labeled postmodern feminist theory to be used in the service of advancing both its own critical tendencies and the most radical aspects of modernism and postmodernism. Finally, I will indicate how these three discourses might contribute to developing some important principles in the construction of a critical pedagogy for democratic struggle. It is to these issues that I will now turn.

Mapping the Politics of Modernism

To invoke the term *modernism* is immediately to place oneself in the precarious position of suggesting a definition that is itself open to enormous debate and little agreement (Groz et al. 7-17; Newman, "Revising Modernism"). Not only is there a disagreement regarding the periodization of the term, there is enormous controversy regarding what it actually refers to.[3] To some it has become synonymous with terroristic claims of reason, science, and totality (Lyotard). To others it embodies, for better or worse, various movements in the arts (Newman, *Post-Modern Aura*). And to some of its more ardent defenders, it represents the progressive rationality of communicative competence and support for the autonomous individual subject (Habermas, "Modernity versus Postmodernity," "Modernity," *Discourse*). It is not possible within the context of this essay to provide a detailed history of the various historical and ideological discourses of modernism, even though such an analysis is essential to provide a sense of the complexity of both the category and the debates that have emerged around modernism.[4] Instead, I want to focus on some of the central assumptions of modernism. The value of this approach is that it not only serves to highlight some of the more important arguments that have been made in the defense of modernism, but also provides a theoretical and political backdrop for understanding some of the central features of various postmodernist and feminist discourses. This is particularly important with respect to postmodernism, which presupposes some idea of the modern and also of various feminist discourses, which have increasingly been forged largely in opposition to some of modernism's major assumptions, particularly as these relate to notions such as rationality, truth, subjectivity, and progress.

The theoretical, ideological, and political complexity of modernism can be grasped through analysis of its diverse vocabularies with respect to three traditions: the social, the aesthetic, and the political. The notion of social modernity corresponds with the tradition of the new, the process of economic and social organization carried out under the growing relations of capitalist production. Social modernity approximates what Matei Calinescu calls the bourgeois idea of modernity, which is characterized by

> the doctrine of progress, the confidence in the beneficial possibilities of science and technology, the concern with time (a measurable time, a time that can be bought and sold and therefore has, like any other commodity, a calculable equivalent in money), the cult of reason, and the ideal of freedom defined within the framework of an abstract humanism, but also the orientation toward pragmatism and the cult of action and success. (41)

Within this notion of modernism, the unfolding of history is linked to the "continual progress of the sciences and of techniques, the rational division of industrial work, [which] introduces into social life a dimension of permanent change, of destruction of customs and traditional culture" (Baudrillard 65). At issue here is a definition of modernity that points to the progressive differentiation and rationalization of the social world through the process of economic growth and administrative rationalization. Another characteristic of social modernism is the epistemological project of elevating reason to an ontological status. Modernism in this view becomes synonymous with civilization itself, and reason is universalized in cognitive and instrumental terms as the basis for a model of industrial, cultural, and social progress. At stake in this notion of modernity is a view of individual and collective identity in which historical memory is devised as a linear process, the human subject becomes the ultimate source of meaning and action, and a notion of geographical and cultural territoriality is constructed in a hierarchy of domination and subordination marked by a center and margin legitimated through the civilizing knowledge/power of a privileged Eurocentric culture (Aronowitz).

The category of aesthetic modernity has a dual characterization that is best exemplified in its traditions of resistance and formal aestheticism (Newman, "Revising Modernism"). But it is in the tradition of opposition, with its all-consuming disgust with bourgeois values and its attempt through various literary and avant-garde movements to define art as a representation of criticism, rebellion, and resistance, that aesthetic modernism first gains a sense of notoriety. Fueling this aesthetic modernism of the nineteenth and early twentieth centuries is an alienation and negative passion whose novelty is perhaps best captured in Bakunin's anarchist maxim, "To destroy is to create" (quoted in Calinescu 117). The cultural and political lineaments of this branch of aesthetic modernism are best expressed in avant-garde movements ranging from the surrealists and the futurists to the conceptualist artists of the 1970s. Within this movement, with its diverse politics and expressions, there is an underlying commonality, an attempt to collapse the distinction between art and politics and to blur the boundaries between life and aesthetics. But in spite of its oppositional tendencies, aesthetic modernism has not fared well in the latter part of the twentieth century. Its critical stance, its aesthetic dependency on the presence of bourgeois norms, and its apocalyptic tone have increasingly become recognized as artistically fashionable by the very class it attacks (Barthes).

The central elements that bring these two traditions of modernism together constitute a powerful force not only for shaping the academic disciplines and the discourse of educational theory and practice, but also for providing a number of points where various ideological positions share a common ground. This is especially true in modernism's claim for the superiority of high culture over popular culture; its affirmation of a centered if not unified subject; its faith in the power of the highly rational, conscious mind; and its belief in the unequivocal ability of human beings to shape a better world. There is a long tradition of support for modernism, and some of its best representatives are as diverse as Marx, Baudelaire, and Dostoevsky. This notion of the self based on the universalization of reason and the totalizing discourses of emancipation have provided a cultural and political script for celebrating Western culture as synonymous with civilization itself, and for regarding progress as a terrain that only needed to be mastered as part of the inexorable march of science and history. Marshall Berman exemplifies the dizzying heights of ecstasy made possible by the script of modernism in his own rendition of the modernist sensibility:

> Modernists, as I portray them, are simultaneously at home in this world and at odds with it. They celebrate and identify with the triumphs of modern science, art, technology, communications, economics, politics—in short, with all the activities, techniques, and sensibilities that enable mankind to do what the Bible said God could do—to "make all things new." At the same time, however, they oppose modernization's betrayal of its own human promise and potential. Modernists demand more profound and radical renewals: modern men and women must become the subjects as well as the objects of modernization; they must learn to change the world that is changing them and to make it their own. The modernist knows this is possible: the fact that the world has changed so much is proof that it can change still more. The modernist can, in Hegel's phrase, "look the negative in the face and live with it." The fact that "all that is solid melts into air" is a source not of despair, but of strength and affirmation. If everything must go, then let it go: modern people have the power to create a better world than the world they have lost. ("Why Modernism" 11)

Of course, for many critics of modernism, the coupling of social and aesthetic modernism reveals itself quite differently. Modernist art is criticized for having become nothing more than a commercial market for the museums and the corporate boardrooms and a depoliticized discourse institutionalized within the universities. In addition, many critics have argued that under the banner of modernism, reason and aesthetics often come together in a technology of self and culture that combines a notion of beauty that is white, male, and European with a notion of mastery that legitimates modern industrial technologies and the exploitation of vast pools of labor from the "margins" of Second and Third World economies. Robert Merrill gives this argument a special twist in claiming that the modernist ego, with its pretensions to infallibility and unending progress, has actually come to doubt its own promises. For example, he argues that many proponents of modernism increasingly recognize that what has been developed by the West in the name of mastery actually indicates the failure of modernism to produce a technology of self and power that can deliver on the promises to provide freedom through science, technology, and control. He writes that a loss of faith in the promises of modernism

> is no less true for corporate and governmental culture in the United States which displays a . . . desperate quest for aestheticization of the self as modernist construct—white, male, Christian, industrialist—through monumentally styled office buildings, the Brooks Brothers suit (for male and female), designer food, business practices which amount only to the exercise of symbolic power, and most of all, the Mercedes Benz which as the unification in design of the good (here functional) and the beautiful and in production of industrial coordination and exploitation of human labor is preeminently the sign that one has finally achieved liberation and mastery, "made it to the top" (even if its stylistic lines thematize what can only be called a fascist aesthetics). (ix)

It is against the claims of social and aesthetic modernism that the diverse discourses of postmodernism and feminism have delivered some of their strongest theoretical and political criticism, and these will be taken up shortly. But there is a third tradition of modernism that has been engaged by feminism but generally ignored by postmodernism. This is the tradition of political modernism. Political modernism, unlike its related aesthetic and social traditions, does not focus on epistemological and cultural issues so much as it develops a project of possibility out of a number of Enlightenment ideals (Laclau, "Politics"; Mouffe, "Radical Democracy" 32-34). It should be noted that political modernism constructs a project that rests on a distinction between political liberalism and economic liberalism. In the latter, freedom is conflated with the dynamics of the capitalist marketplace, whereas in the former, freedom is associated with the principles and rights embodied in the democratic revolution that has progressed in the

West over the last three centuries. The ideals that have emerged out of this revolution include "the notion that human beings ought to use their reason to decide on courses of action, control their futures, enter into reciprocal agreements, and be responsible for what they do and who they are" (Warren ix-x). In general terms, the political project of modernism is rooted in the capacity of individuals to be moved by human suffering so as to remove its causes; to give meaning to the principles of equality, liberty, and justice; and to increase those social forms that enable human beings to develop the capacities needed to overcome ideologies and material forms that legitimate and are embedded in relations of domination.

The tradition of political modernism has largely been taken up and defended in opposition to and against the discourse of postmodernism. Consequently, when postmodernism is defined in relation to the discourse of democracy, it is either pitted against the Enlightenment project and seen as reactionary in its political tendencies (Berman, *Air*; Habermas, "Modernity," *Discourse*), grafted onto a notion of economic liberalism that converts it into an apology for rich Western democracies (Rorty, "Habermas" 174-75), or portrayed in opposition to the emancipatory projects of Marxism (Eagleton; Anderson) and feminism (Hartsock 190-91; Christian). In what follows, I want to examine some of the challenges that Habermas presents to various versions of postmodernism and feminism through his defense of modernity as an unfinished emancipatory project.

Habermas and the Challenge of Modernism

Habermas has been one of the most vigorous defenders of the legacy of modernism. His work is important because in forging his defense of modernism as part of a critique of the postmodernist and poststructuralist discourses that have emerged in France since 1968, he has opened up a debate between these seemingly opposing positions. Moreover, Habermas has attempted to revise and reconstruct the earlier work of his Frankfurt school colleagues, Theodor Adorno and Max Horkheimer, by revising their pessimistic views of rationality and democratic struggle.

Habermas identifies postmodernity less as a question of style and culture than as one of politics. Postmodernism's rejection of grand narratives, its denial of epistemological foundations, and its charge that reason and truth are always implicated in relations of power are viewed by Habermas as both a retreat from and a threat to modernity. For him, postmodernism has a paradoxical relation with modernism. On the one hand, it embodies the worst dimensions of an aesthetic modernism. That is, it extends those aspects of the avant-garde that "live [in] the experience of rebelling against all that is normative" ("Modernity" 5). In this sense, postmodernism echoes surrealism's attempt to undermine the cultural autonomy of art by removing the boundaries that separate it from everyday life. On the other hand, postmodernism represents the negation of the project of social modernity by rejecting the latter's language of universal reason, rights, and autonomy as a foundation for modern social life. According to Habermas, postmodernism's argument that realism, consensus, and totality are synonymous with terror represents a form of political and ethical exhaustion that unjustifiably renounces the unfinished task of the rule of reason (*Communication* 3-13).

In Habermas's terms, the postmodernist thinkers are conservatives whose philosophical roots are to be found in various irrationalist and counter-Enlightenment theories that suggest a peculiar political kinship with fascism. Hence postmodernism undermines the still unfolding project of modernity, with its promise of democracy through the rule of reason, communicative competence, and cultural differentiation. Postmodernism is guilty of the dual crime, in this case, of rejecting the most basic tenets of the modernist ethos and failing to recognize its most emancipatory contributions to contemporary life. In the first instance, postmodernism recklessly overemphasizes the play of difference, contingency, and language against all appeals to universalized and transcendental claims. For the postmodernist, theory without the guarantee of truth redefines the relationship between discourse and power and in doing so destabilizes the modernist faith in consensus and reason. For Habermas, postmodernism represents a revolt against a substantive view of reason and subjectivity and negates the productive features of modernism.

Modernity offers Habermas the promise of integrating the differentiating spheres of science, morality, and art back into society, not through an appeal to power, but through the rule of reason, the application of a universal pragmatics of language, and the development of forms of learning based on dictates of communicative competence. While he accepts the excesses of technological rationality and substantive reason, he believes that only through reason can the logic of scientific/technological rationality and domination be subordinated to the imperatives of modernist justice and morality (Kellner 262-66). Habermas admires Western culture and argues that "bourgeois ideals" contain elements of reason that should be at the center of a democratic society. By these ideals, he writes,

> I mean the internal theoretical dynamic which constantly propels the sciences—and the self-reflection of the sciences as well—beyond the creation of merely technologically exploitable knowledge; furthermore, I mean the universalist foundations of law and morality which have also been embodied (in no matter how distorted and imperfect a form) in the institutions of constitutional states, in the forms of democratic decision-making, and in individualistic patterns of identity formation; finally, I mean the productivity and the liberating force of an aesthetic experience with a subjectivity set free from the imperatives of purposive activity and from the conventions of everyday perception. ("Entwinement" 18)

Central to Habermas's defense of modernity is his important distinction between instrumental and communicative rationality. Instrumental rationality represents those systems or practices embodied in the state, money, and various forms of power that work through "steering mechanisms" to stabilize society. Communicative rationality refers to the world of common experience and discursive intersubjective interaction, a world characterized by various forms of socialization mediated through language and oriented toward social integration and consensus. Habermas accepts various criticisms of instrumental rationality, but he largely agrees that capitalism, in spite of its problems, represents more acceptable forms of social differentiation, rationalization, and modernization than have characterized past stages of social and instrumental development. On the other hand, he is adamant about the virtues of communicative rationality, with its emphasis on the rules of mutual understanding, clarity, consensus, and the force of argument. Habermas views any serious attack on this form of rationality as in itself irrational. In effect, his notion of communicative rationality provides the basis not only for his ideal speech situation but also for his broader view of social reconstruction. Rationality, in this case, with its distinctions between an outer world of systemic steering practices and a privileged inner world of communicative process, represents in part a division between a world saturated with material power expressed in the evolution of ever-growing and complex subsystems of rational modernization and one shaped by universal reason and communicative action. At the core of this distinction is a notion of democracy in which struggle and conflict are not based on a politics of difference and power, but on a conceptual and linguistic search for defining the content of what is rational (Ryan 27-45).

Habermas's defense of modernity is not rooted in a rigorous questioning of the relationship among discourses, institutional structures, and the interests they produce and legitimate within specific social conditions. Instead he focuses on linguistic competence and the principle of consensus, with its guiding problematic defined by the need to uproot the obstacles to "distorted communication." This not only points to a particular view of power, politics, and modernity; it also legitimates, as Stanley Aronowitz points out, a specific notion of reason and learning:

> He [Habermas] admonishes us to recognize [modernity's] unfinished tasks: the rule of reason. Rather than rules of governance based on power or discursive hegemonies, we are exhorted to create a new imaginary, one that would recognize societies able to resolve social conflicts, at least provisionally, so as to permit a kind of collective reflexivity. Characteristically, Habermas finds that the barriers to learning are not found in the exigencies of class interest, but in distorted communication. The mediation of communication by interest constitutes here an obstacle to reflexive knowledge. "Progressive" societies are those capable of learning—that is, acquiring knowledge that overcomes the limits of strategic or instrumental action. (103)

Habermas's work has been both opposed and taken up by a number of critical and radical groups. He has been criticized by feminists such as Nancy Fraser ("Critical Theory") and embraced by radicals who believe that his search for universal values represents a necessary ingredient in the struggle for human emancipation (Epstein 54-56). In many respects his writing provides a theoretical marker for examining how the debate over foundationalism and democracy on the one hand, and over a politics of difference and contingency on the other, has manifested itself on the left as a debate among those who line up for or against different versions of modernism or postmodernism.

A more constructive approach, both to the specifics of Habermas's work and to the larger issue of modernism, is that neither should be accepted or rejected as if the only choice is complete denial or conversion. Habermas, for example, is both right and wrong in his analyses of modernism and postmodernism. He is right in attempting to salvage the productive and emancipatory aspects of modernism and to develop a unifying principle that provides a referent point for engaging and advancing a democratic society. He is also right in claiming that postmodernism is as much about politics and culture as it is about aesthetics and style (Huyssen). In this sense, Habermas provides a theoretical service by trying to keep alive as part of a modernist discourse the categories of critique, agency, and democracy. For better or worse, Habermas injects into the modernist-versus-postmodernist debate the primacy of politics and of the role that rationality might play in the service of human freedom and the imperatives of democratic ideology and struggle. As Thomas McCarthy points out, Habermas

> believes that the defects of the Enlightenment can only be made good by further enlightenment. The totalized critique of reason undercuts the capacity of reason to be critical. It refuses to acknowledge that modernization bears developments as well as distortions of reason. Among the former, he mentions the "unthawing" and "reflective refraction" of cultural traditions, the universalization of norms and generalization of values, and the growing individuation of personal identities—all prerequisites for that effectively democratic organization of society through which alone reason can, in the end, become practical. (xvii)

It is around these concerns that postmodern theorists have challenged some of the basic assumptions of modernism. For Habermas, these challenges weaken rather than mobilize the democratic tendencies of modernism. But, as I hope to demonstrate in the remainder of this essay, Habermas is wrong in simply dismissing all forms of postmodernism as antimodernist and neoconservative. Moreover, given his own notions of consensus and social action, coupled with his defense of Western tradition, his view of modernity is too complicitous with a notion of reason that is used to legitimate the superiority of a culture primarily white, male, and Eurocentric. Habermas's position is susceptible to the charge not only of being patriarchal but also of not adequately engaging the relationship between discourse and power and the messy material relations of class, race, and gender. Postmodern and feminist critiques of his work cannot be dismissed simply because they might be labeled antimodern or antirationalist. In what follows, I want to take up some of the challenges that postmodernism has developed in opposition to some of the central assumptions of modernism.

Postmodern Negations

> If postmodernism means putting the Word in its place . . . if it means the opening up to critical discourse of lines of enquiry which were formerly prohibited, of evidence which was previously inadmissible so that new and different questions can be asked and new and other voices can begin asking them; if it means the opening up of institutional and discursive spaces within which more fluid and plural social and sexual identities may develop; if it means the erosion of triangular formations of power and knowledge with the expert at the apex and the "masses" at the base, if, in a word, it enhances our collective (and democratic) sense of *possibility*, then I for one am a postmodernist. (Hebdige, *Hiding* 226)

Dick Hebdige's guarded comments regarding his own relationship to postmodernism suggest some of the problems that have to be faced in using the term. As the term is increasingly employed both in and out of the academy to designate a variety of discourses, its political and semantic currency repeatedly becomes an object of conflicting forces and divergent tendencies. Postmodernism has not only become a site of conflicting ideological struggles—denounced by different factions on both the left and the right, supported by an equal number of diverse progressive groups, and appropriated by interests that would renounce any claim to politics—its varied forms also produce both radical and reactionary elements. Postmodernism's diffuse influence and contradictory character are evident within many cultural fields—painting, architecture, photography, video, dance, literature, education, music, mass communications—and in the varied contexts of its production and exhibition. Such a term does not lend itself to the usual topology of categories that serve to inscribe it ideologically and politically within traditional binary oppositions. In this case the politics of postmodernism cannot be neatly labeled under the traditional categories of left and right.

That many groups are making a claim for its use should not suggest that the term has no value except as a buzzword for the latest intellectual fashions. On the contrary, its widespread appeal and conflict-ridden terrain indicate that something important is being fought over, that new forms of social discourse are being constructed at a time when the intellectual, political, and cultural boundaries of the age are being refigured amidst significant historical shifts, changing power structures, and emergent alternative forms of political struggle. Of course, whether these new postmodernist discourses adequately articulate rather than simply reflect these changes is the important question.

I believe that the discourse of postmodernism is worth struggling over, and not merely as a semantic category that needs to be subjected to ever more precise definitional rigor. As a discourse of plurality, difference, and multinarratives, postmodernism resists being inscribed in any single articulating principle in order to explain either the mechanics of domination or the dynamic of emancipation. At issue here is the need to mine its contradictory and oppositional insights so that they might be appropriated in the service of a radical project of democratic struggle. The value of postmodernism lies in its role as a shifting signifier that both reflects and contributes to the unstable cultural and structural relationships that increasingly characterize the advanced industrial countries of the West. The important point here is not whether postmodernism can be defined within the parameters of particular politics, but how its best insights might be appropriated within a progressive and emancipatory democratic politics.

I want to argue that although postmodernism does not suggest a particular ordering principle for defining a particular political project, it does have a rudimentary coherence with respect to the set of "problems and basic issues that have been created by the various discourses of postmodernism, issues that were not particularly problematic before but certainly are now" (Hutcheon, "Problematic" 5). Postmodernism raises questions and problems so as to redraw and re-present the boundaries of discourse and cultural criticism. The issues that postmodernism has brought into view can be seen, in part, through its various refusals of all "natural laws" and transcendental claims that by definition attempt to "escape" from any type of historical and normative grounding. In fact, if there is any underlying harmony to various discourses of postmodernism, it is in their rejection of absolute essences. Arguing along similar lines, Laclau claims that postmodernity as a discourse of social and cultural criticism begins with a form of epistemological, ethical, and political awareness based on three fundamental negations:

> The beginning of postmodernity can . . . be conceived as the achievement of multiple awareness: epistemological awareness, insofar as scientific progress appears as a succession of paradigms whose transformation and replacement is not grounded in any algorithmic certainty; ethical awareness, insofar as the defense and assertion of values is grounded on argumentative movements (conservational movements, according to Rorty), which do not lead back to any absolute foundation; political awareness, insofar as historical achievements appear as the product of hegemonic and contingent—and as such, always reversible—articulations and not as the result of immanent laws of history. ("Building" 21)

Laclau's list does not exhaust the range of negations that postmodernism has taken up as part of the increasing resistance to all totalizing explanatory systems and as part of the growing call for a language that offers the possibility of addressing the changing ideological and structural conditions of our time. In what follows, I will address some of the important thematic considerations that cut across postmodernism, what I define as a series of postmodern negations. I will address these negations in terms of the challenge they present to what can be problematized as either oppressive or productive features of modernism.

Postmodernism and the Negation of Totality, Reason, and Foundationalism

A central feature of postmodernism has been its critique of totality, reason, and universality. This critique has been most powerfully developed in the work of Jean-François Lyotard. In developing his attack on Enlightenment notions of totality, Lyotard argues that the very notion of the postmodern is inseparable from an incredulity toward metanarratives. In Lyotard's view, "The narrative view is losing its functors, its great hero, its great dangers, its great voyages, its great goal. It is being dispersed in clouds of narrative language elements—narrative, but also denotative, prescriptive, descriptive, and so on" (xxiv). For Lyotard, grand narratives do not problematize their own legitimacy; they deny the historical and social construction of their own first principles, and in doing so wage war on difference, contingency, and particularity. Against Habermas and others, Lyotard argues that appeals to reason and consensus, when inserted within grand narratives that unify history, emancipation, and knowledge, deny their own implications in the production of knowledge and power. More emphatically, Lyotard claims that within such narratives are elements of mastery and control in which "we can hear the mutterings of the desire for a return of terror, for the realization of the fantasy to seize reality" (82). Against metanarratives that totalize historical experience by reducing its diversity to a one-dimensional, all-encompassing logic, he posits a discourse of multiple horizons, the play of language games, and the terrain of micropolitics. Against the formal logic of identity and the transhistorical subject, he invokes a dialectics of indeterminacy, varied discourses of legitimation, and a politics based on the "permanence of difference."

Lyotard's attack on metanarratives represents both a trenchant form of social criticism and a philosophical challenge to all forms of foundationalism that deny the historical, the normative, and the contingent. Fraser and Linda Nicholson articulate this connection well:

> For Lyotard, postmodernism designates a general condition of contemporary Western civilization. The postmodern condition is one in which "grand narratives of legitimation" are no longer credible. By "grand narratives" he means, in the first instance, overarching philosophies of history like the

> Enlightenment story of the gradual but steady progress of reason and freedom, Hegel's dialectic of Spirit coming to know itself, and, most important, Marx's drama of the forward march of human productive capacities via class conflict culminating in proletarian revolution. . . . For what most interests [Lyotard] about the Enlightenment, Hegelian, and Marxist stories is what they share with other nonnarrative forms of philosophy. Like ahistorical epistemologies and moral theories, they aim to show that specific first-order discursive practices are well formed and capable of yielding true and just results. True and just here mean something more than results reached by adhering scrupulously to the constitutive rules of some given scientific and political games. They mean, rather, results that correspond to Truth and Justice as they really are in themselves independent of contingent, historical social practices. Thus, in Lyotard's view, a metanarrative . . . purports to be a privileged discourse capable of situating, characterizing, and evaluating all other discourses, but not itself infected by the historicity and contingency that render first-order discourses potentially distorted and in need of legitimation. (86-87)

What Fraser and Nicholson point out by implication is that postmodernism does more than wage war on totality; it also calls into question the use of reason in the service of power, the role of intellectuals who speak through authority invested in a science of truth and history, and the forms of leadership that demand unification and consensus within centrally administered chains of command. Postmodernism rejects a notion of reason that is disinterested, transcendent, and universal. Rather than separating reason from the terrain of history, place, and desire, postmodernism argues that reason and science can be understood only as part of a broader historical, political, and social struggle over the relationship between language and power. Within this context, the distinctions between passion and reason, objectivity and interpretation no longer exist as separate entities, but represent instead the effects of particular discourses and forms of social power. This issue is not merely epistemological, but deeply political and normative. Gary Peller makes this point clear by arguing that what is at stake in this form of criticism is nothing less than the dominant and liberal commitment to Enlightenment culture. He writes:

> Indeed the whole way that we conceive of liberal progress (overcoming prejudice in the name of truth, seeing through the distortions of ideology to get at reality, surmounting ignorance and superstition with the acquisition of knowledge) is called into question. [Postmodernism] suggests that what has been presented in our social-political and our intellectual traditions as knowledge, truth, objectivity, and reason are actually merely the effects of a

> particular form of social world that then presents itself as beyond mere interpretation, as truth itself. (30)

By asserting the primacy of the historical and the contingent in the construction of reason, authority, truth, ethics, and identity, postmodernism provides a politics of representation and a basis for social struggle. Laclau argues that the postmodern attack on foundationalism is an eminently political act, because it expands the possibility for argumentation and dialogue. Moreover, by acknowledging questions of power and value in the construction of knowledge and subjectivities, postmodernism helps to make visible important ideological and structural forces, such as race, gender, and class. For theorists such as Laclau, the collapse of foundationalism does not suggest a banal relativism or the onset of a dangerous nihilism. On the contrary, he argues that the lack of ultimate meaning radicalizes the possibilities for human agency and a democratic politics:

> Abandoning the myth of foundations does not lead to nihilism, just as uncertainty as to how an enemy will attack does not lead to passivity. It leads, rather, to a proliferation of discursive interventions and arguments that are necessary, because there is no extradiscursive reality that discourse might simply reflect. Inasmuch as argument and discourse constitute the social, their open-ended character becomes the source of a greater activism and a more radical libertarianism. Humankind, having always bowed to external forces—God, Nature, the necessary laws of History—can now, at the threshold of postmodernity, consider itself for the first time the creator and constructor of its own history. ("Politics" 79-80)

The postmodern attack on totality and foundationalism is not without its drawbacks. While it rightly focuses on the importance of local narratives and rejects the notion that truth precedes the notion of representation, it also runs the risk of blurring the distinction between master narratives that are monocausal and formative narratives that provide the basis for historically and relationally placing different groups or local narratives within some common project. To draw out this point further, it is difficult to imagine any politics of difference as a form of radical social theory if it does not offer a formative narrative capable of analyzing difference within rather than against unity. I will develop these criticisms in more detail in another section.

Postmodernism as the Negation of Border Cultures

Postmodernism offers a challenge to the cultural politics of modernism at a number of different levels. That is, it not only provides a discourse for retheorizing culture as fundamental to the construction of political subjects and collective struggle, it also theorizes culture as a politics of representation and power. Emily Hicks has presented the postmodern challenge to modernist culture as one framed within the contexts of shifting identities, the remapping of borders, and nonsynchronous memory. In her terms, modernist culture negates the possibility of identities created within the experience of multiple narratives and "border" crossings; instead, modernism frames culture within rigid boundaries that both privilege and exclude around the categories of race, class, gender, and ethnicity. Within the discourse of modernism, culture in large part becomes an organizing principle for constructing borders that reproduce relations of domination, subordination, and inequality. In this case, borders do not offer the possibility of experiencing and positioning ourselves within a productive exchange of narratives. Instead, modernism constructs borders framed in the language of universals and oppositions. Within the cultural politics of modernism, European culture becomes identified with the center of civilization, high culture is defined in essentialist terms against the popular culture of the everyday, and history as the reclaiming of critical memory is displaced by the proliferation of images. In effect, postmodernism constitutes a general attempt to transgress the borders sealed by modernism, to proclaim the arbitrariness of all boundaries, and to call attention to the sphere of culture as a shifting social and historical construction.

I want to approach the postmodern challenge to a modernist cultural politics by focusing briefly on a number of issues. First, postmodernism has broadened the discussion regarding the relationship between culture and power by illuminating the changing conditions of knowledge embedded in the age of electronically mediated information systems, cybernetic technologies, and computer engineering (Lyotard). In doing so, it has pointed to the development of new forms of knowledge that significantly shape traditional analyses relevant to the intersection of culture, power, and politics. Second, postmodernism raises a new set of questions about how culture is inscribed in the production of center/margin hierarchies and the reproduction of postcolonial forms of subjugation. At stake here is not only a reconsideration of the intersection of race, gender, and class, but also a new way of reading history; that is, postmodernism provides forms of historical knowledge as a way of reclaiming power and identity for subordinate groups (Spivak; Minh-ha). Third, postmodernism breaks down the distinction between high and low culture and makes the everyday an object of serious study (Collins).

In the first instance, postmodernism points to the increasingly powerful and complex role of the new electronic medium in constituting individual identities, cultural languages, and new social formations. In effect, postmodernism has provided a new discourse that enables us to understand the changing nature of domination and resistance in late capitalist societies (Lash and Urry). This is particularly true in its analyses of how the conditions for the production of knowledge have changed within the last two decades with respect to the electronic information technologies of production, the types of knowledge produced, and the impact they have had at both the level of everyday life and in larger global terms (Poster). Postmodern discourse highlights radical changes in the ways in which culture is produced, circulated, read, and consumed; moreover, it seriously challenges those theoretical models that have inadequately analyzed culture as a productive and constituting force within an increasingly global network of scientific, technological, and information-producing apparatuses.

In the second instance, postmodernism has provided an important theoretical service in mapping the relations of the center and the periphery with respect to three related interventions into cultural politics. First, it has offered a powerful challenge to the hegemonic notion that Eurocentric culture is superior to other cultures and traditions by virtue of its canonical status as a universal measure of Western civilization. In exposing the particularity of the alleged universals that constitute Eurocentric culture, postmodernism has revealed that the "truth" of Western culture is by design a metanarrative that ruthlessly expunges the stories, traditions, and voices of those who by virtue of race, class, and gender constitute the "Other." Postmodernism's war on totality is defined, in this case, as a campaign against Western patriarchal culture and ethnocentricity (McLaren and Hammer). To the extent that postmodernism has rejected the ethnocentrism of Western culture, it has also waged a battle against those forms of academic knowledge that serve to reproduce the dominant Western culture as a privileged canon and tradition immune from history, ideology, and social criticism (Aronowitz and Giroux, *Education*). Central to such a challenge is a second aspect of postmodernism's refiguring of the politics of the center and the margins. That is, postmodernism not only challenges the form and content of dominant models of knowledge, it also produces new forms of knowledge through its emphasis on breaking down disciplines and taking up objects of study that were unrepresentable in the dominant discourses of the Western canon.

Postmodern criticism provides an important theoretical and political service in assisting those deemed "Other" in reclaiming their own histories and voices. By problematizing the dominant notion of tradition, postmodernism has developed a power-sensitive discourse that helps subordinated and excluded groups to make sense out of their own social worlds and histories while simultaneously offering new opportunities to produce political and cultural vocabularies by which to define and shape their individual and collective identities (Lipsitz 211-31). At stake here is the rewriting of history within a politics of difference that substitutes for totalizing narratives of oppression local and multiple narratives that assert their identities and interests as part of a broader reconstruction of democratic public life. Craig Owens captures the project of possibility that is part of reclaiming voices that have been relegated to the marginal and therefore seem to be unrepresentable. Although women emerge as the privileged force of the marginal in this account, his analysis is equally true for a number of subordinated groups:

> It is precisely at the legislative frontier between what can be represented and what cannot that the postmodernist operation is being staged—not in order

to transcend representation, but in order to expose that system of power that authorizes certain representations while blocking, prohibiting or invalidating others. Among those prohibited from Western representation, whose representations are denied all legitimacy, are women. Excluded from representation by its very structure, they return within it as a figure for—a presentation of—the unrepresentable. (59)

Postmodernism's attempt to explore and articulate new spaces is not without its problems. Marginality as difference is not an unproblematic issue, and differences have to be weighed against the implications they have for constructing multiple relations between the self and the "Other." Moreover, resistance not only takes place on the margins but also at various points of entry within dominant institutions. Needless to say, any notion of difference and marginality runs the risk of mystifying as well as enabling a radical cultural politics. But what is crucial is that postmodernism does offer the possibility for developing a cultural politics that focuses on the margins, for reclaiming, as Edward Said points out, "the right of formerly un- or mis-represented human groups to speak for and represent themselves in domains defined, politically and intellectually, as normally excluding them, usurping their signifying and representing functions, overriding their historical reality" (quoted in Connor 233).

This leads to a third dimension of a postmodern cultural politics. As part of a broader politics of difference, postmodernism has also focused on the ways in which modernity functions as an imperialist master narrative that links Western models of industrial progress with hegemonic forms of culture, identity, and consumption. Within this context, the project of modernity relegates all non-Western cultures to the periphery of civilization, outposts of insignificant histories, cultures, and narratives.

In the discourse of postcolonial modernism, the culture of the "Other" is no longer inscribed in imperialist relations of domination and subordination through the raw exercise of military or bureaucratic power. Power now inscribes itself in apparatuses of cultural production that easily transgress national and cultural borders. Data banks, radio transmissions, and international communications systems become part of the vanguard of a new global network of cultural and economic imperialism. Modernity now parades its universal message of progress through the experts and intellectuals it sends to Third World universities, through the systems of representations that it produces to saturate billboards all over Latin America, and/or through the advertising images it sends out from satellites to the television sets of inhabitants of Africa, India, and Asia.

Postmodernism makes visible both the changing technological nature of postcolonial imperialism and the new forms of emerging resistance that it encounters. On the one hand, it rejects the notion that the colonial relationship is an "uninterrupted psychodrama of repression and subjugation" (Roth 250). In this perspective, there is an attempt to understand how power is not only administered, but also taken up, resisted, and struggled over. The "Other" in this scenario does not suffer the fate of being generalized out of existence, but bears the weight of historical and cultural specificity. In part, this has resulted in a radical attempt to read the culture of the "Other" as a construction rather than a description, as a form of text that evokes rather than merely represents (Tyler; Clifford and Marcus; Clifford). Within this scenario, the relationship between the subject and the object, between invention and construction, is never innocent and is always implicated in theorizing about the margins and the center. At issue here is an attempt to make problematic the voices of those who try to describe the margins, even when they do so in the interests of emancipation and social justice (Minh-ha). This suggests yet another aspect of postcolonial discourse that postmodernism has begun to analyze as part of its own cultural politics.

In the postmodern age, the boundaries that once held back diversity, otherness, and difference, whether in domestic ghettos or through national borders policed by custom officials, have begun to break down. The Eurocentric center can no longer absorb or contain the culture of the "Other" as something threatening and dangerous. As Renato Rosaldo points out, "The Third World has imploded into the metropolis. Even the conservative national politics of containment, designed to shield 'us' from 'them,' betray the impossibility of maintaining hermetically sealed cultures" (44). Culture in postcolonial discourse becomes something that "Others" have; it is the mark of ethnicity and difference. What has changed in this hegemonic formulation/strategy is that diversity is not ignored in the dominant cultural apparatus, but promoted in order to be narrowly and reductively defined through dominant stereotypes. Representation does not merely exclude, it also defines cultural difference by *actively* constructing the identity of the "Other" for dominant and subordinate groups. Postmodernism challenges postcolonial discourse by bringing the margins to the center in terms of their own voices and histories. Representation, in this sense, gives way to opposition and the struggle over questions of identity, place, and values (Spivak; Minh-ha). Difference in this context holds out the possibility of not only bringing the voices and politics of the "Other" to the centers of power, but also understanding how the center is implicated in the margins. It is an attempt to understand how the radicalizing of difference can produce new forms of displacement and more refined forms of racism and sexism. Understandably, the best work in this field is being done by writers from the "margins."

Finally, it is well known that postmodernism breaks with dominant forms of representation by rejecting the distinction between elite and popular culture and by arguing for alternative sites of artistic engagement and forms of experimentation (Hebdige, *Hiding* 116-43). As an anti-aesthetic, postmodernism rejects the modernist notion of privileged culture or art; it renounces "official" centers for "housing" and displaying art and culture along with their interests in origins, periodization, and authenticity (Foster xv-xvi; Crimp). Moreover, postmodernism's challenge to the boundaries of modernist art and culture has, in part, resulted in new forms of art, writing, filmmaking, and various types of aesthetic and social criticism. For example, films such as *Wetherby* (1985) deny the structure of plot and seem to have no recognizable beginning or end; photographer Sherrie Levine uses a "discourse of copy" in her work to transgress the notions of origin and originality. Writer James Sculley blurs the lines between writing poetry and producing it within a variety of representational forms. The American band Talking Heads adopts an eclectic range of aural and visual signifiers to produce a pastiche of styles in which genres are mixed, identities shift, and the lines between reality and image are purposely blurred (Hebdige, *Hiding* 233-44).

Most important, postmodernism conceives of the everyday and the popular as worthy of serious *and* playful consideration. In the first instance, popular culture is analyzed as an important sphere of contestation, struggle, and resistance. In doing so, postmodernism does not abandon the distinctions that structure varied cultural forms within and among different levels of social practice; instead it deepens the possibility for understanding the social, historical, and political foundations for such distinctions as they are played out within the intersection of power, culture, and politics. In the second instance, postmodernism cultivates a tone of irony, parody, and playfulness as part of an aesthetic that desacralizes cultural aura and "greatness" while simultaneously demonstrating that "contingency penetrates all identity" and that "the primary and constitutive character of the discursive is . . . the condition of any practice" (Laclau, "Building" 17). Richard Kearney has noted that the postmodern notion of play, with its elements of undecidability and poetical imagining, challenges constricted and egocentric levels of selfhood and allows us to move toward a greater understanding of the "Other":

> The ex-centric characteristics of the play paradigm may be construed as tokens of the poetical power of imagination to transcend the limits of egocentric, and indeed anthropocentric, consciousness—thereby exploring different possibilities of existence. Such "possibilities" may well be deemed impossible at the level of the established reality. (366-67)

Central to the postmodern rejection of elite culture as a privileged domain of cultural production and repository of "truth" and civilization is an attempt to understand modernist cultural practices in their hegemonic and contradictory manifestations. Similarly, postmodernism rejects the notion of popular culture as structured exclusively through a combination of commodity production and audience passivity, a site both for dumping commercial junk and for creating consumer robots. Instead, postmodernism views popular culture as a terrain of accommodation and struggle, a terrain whose structuring principles should not be analyzed in the reductionistic language of aesthetic standards but rather through the discourse of power and politics (Giroux and Simon, *Popular*). Of course, it must be stated that the postmodern elements of a cultural politics that I have provided need to be interrogated more closely for their excesses and absences, and I will take up this issue in another section; but in what follows I will analyze the third postmodern negation, that regarding language and subjectivity.

Postmodernism, Language, and the Negation of the Humanist Subject

Within the discourse of postmodernism, the new social agents become plural; that is, the universal agent, such as the working class, is replaced by multiple agents forged in a variety of struggles and social movements. Here we have a politics that stresses differences among groups. But it is worth noting that subjectivities are also constituted within difference. This is an important distinction and offers an important challenge to the humanist notion of the subject as a free, unified, stable, and coherent self. In fact, one of the most important theoretical and political advances of postmodernism is its stress on the centrality of language and subjectivity as new fronts from which to rethink the issues of meaning, identity, and politics. This issue can best be approached through an analysis of the ways in which postmodernism has challenged the conventional view of language.

Postmodern discourse has retheorized the nature of language as a system of signs structured in the infinite play of difference, and in doing so has undermined the dominant, positivist notion of language as either a genetic code structured in permanence or simply a linguistic, transparent medium for transmitting ideas and meaning. Theorists such as Jacques Derrida, Michel Foucault, Jacques Lacan, and Laclau and Mouffe, in particular, have played a major role in retheorizing the relationships among discourse, power, and difference. For example, Derrida has brilliantly analyzed the issue of language through the principle of what he calls "*différance*." This view suggests that meaning is the product of a language constructed out of and subject to the endless play of differences among signifiers. What constitutes the meaning of a signifier is defined by the shifting, changing relations of difference that characterize the referential play of language. What Derrida, Laclau and Mouffe, and a host of other critics have demonstrated is "the increasing difficulty of defining the limits of language, or, more accurately, of defining the specific identity of the linguistic object" (Laclau, "Politics" 67). But more is at stake here than theoretically demonstrating that meaning can never be fixed once and for all.

The postmodern emphasis on the importance of discourse has also resulted in a major rethinking of the notion of subjectivity. In particular, various postmodern discourses have offered a major critique of the liberal humanist notion of subjectivity, which is predicated on the notion of a unified, rational, self-determining consciousness. In this view, the individual subject is the source of self-knowledge, and his or her view of the world is constituted through the exercise of a rational and autonomous mode of understanding and knowing. What postmodern discourse challenges is liberal humanism's notion of the subject "as a kind of free, autonomous, universal sensibility, indifferent to any particular or moral contents" (Eagleton 101). Teresa Ebert, in her discussion of the construction of gender differences, offers a succinct commentary on the humanist notion of identity:

> Postmodern feminist cultural theory breaks with the dominant humanist view . . . in which the subject is still considered to be an autonomous individual with a coherent, stable self constituted by a set of natural and pre-given elements such as biological sex. It theorizes the subject as produced through signifying practices which precede her and not as the originator of meaning. One acquires specific subject positions—that is, existence in meaning, in social relations—being constituted in ideologically structured discursive acts. Subjectivity is thus the effect of a set of ideologically organized signifying practices through which the individual is situated in the world and in terms of which the world and one's self are made intelligible. (22-23)

The importance of postmodernism's retheorizing of subjectivity cannot be overemphasized. In this view, subjectivity is no longer assigned to the apolitical wasteland of essences and essentialism. Subjectivity is now read as multiple, layered, and nonunitary; rather than being constituted in a unified and integrated ego, the "self" is seen as being "constituted out of and by difference and remains contradictory" (quoted in Grossberg 56). No longer viewed as merely the repository of consciousness and creativity, the self is constructed as a terrain of conflict and struggle, and subjectivity is seen as site of both liberation and subjugation. How subjectivity relates to issues of identity, intentionality, and desire is a deeply political issue that is inextricably related to social and cultural forces that extend far beyond the self-consciousness of the so-called humanist subject. Both the very nature of subjectivity and its capacities for self- and social determination can no longer be situated within the guarantees of transcendent phenomena or metaphysical essences. Within this postmodern perspective, the basis for a cultural politics and the struggle for power has been opened up to include the issues of language and identity. In what follows, I want to take up how various feminist discourses reinscribe some of the central assumptions of modernism and postmodernism as part of a broader cultural practice and political project.

Postmodern Feminism as Political and Ethical Practice

Feminist theory has always engaged in a dialectical relationship with modernism. On the one hand, it has stressed modernist concerns with equality, social justice, and freedom through an ongoing engagement with substantive political issues, specifically the rewriting of the historical and social construction of gender in the interest of an emancipatory cultural politics. In other words, feminism has been quite discriminating in its ability to sift through the wreckage of modernism in order to liberate modernism's victories, particularly the unrealized potentialities that reside in its categories of agency, justice, and politics. On the other hand, postmodern feminism has rejected those aspects of modernism that exalt universal laws at the expense of specificity and contingency. More specifically, postmodern feminism opposes a linear view of history that legitimates patriarchal notions of subjectivity and society; moreover, it rejects the notion that science and reason have a direct correspondence with objectivity and truth. In effect, postmodern feminism rejects the binary opposition between modernism and postmodernism in favor of a broader theoretical attempt to situate both discourses critically within a feminist political project.

Feminist theory has both produced and profited from a critical appropriation of a number of assumptions central to modernism and postmodernism. The feminist engagement with modernism has been primarily a discourse of self-criticism and has served to expand radically a plurality of positions within feminism itself. Women of color, lesbians, and poor and working-class women have challenged the essentialism, separatism, and ethnocentrism that have been expressed in feminist theorizing, and in doing so have seriously undermined the Eurocentrist and totalizing discourse that has become a political straitjacket within the movement. Fraser and Nicholson offer a succinct analysis of some of the issues involved in this debate, particularly in relation to the appropriation by some feminists of "quasi metanarratives":

> They tacitly presuppose some commonly held but unwarranted and essentialist assumptions about the nature of human beings and the conditions for social life. In addition, they assume methods and/or concepts that are uninflected by temporality or historicity and that therefore function de facto as permanent, neutral matrices for inquiry. Such theories, then, share some of the essentialist and ahistorical features of metanarratives: they are insufficiently attentive to historical and cultural diversity; and they falsely universalize features of the theorist's own era, society, culture, class, sexual orientation, and/or ethnic or racial group. . . . It has become clear that quasi metanarratives hamper, rather than promote, sisterhood, since they elide differences among women and among the forms of sexism to which different women are differentially subject. Likewise, it is increasingly apparent that such theories hinder alliances with other progressive movements, since they tend to occlude axes of domination other than gender. In sum, there is a growing interest among feminists in modes of theorizing that are attentive to differences and to cultural and historical specificity. (92, 99)

Fashioning a language that has been highly critical of modernism has not only served to make problematic what can be called *totalizing feminisms*; it has also called into question the notion that sexist oppression is at the root of all forms of domination (Malson et al. 5-9). Implicit in this position are two assumptions that have significantly shaped the arguments of mostly white, Western women. The first argument inverts the orthodox Marxist position that regards class as the primary category of domination, with all other modes of oppression being relegated to second place. In this instance, patriarchy becomes the primary form of domination, while race and class are reduced to its distorted reflection. The second assumption recycles another aspect of orthodox Marxism, which assumes that the struggle over power is exclusively waged among opposing social classes. The feminist version of this argument simply substitutes gender for class, and in doing so reproduces a form of "us-against-them" politics that is antithetical to developing community within a broad and diversified public culture. Both of these arguments represent the ideological baggage of modernism. In both cases, domination is framed in binary oppositions that suggest that workers or women cannot be complicit in their own oppression and that domination assumes a form that is singular and uncomplicated. The feminist challenge to this ideological straitjacket of modernism is well expressed by bell hooks, who avoids the politics of separatism by invoking an important distinction between the role feminists might play in asserting their own particular struggle against patriarchy and the role they can play as part of a broader struggle for liberation:

> Feminist effort to end patriarchal domination should be of primary concern precisely because it insists on the eradication of exploitation and oppression in the family context and in all other intimate relationships. . . . Feminism, as liberation struggle, must exist apart from and as a part of the larger struggle to eradicate domination in all of its forms. We must understand that patriarchal domination shares an ideological foundation with racism and other forms of group oppression, that there is no hope that it can be eradicated while these systems remain intact. This knowledge should consistently inform the direction of feminist theory and practice. Unfortunately, racism and class elitism among women [have] frequently led to the suppression and distortion of this connection so that it is now necessary for feminist thinkers to critique and revise much feminist theory and the direction of the feminist movement. This effort at revision is perhaps most evident in the current widespread acknowledgement that sexism, racism, and class exploitation constitute interlocking systems of domination—that sex, race, and class, and not sex alone, determine the nature of any female's identity, status, and circumstance, the degree to which she will or will not be dominated, the extent to which she will have the power to dominate. (22)

I invoke the feminist critique of modernism to make visible some of the ideological territory it shares with certain versions of postmodernism and to suggest the wider implications that a postmodern feminism has for developing and broadening the terrain of political struggle and transformation. It is important to note that this encounter between feminism and postmodernism should not be seen as an effort to displace a feminist politics with a politics and pedagogy of postmodernism. On the contrary, I think feminism provides postmodernism with a politics, and with a great deal more. What is at stake here is using feminism, in the words of Meaghan Morris, as "a context in which debates about postmodernism might further be considered, developed, transformed (or abandoned)" (16). Critical to such a project is the need to analyze the ways in which feminist theorists have used postmodernism to fashion a form of social criticism whose value lies in its critical approach to gender issues and in the theoretical insights it provides for developing broader democratic and pedagogical struggles.

The theoretical status and political viability of various postmodern discourses regarding the issues of totality, foundationalism, culture, subjectivity, and language are a matter of intense debate among diverse feminist groups. I am little concerned with charting this debate or focusing on those positions that dismiss postmodernism as antithetical to feminism. Instead I want to focus primarily on those feminist discourses that acknowledge being influenced by postmodernism but at the same time deepen and radicalize the assumptions most important in the interest of a theory and practice of transformative feminist, democratic struggles.[5]

Feminism's relationship with postmodernism has been fruitful but problematic (E. Kaplan 1-6). Postmodernism shares a number of assumptions with various feminist theories and practices. For example, both discourses view reason as plural and partial, define subjectivity as multilayered and contradictory, and posit contingency and difference against various forms of essentialism.

At the same time, postmodern feminism has criticized and extended a number of assumptions central to postmodernism. First, it has asserted the primacy of social criticism, and in doing so has redefined the significance of the postmodern challenge to founding discourses and universal principles in terms that prioritize political struggles over epistemological engagements. Donna Haraway puts it well in her comment that "the issue is ethics and politics perhaps more than epistemology" (579). Second, postmodern feminism has refused to accept the postmodern view of totality as a wholesale rejection of all forms of totality or metanarratives. Third, it has rejected the postmodern emphasis on erasing human agency by decentering the subject; in related fashion, it has resisted defining language as the only source of meaning, and in doing so has linked power not merely to discourse but also to material practices and struggles. Fourth, it has asserted the importance of difference as part of a broader struggle for ideological and institutional change rather than emphasized the postmodern approach to difference as either an aesthetic (pastiche) or an expression of liberal pluralism (the proliferation of difference without recourse to the language of power). As it is impossible within this essay to analyze all of these issues in great detail, I will take up some of the more important tendencies implied in these positions.

Postmodern Feminism and the Primacy of the Political

> Working collectively to confront difference, to expand our awareness of sex, race, and class as interlocking systems of domination, of the ways we reinforce and perpetuate these structures, is the context in which we learn the true meaning of solidarity. It is this work that must be the foundation of feminist movement. Without it, we cannot effectively resist patriarchal domination; without it, we remain estranged and alienated from one another. Fear of painful confrontation often leads women and men active in feminist movement to avoid rigorous critical encounter, yet if we cannot engage dialectically in a committed, rigorous, humanizing manner, we cannot hope to change the world. . . . While the struggle to eradicate sexism and sexist oppression is and should be the primary thrust of feminist movement, to prepare ourselves politically for this effort we must first learn how to be in solidarity, how to struggle with one another. (hooks 25)

Hooks speaks eloquently to the issue of constructing a feminism that is self-consciously political. In solidarity with a number of feminists, she provides a much-needed corrective to the postmodern tendency to eclipse the political and ethical in favor of epistemological and aesthetic concerns. Not only does she assert that intellectual and cultural work must be driven by political questions and issues, she also performs the theoretically important task of affirming a feminist politics that attempts to understand and contest the various ways in which patriarchy is inscribed at every level of daily life. But what is different and postmodern about hooks's commentary is that she not only argues for a postmodern feminist practice that is oppositional in its appeal "to end sexism and sexist oppression" (23), she also calls into question those feminisms that reduce domination to a single cause, focus exclusively on sexual difference, and ignore women's differences as they intersect across other vectors of power, particularly with regard to race and class. What is at stake in this version of postmodern feminist politics is an attempt to reaffirm the centrality of gender struggles while simultaneously broadening the issues associated with such struggles. Similarly, there is an attempt to connect gender politics to a broader politics of solidarity. Let me be more specific about some of these issues.

Central to the feminist movement in the United States since the 1970s has been the important notion that the personal is political. This argument suggests a complex relationship between material social practices and the construction of subjectivity through the use of language. Within this context, subjectivity was analyzed as a historical and social construction, en-gendered through the historically weighted configurations of power, language, and social formations. The problematization of gender relations in this case has often been described as the most important theoretical advance made by feminists (Showalter). Postmodern feminism has extended the political significance of this issue in important ways.

First, it has strongly argued that feminist analyses cannot downplay the dialectical significance of gender relations. That is, such relations have to focus not only on the various ways in which women are inscribed in patriarchal representations and relations of power, but also on how gender relations can be used to problematize the sexual identities, differences, and commonalities of both men and women. To suggest that masculinity is an unproblematic category is to adopt an essentialist position that ultimately reinforces the power of patriarchal discourse (Showalter 1-3).

Second, feminist theorists have redefined the relationship between the personal and the political in ways that advance some important postmodern assumptions. In part, this redefinition has emerged out of a growing feminist criticism that rejects the notions that sexuality is the only axis of domination and that the study of sexuality should be limited theoretically to an exclusive focus on how women's subjectivities are constructed. For example, theorists such as Teresa de Lauretis have argued that central to feminist social criticism is the need for feminists to maintain a "tension between [the personal and the political] precisely through the understanding of identity as multiple and even self-contradictory" ("Feminist" 9). To ignore such a tension often leads to the trap of collapsing the political into the personal and limiting the sphere of politics to the language of pain, anger, and separatism. Hooks elaborates on this point by arguing that when feminists reduce the relationship between the personal and the political to the mere naming of one's pain in relation to structures of domination, they often undercut the possibilities of understanding domination's multifaceted nature and creating a politics of possibility. She writes:

> That powerful slogan, "the personal is political," addresses the connection between the self and political reality. Yet it was often interpreted as meaning that to name one's personal pain in relation to structures of domination was not just a beginning stage in the process of coming to political consciousness, to awareness, but all that was necessary. In most cases, naming one's personal pain was not sufficiently linked to overall education for critical consciousness of collective political resistance. Focussing on the personal in a framework that did not compel acknowledgement of the complexity of structures of domination could easily lead to misnaming, to the creation of yet another sophisticated level of non or distorted awareness. This often happens in a feminist context when race and/or class are not seen as factors determining the social construction of one's gendered reality and most importantly, the extent to which one will suffer exploitation and domination. (32)

In this case, the construction of gender must be seen in the context of the wider relations in which it is structured. At issue here is the need to deepen the postmodern notion of difference by radicalizing the notion of gender through a refusal to isolate it as a social category while simultaneously engaging in a politics that aims at transforming self, community, and society. Within this context, postmodern feminism offers the possibility of going beyond the language of domination, anger, and critique.

Third, postmodern feminism attempts to understand the broader workings of power by examining how it functions through means other than specific technologies of control and mastery (de Lauretis, *Technologies*). At issue here is understanding how power is constituted productively. De Lauretis develops this insight by arguing that while postmodernism provides a theoretical service in recognizing that power is "productive of knowledges, meanings, and values, it seems obvious enough that we have to make distinctions between the positive effects and the oppressive effects of such production" ("Feminist" 18). Her point is important because it suggests that power can work in the interests of a politics of possibility, that it can be used to rewrite the narratives of subordinate groups not merely in reaction to the forces of domination but in response to the construction of alternative visions and futures. The exclusive emphasis on power as oppressive always runs the risk of developing as its political equivalent a version of radical cynicism and antiutopianism. Postmodern feminism offers the possibility for redefining both a negative feminist politics (Kristeva) and a more general postmodern inclination toward a despair that dresses itself up in irony, parody, and pastiche. Linda Alcoff puts it well in arguing, "As the Left should by now have learned, you cannot mobilize a movement that is only and always against: you must have a positive alternative, a vision of a better future that can motivate people to sacrifice their time and energy toward its realization" (418-19). Central to this call for a language of possibility are the ways in which a postmodern feminism has taken up the issue of power in more expansive and productive terms, one that is attentive to the ways in which power inscribes itself through the force of reason, and constructs itself at the levels of intimate and local associations (Diamond and Quinby).

Postmodern Feminism and the Politics of Reason and Totality

Various feminist discourses have provided a theoretical context and politics for enriching postmodernism's analyses of reason and totality. Whereas postmodern theorists have stressed the historical, contingent, and cultural construction of reason, they have failed to show how reason has been constructed as part of a masculine discourse (Diamond and Quinby 194-97). Postmodern feminists have provided a powerful challenge to this position, particularly in their analyses of the ways in which reason, language, and representation have produced knowledge/power relations, legitimated in the discourse of science and objectivity, to silence, marginalize, and misrepresent women

(Jagger; Keller; Harding; Birke). Feminist theorists have also modified the postmodern discussion of reason in two other important ways. First, while recognizing that all claims to reason are partial, they have argued for the emancipatory possibilities that exist in reflective consciousness and critical reason as a basis for social criticism (Welch; de Lauretis, "Feminist"). In these terms, reason is not merely about a politics of representation structured in domination or a relativist discourse that abstracts itself from the dynamics of power and struggle; it also offers the possibility for self-representation and social reconstruction. For example, Haraway has qualified the postmodern turn toward relativism by theorizing reason within a discourse of partiality that "privileges contestation, deconstruction, passionate construction, webbed connections, and hope for transformation of systems of knowledge and ways of seeing" (585). Similarly, hooks (105-19) and others have argued that feminists who deny the power of critical reason and abstract discourse often reproduce a cultural practice that operates in the interest of patriarchy. That is, this culture serves to silence women and others by positioning them in ways that cultivate a fear of theory, which positions in turn often produce a form of powerlessness buttressed by a powerful anti-intellectualism. Second, feminists such as Jane Flax have modified postmodernism's approach to reason by arguing that reason is not the only locus of meaning:

> I cannot agree . . . that liberation, stable meaning, insight, self-understanding and justice depend above all on the "primacy of reason and intelligence." There are many ways in which such qualities may be attained—for example, political practices; economic, racial and gender equality; good childrearing; empathy; fantasy; feelings; imagination; and embodiment. On what grounds can we claim reason is privileged or primary for the self or justice? ("Reply" 202)

At issue here is the rejection not of reason but of a modernist version of reason that is totalizing, essentialist, and politically repressive. Postmodern feminism has challenged and modified the postmodern approach to totality or master narratives on similar terms. While accepting the postmodern critique of master narratives that employ a single standard and claim to embody a universal experience, postmodern feminism does not define all large or formative narratives as oppressive. At the same time, postmodern feminism recognizes the importance of grounding narratives in the contexts and specificities of people's lives, communities, and cultures, but supplements this distinctly postmodern emphasis on the contextual with an argument for metanarratives that employ forms of social criticism that are dialectical, relational, and holistic. Metanarratives play an important theoretical role in placing the particular and the specific in broader historical and relational contexts. To reject all notions of totality is to risk being trapped in particularistic theories that cannot explain how the various diverse relations that constitute larger social, political, and global systems interrelate or mutually determine and constrain one another. Postmodern feminism recognizes that we need a notion of large narratives that privileges forms of analyses in which it is possible to make visible those mediations, interrelations, and interdependencies that give shape and power to larger political and social systems. Fraser and Nicholson make very clear the importance of such narratives to social criticism:

> Effective criticism . . . requires an array of different methods and genres. It requires, at minimum, large narratives about changes in social organization and ideology, empirical and social-theoretical analyses of macrostructures and institutions, interactionist analyses of the micropolitics of everyday life, critical-hermeneutical and institutional analyses of cultural production, historically and culturally specific sociologies of gender. . . . The list could go on. (91)

Postmodern Feminism and the Politics of Difference and Agency

Feminists share a healthy skepticism about the postmodern celebration of difference. Many feminist theorists welcome the postmodern emphasis on the proliferation of local narratives, the opening up of the world to cultural and ethnic differences, and the positing of difference as a challenge to hegemonic power relations parading as universals (Flax, "Reply"; McRobbie; Nicholson; E. Kaplan; Lather). But at the same time, postmodern feminists have raised serious questions about how differences are to be understood so as to change rather than reproduce prevailing power relations. This is particularly important because difference in the postmodern sense often slips into a theoretically harmless and politically deracinated notion of pastiche. For many postmodern feminists, the issue of difference has to be interrogated around a number of concerns. These include questions about how a politics of difference can be constructed that will not simply reproduce forms of liberal individualism, or how a politics of difference can be "re-written as a refusal of the terms of radical separation" (C. Kaplan 194). Also at issue is how to develop a theory of difference that is not at odds with a politics of solidarity. Equally important is how a theory of the subject constructed in difference might sustain or negate a politics of human agency. Relatedly, there is the question of how a postmodern feminism can redefine the knowledge/power relationship in order to develop a theory of difference that is not static, one that is able to make distinctions between differences that matter and those that do not. All these questions have been addressed in a variety of feminist discourses, not all of which support postmodernism. What has increasingly emerged out of this engagement is a discourse that radically complicates and amplifies the possibilities for reconstructing difference within a radical political project and set of transformative practices.

In the most general sense, the postmodern emphasis on difference serves to dissolve all pretensions to an undifferentiated concept of truth, man, woman, and subjectivity, while at the same time refusing to reduce difference to "opposition, exclusion, and hierarchic arrangement" (Malson et al. 4). Postmodern feminism has gone a long way in framing the issue of difference in terms that give it an emancipatory grounding, that identify the "differences that make a difference" as an important political act. In what follows, I want to take up briefly the issues of difference and agency that have been developed within a postmodern feminist discourse.

Joan Wallach Scott has provided a major theoretical service in dismantling one of the crippling dichotomies in which the issue of difference has been situated. Rejecting the idea that difference and equality constitute an opposition, she argues that the opposite of equality is inequality. In this sense, the issue of equality depends on an acknowledgment of which differences promote inequality and which do not. In this case, the category of difference is central as a political construct to the notion of equality itself. The implication this has for a feminist politics of difference, according to Scott, involves two important theoretical moves:

> In histories of feminism and in feminist political strategies there needs to be at once attention to the operations of difference and an insistence on differences, but not a simple substitution of multiple for binary difference, for it is not a happy pluralism we ought to invoke. The resolution of the "difference dilemma" comes neither from ignoring nor embracing difference as it is normatively constituted. Instead it seems to me that the critical feminist position must always involve two moves: the first, systematic criticism of the operations of categorical difference, exposure of the kinds of exclusions and inclusions—the hierarchies—it constructs, and a refusal of their ultimate "truth." A refusal, however, not in the name of an equality that implies sameness or identity but rather (and this is the second move) of an equality that rests on differences—differences that confound, disrupt, and render ambiguous the meaning of any fixed binary opposition. To do anything else is to buy into the political argument that sameness is a requirement for equality, an untenable position for feminists (and historians) who know that power is constructed on, and so must be challenged from, the ground of difference. (176-77)

According to Scott, to challenge power from the ground of difference by focusing on both exclusions and inclusions is to avoid slipping into a facile and simple elaboration or romanticization of difference. In more concrete terms, E. Ann Kaplan takes up this issue in arguing that the postmodern elimination of all distinctions between high and low culture is important but erases the important differences at work in the production and exhibition of specific cultural works. By not discriminating among differences of context, production, and consumption, postmodern discourses run the risk of suppressing the differences at work in the power relations that characterize these different spheres of cultural production. For example, treating all cultural products as texts may situate them as historical and social constructions, but it is imperative that the institutional mechanisms and power relations in which different texts are produced be distinguished so that it becomes possible to understand how such texts, in part, make a difference in terms of reproducing particular meanings, social relations, and values.

A similar issue is at work regarding the postmodern notion of subjectivity. The postmodern notion that human subjectivities and bodies are constructed in the endless play of difference threatens to erase not only any possibility for human agency or choice, but also the theoretical means for understanding how the body becomes a site of power and struggle around specific differences that do matter with respect to the issues of race, class, and gender. There is little sense in many postmodern accounts of the ways in which different historical, social, and gendered representations of meaning and desire are actually mediated and taken up subjectively by real individuals. Individuals are positioned within a variety of "subject positions," but there is no sense of how they actually make choices, promote effective resistance, or mediate between themselves and others. Feminist theorists have extended the most radical principles of modernism in modifying the postmodern view of the subject. Theorists such as de Lauretis (*Alice*, "Feminist," *Technologies*) insist that the construction of female experience is not constructed outside of human intentions and choices, however limited. She argues that the agency of subjects is made possible through shifting and multiple forms of consciousness, which are constructed through available discourses and practices but are always open to interrogation through self-analysis. For de Lauretis and others, such as Alcoff, such a practice is theoretical and political. Alcoff's own attempt to construct a feminist identity-politics draws on de Lauretis's work and is insightful in its attempt to develop a theory of positionality:

> The identity of a woman is the product of her own interpretation and reconstruction of her history, as mediated through a cultural discursive context to which she has access. Therefore, the concept of positionality includes two points: First . . . the concept of woman is a relational term identifiable only with a (constantly moving) context; but second . . . the position that women find themselves in can be actively utilized (rather than transcended) as a location for the construction of meaning, a place where a meaning can be discovered (the meaning of femaleness). The concept . . . of positionality shows how women use their positional perspective as a place from which values are interpreted and constructed rather than as a locus of an already determined set of values. (434)

Feminists have also voiced concern about the postmodern tendency to portray the body as so fragmented, mobile, and boundaryless that it invites confusion over how the body is actually engendered and positioned within concrete configurations of power and forms of material oppression. The postmodern emphasis on the proliferation of ideas, discourses, and representations underplays both the different ways in which bodies are oppressed and the manner in which bodies are constructed differently through specific material relations. Feminists such as Sandra Lee Bartky have provided a postmodern reading of the politics of the body by extending Foucault's notion in *Discipline and Punish* and *The History of Sexuality* of how the growth of the modern state has been accompanied by an unprecedented attempt to discipline the body. Bartky differs from Foucault in that she employs a discriminating notion of difference by showing how gender is implicated in the production of the body as a site of domination, struggle, and resistance. For example, Bartky points to the disciplinary measures of dieting, the tyranny of fashion and the insistence on slenderness, the discourse of exercise, and other technologies of control. She also goes beyond Foucault in arguing that the body must be seen as a site of resistance and linked to a broader theory of agency.

Postmodern feminism provides a grounded politics that employs the most progressive aspects of modernism and postmodernism. In the most general sense, it reaffirms the importance of difference as part of a broader political struggle for the reconstruction of public life. It rejects all forms of essentialism but recognizes the importance of certain formative narratives. Similarly, it provides a language of power that engages the issues of inequality and struggle. In recognizing the importance of institutional structures and language in the construction of subjectivities and political life, it promotes social criticism that acknowledges the interrelationship between human agents and social structures, rather than succumbing to a social theory that lacks agents or one in which agents are simply the product of broad structural and ideological forces. Finally, postmodern feminism provides a radical social theory imbued with a language of critique and possibility. Implicit in its various discourses are new relations of parenting, work, schooling, play, citizenship, and joy. These relations link a politics of intimacy and solidarity, the concrete and the general; it is a politics that in its various forms needs to be taken up as central to the development of a critical pedagogy. That is, critical educators need to provide a sense of how the most critical elements of modernism, postmodernism, and postmodern feminism might be taken up by teachers and educators so as to create a postmodern pedagogical practice. In ending, I want to outline briefly what some of the principles are that inform such a practice.

Toward a Postmodern Pedagogy

> As long as people are people, democracy in the full sense of the word will always be no more than an ideal. One may approach it as one would a horizon, in ways that may be better or worse, but it can never be fully attained. In this sense, you, too, are merely approaching democracy. You have thousands of problems of all kinds, as other countries do. But you have

> one great advantage: You have been approaching democracy uninterrupted for more than 200 years. (Vaclav Havel, quoted in Oreskes 16)

> How on earth can these prestigious persons in Washington ramble on in their sub-intellectual way about the "end of history"? As I look forward into the twenty-first century I sometimes agonize about the times in which my grandchildren and their children will live. It is not so much the rise in population as the rise in universal material expectations of the globe's huge population that will be straining its resources to the very limits. North-South antagonisms will certainly sharpen, and religious and national fundamentalisms will become more intransigent. The struggle to bring consumer greed within moderate control, to find a level of low growth and satisfaction that is not at the expense of the disadvantaged and poor, to defend the environment and to prevent ecological disasters, to share more equitably the world's resources and to insure their renewal—all this is agenda enough for the continuation of "history" (Thompson 120).

> A striking characteristic of the totalitarian system is its peculiar coupling of human demoralization and mass depoliticizing. Consequently, battling this system requires a conscious appeal to morality and an inevitable involvement in politics. (Michnik 44)

All these quotations stress, implicitly or explicitly, the importance of politics and ethics to democracy. In the first, the newly elected president of Czechoslovakia, Vaclav Havel, reminds the American people while addressing a joint session of Congress that democracy is an ideal that is filled with possibilities but that always has to be seen as part of an ongoing struggle for freedom and human dignity. As a playwright and former political prisoner, Havel is a living embodiment of such a struggle. In the second, E. P. Thompson, the English peace activist and historian, reminds the American public that history has not ended but needs to be opened up in order to engage the many problems and possibilities that human beings will have to face in the twenty-first century. And in the third, Adam Michnik, a founder of Poland's Workers' Defense Committee and an elected member of the Polish parliament, provides an ominous insight into one of the central features of totalitarianism, whether of the Right or the Left. He points to a society that fears democratic politics while simultaneously reproducing in people a sense of massive collective despair. None of these writers is from the United States, and all of them are caught up in the struggle to recapture the Enlightenment model of freedom, agency, and democracy while at the same time attempting to deal with the conditions of a postmodern world.

All these statements serve to highlight the inability of the American public to grasp the full significance of the democraticization of Eastern Europe in terms of what it reveals about the nature of our own democracy. In Eastern Europe and elsewhere there is a strong call for the primacy of the political and the ethical as a foundation for democratic public life, whereas in the United States there is an ongoing refusal of the discourse of politics and ethics. Elected politicians from both established parties in Congress complain that American politics is about "trivialization, atomization, and paralysis." Politicians as diverse as Lee Atwater, the Republican party chairman, and Walter Mondale, the former vice president, agree that we have entered into a time in which much of the American public believes that "bull permeates everything [and that] we've got a kind of politics of irrelevance" (Oreskes 16). At the same time, a number of polls indicate that while the youth of Poland, Czechoslovakia, and the former East Germany are extending the frontiers of democracy, American youth are both poorly motivated and largely ill prepared to struggle for and keep democracy alive in the twenty-first century.

Rather than being a model of democracy, the United States has become indifferent to the need to struggle for the conditions that make democracy a substantive rather than lifeless activity. At all levels of national and daily life, the breadth and depth of democratic relations are being rolled back. We have become a society that appears to demand less rather than more of democracy. In some quarters, democracy has actually become subversive. What does this suggest for developing some guiding principles in order to rethink the purpose and meaning of education and critical pedagogy within the present crises? In what follows, I want to situate some of the work I have been developing on critical pedagogy over the last decade by placing it within a broader political context. That is, the principles that I develop below represent educational issues that must be located in a larger framework of politics. Moreover, these principles emerge out of a convergence of various tendencies within modernism, postmodernism, and postmodern feminism. What is important to note here is the refusal simply to play off these various theoretical tendencies against each other. Instead, I try to appropriate critically the most important aspects of these theoretical movements by raising the question of how they contribute to creating the conditions for deepening the possibilities for a radical pedagogy and a political project that aims at reconstructing democratic public life so as to extend the principles of freedom, justice, and equality to all spheres of society.

At stake here is the issue of retaining modernism's commitment to critical reason, agency, and the power of human beings to overcome human suffering. Modernism reminds us of the importance of constructing a discourse that is ethical, historical, and political (Giddens 151-73). At the same time, postmodernism provides a powerful challenge to all totalizing discourses, places an important emphasis on the contingent and the specific, and provides a new theoretical language for developing a politics of difference. Finally, postmodern feminism makes visible the importance of grounding our visions in a political project, redefines the relationship between the margins and the center around concrete political struggles, and offers the opportunity for a politics of voice that links rather than severs the relationship between the personal and the political as part of a broader struggle for justice and social transformation. All the principles developed below touch on these issues and recast the relationship between the pedagogical and the political as central to any social movement that attempts to effect emancipatory struggles and social transformations.

1. Education must be understood as producing not only knowledge but also political subjects. Rather than rejecting the language of politics, critical pedagogy must link public education to the imperatives of a critical democracy (Dewey; Giroux). Critical pedagogy needs to be informed by a public philosophy dedicated to returning schools to their primary task: furnishing places of critical education that serve to create a public sphere of citizens who are able to exercise power over their own lives and especially over the conditions of knowledge production and acquisition. This is a critical pedagogy defined, in part, by the attempt to create the lived experience of empowerment for the vast majority. In other words, the language of critical pedagogy needs to construct schools as democratic public spheres. In part, this means that educators need to develop a critical pedagogy in which the knowledge, habits, and skills of critical rather than simply good citizenship are taught and practiced. This means providing students with the opportunity to develop the critical capacity to challenge and transform existing social and political forms, rather than simply adapt to them. It also means providing students with the skills they will need to locate themselves in history, find their own voices, and provide the convictions and compassion necessary for exercising civic courage, taking risks, and furthering the habits, customs, and social relations that are essential to democratic public forms.

In effect, critical pedagogy needs to be grounded in a keen sense of the importance of constructing a political vision from which to develop an educational project as part of a wider discourse for revitalizing democratic public life. A critical pedagogy for democracy cannot be reduced, as some educators, politicians, and groups have argued, to forcing students to say the pledge of allegiance at the beginning of every school day or to speak and think only in the dominant English (Hirsch). A critical pedagogy for democracy does not begin with test scores but with these questions: What kinds of citizens do we hope to produce through public education in a postmodern culture? What kind of society do we want to create in the context of the present shifting cultural and ethnic borders? How can we reconcile the notions of difference and equality with the imperatives of freedom and justice?

2. Ethics must be seen as a central concern of critical pedagogy. This suggests that educators should attempt to understand more fully how different discourses offer students diverse ethical referents for structuring their relationship to the wider society. But it also suggests that educators should go beyond the postmodern notion of understanding how student experiences are shaped within different ethical discourses. Educators must also come to view ethics and politics as a relationship between the self and the other. Ethics, in this case, is not a matter of individual choice or relativism but a social discourse grounded in struggles that refuse to accept needless human suffering

and exploitation. Thus ethics is taken up as a struggle against inequality and as a discourse for expanding basic human rights. This points to a notion of ethics attentive to both the issue of abstract rights and those contexts that produce particular stories, struggles, and histories. In pedagogical terms, an ethical discourse needs to regard the relations of power, subject positions, and social practices it activates (Simon). This is an ethics of neither essentialism nor relativism. It is an ethical discourse rooted in historical struggles and attentive to the construction of social relations free of injustice. The quality of ethical discourse, in this case, is not grounded simply in difference but in the issue of how justice arises out of concrete historical circumstances (Shapiro).

3. Critical pedagogy needs to focus on the issue of difference in an ethically challenging and politically transformative way. There are at least two notions of difference at work here. First, difference can be incorporated into a critical pedagogy as part of an attempt to understand how student identities and subjectivities are constructed in multiple and contradictory ways. In this case, identity is explored through its own historicity and complex subject positions. The category of student experience should not be limited pedagogically to students exercising self-reflection, but opened up as a race-, gender-, and class-specific construct to include the diverse historical and social ways in which their experiences and identities have been constructed. Second, critical pedagogy can focus on how differences among groups develop and are sustained around both enabling and disempowering sets of relations. In this instance, difference becomes a marker for understanding how social groups are constituted in ways that are integral to the functioning of any democratic society. Examining difference in this context does not mean only charting spatial, racial, ethnic, or cultural differences, but also analyzing historical differences that manifest themselves in public struggles.

As part of their use of a language of critique, teachers can make problematic how different subjectivities are positioned within a historically specific range of ideologies and social practices that inscribe students in modes of behavior that subjugate, infantilize, and corrupt. Similarly, such a language can analyze how differences within and among social groups are constructed and sustained both within and outside schools in webs of domination, subordination, hierarchy, and exploitation. As part of their use of a language of possibility, teachers can explore creating knowledge/power relations in which multiple narratives and social practices are constructed around a politics and pedagogy of difference that offers students the opportunity to read the world differently, resist the abuse of power and privilege, and envision alternative democratic communities. Difference in this case cannot be seen as simply a politics of assertion, of simply affirming one's voice or sense of the common good; it must be developed within practices in which differences can be affirmed *and* transformed in their articulation with categories central to public life: democracy, citizenship, public spheres. In both political and pedagogical terms, the category of difference must be central to the notion of democratic community.

4. Critical pedagogy needs a language that allows for competing solidarities and political vocabularies that do not reduce the issues of power, justice, struggle, and inequality to a single script, a master narrative that suppresses the contingent, the historical, and the everyday as serious objects of study (Cherryholmes). This suggests that curriculum knowledge should not be treated as a sacred text but developed as part of an ongoing engagement with a variety of narratives and traditions that can be reread and reformulated in politically different terms. At issue here is construction of a discourse of textual authority that is power sensitive and that has developed as part of a wider analysis of the struggle over culture fought out at the levels of curricula knowledge, pedagogy, and the exercise of institutional power (Aronowitz and Giroux, "Schooling"). This is not merely an argument against a canon, but one that disavows the very category. Knowledge has to be reexamined constantly in terms of its limits and rejected as a body of information that only has to be passed down to students. As Laclau has pointed out, setting limits to the answers given by what can be judged as a valued tradition (a matter of argument also) is an important political act ("Politics" 77-78). What Laclau is suggesting is the possibility for students to appropriate the past creatively as part of a living dialogue, an affirmation of the multiplicity of narratives, and the need to judge these narratives not as timeless or monolithic discourses, but as social and historical inventions that can be refigured in the interests of creating more democratic forms of public life. This points to the possibility of creating pedagogical practices characterized by the open exchange of ideas, the proliferation of dialogue, and the material conditions for the expression of individual and social freedom.

5. Critical pedagogy needs to create new forms of knowledge through its emphasis on breaking down disciplinary boundaries and creating new spaces where knowledge can be produced. In this sense, critical pedagogy must be reclaimed as a cultural politics and a form of countermemory. This is not merely an epistemological issue, but one of power, ethics, and politics. Critical pedagogy as a cultural politics points to the necessity of inserting the struggle over the production and creation of knowledge into a broader attempt to create a public sphere of citizens who are able to exercise power over their lives and especially over the conditions of knowledge production and acquisition. As a form of countermemory, critical pedagogy starts with the everyday and the particular as a basis for learning; it reclaims the historical and the popular as part of an ongoing effort to legitimate the voices of those who have been silenced, and to inform the voices of those who have been located within monolithic and totalizing narratives. At stake here is a pedagogy that provides the knowledge, skills, and habits for students and others to read history in ways that enable them to reclaim their identities in the interest of constructing forms of life that are more democratic and more just.

This struggle deepens the pedagogical meaning of the political and the political meaning of the pedagogical. In the first instance, it raises important questions about how students and others are constructed as agents within particular histories, cultures, and social relations. Against the monolith of culture, it posits the conflicting terrain of cultures shaped within asymmetrical relations of power, grounded in diverse historical struggles. Similarly, culture has to be understood as part of the discourse of power and inequality. As a pedagogical issue, the relationship between culture and power is evident in questions such as "Whose cultures are appropriated as our own? How is marginality normalized?" (Popkewitz 77). To insert the primacy of culture as a pedagogical and political issue is to make central how schools function in the shaping of particular identities, values, and histories by producing and legitimating specific cultural narratives and resources. In the second instance, asserting the pedagogical aspects of the political raises the issue of how difference and culture can be taken up as pedagogical practices and not merely as political categories. For example, how does difference matter as a pedagogical category if educators and cultural workers have to make knowledge meaningful before it can become critical and transformative? Or what does it mean to engage the tension between being theoretically correct and being pedagogically wrong? These concerns and tensions offer the possibility for making the relationship between the political and the pedagogical mutually informing and problematic.

6. The Enlightenment notion of reason needs to be reformulated within a critical pedagogy. First, educators need to be skeptical regarding any notion of reason that purports to reveal the truth by denying its own historical construction and ideological principles. Reason is not innocent, and any viable notion of critical pedagogy cannot exercise forms of authority that emulate totalizing forms of reason that appear to be beyond criticism and dialogue. This suggests that we reject claims to objectivity in favor of partial epistemologies that recognize the historical and socially constructed nature of their own knowledge claims and methodologies. In this way, curriculum can be viewed as a cultural script that introduces students to particular forms of reason that structure specific stories and ways of life. Reason in this sense implicates and is implicated in the intersection of power, knowledge, and politics. Second, it is not enough to reject an essentialist or universalist defense of reason. Instead, the limits of reason must be extended to recognizing other ways in which people learn or take up particular subject positions. In this case, educators need to understand more fully how people learn through concrete social relations, through the ways in which the body is positioned (Grumet), through the construction of habit and intuition, and through the production and investment of desire and affect.

7. Critical pedagogy needs to regain a sense of alternatives by combining the languages of critique and possibility. Postmodern feminism exemplifies this combination in its critique of patriarchy and its search to construct new forms of identity and social relations. It is worth noting that teachers can take up this issue around a number of considerations. First, educators need to construct a language of critique that combines the issue of limits with the discourse of freedom and social responsibility. In other words, the question of freedom needs to be engaged dialectically, not only as a matter of individual rights but also as part of the discourse of social responsibility. That is,

whereas freedom remains an essential category in establishing the conditions for ethical and political rights, it must also be seen as a force to be checked if it is expressed in modes of individual and collective behavior that threaten the ecosystem or produce forms of violence and oppression against individuals and social groups. Second, critical pedagogy needs to explore in programmatic terms a language of possibility that is capable of thinking risky thoughts, engages a project of hope, and points to the horizon of the "not yet." A language of possibility does not have to dissolve into a reified form of utopianism; instead, it can develop as a precondition for nourishing the courage to imagine a different and more just world and to struggle for it. A language of moral and political possibility is more than an outmoded vestige of humanist discourse. It is central to responding not only with compassion to human beings who suffer and agonize but also with a politics and a set of pedagogical practices that can refigure and change existing narratives of domination into images and concrete instances of a future worth fighting for.

A certain cynicism characterizes the language of the Left at the present moment. Central to this mind-set is the refusal of all utopian images, all appeals of "a language of possibility." Such refusals are often made on the grounds that "utopian discourse" is a strategy employed by the Right and therefore is ideologically tainted. Or the very notion of possibility is dismissed as an impractical and therefore useless category. To my mind, this dismissiveness represents less a serious critique than a refusal to move beyond the language of exhaustion and despair. What it is essential to develop in response to this position is a discriminating notion of possibility, one that makes a distinction between "dystopian" and utopian language. In the former, the appeal to the future is grounded in a form of nostalgic romanticism, with its call for a return to a past, which more often than not serves to legitimate relations of domination and oppression. Similarly, in Constance Penley's terms a "dystopian" discourse often "limits itself to solutions that are either individualist or bound to a romanticized notion of guerrilla-like small-group resistance. The true atrophy of the utopian imagination is this: we can imagine the future but we *cannot* conceive the kind of collective political strategies necessary to change or ensure that future" (122). In contrast to the language of dystopia, a discourse of possibility rejects apocalyptic emptiness and nostalgic imperialism and sees history as open and society worth struggling for in the image of an alternative future. This is the language of the "not yet," one in which the imagination is redeemed and nourished in the effort to construct new relationships fashioned out of strategies of collective resistance based on a critical recognition of both what society is and what it might become. Paraphrasing Walter Benjamin, this is a discourse of imagination and hope that pushes history against the grain. Fraser illuminates this sentiment by emphasizing the importance of a language of possibility to the project of social change: "It allows for the possibility of a radical democratic politics in which immanent critique and transfigurative desire mingle with one another" (*Unruly Practices* 107).

8. Critical pedagogy needs to develop a theory of teachers as transformative intellectuals who occupy specifiable political and social locations. Rather than defining teachers' work through the narrow language of professionalism, a critical pedagogy needs to ascertain more carefully what the role of teachers might be as cultural workers engaged in the production of ideologies and social practices. This is not a call for teachers to become wedded to some abstract ideal that removes them from everyday life or turns them into prophets of perfection and certainty; on the contrary, it is a call for teachers to undertake social criticism not as outsiders but as public intellectuals who address the social and political issues of their neighborhoods, their nation, and the wider global world. As public and transformative intellectuals, teachers have an opportunity to make organic connections with the historical traditions that provide them and their students with a voice, history, and sense of belonging. It is a position marked by a moral courage and criticism that does not require educators to step back from society in the manner of the "objective" teacher, but to distance themselves from those power relations that subjugate, oppress, and diminish other human beings. Teachers need to take up criticism from within, to develop pedagogical practices that heighten the possibilities not only for critical consciousness but also for transformative action. In this perspective, teachers would be involved in the invention of critical discourses and democratic social relations. Critical pedagogy would represent itself as the active construction rather than the transmission of particular ways of life. More specifically, as transformative intellectuals, teachers could engage in the invention of languages so as to provide spaces for themselves and their students to rethink their experiences in terms that both name relations of oppression and offer ways in which to overcome them.

9. Central to the notion of critical pedagogy is a politics of voice that combines a postmodern notion of difference with a feminist emphasis on the primacy of the political. This politics entails taking up the relationship between the personal and the political in a way that does not collapse the political into the personal but strengthens the relationship between the two so as to engage in rather than withdraw from addressing those institutional forms and structures that contribute to forms of racism, sexism, and class exploitation. This engagement suggests some important pedagogical interventions. First, the self must be seen as a primary site of politicization. That is, the issue of how the self is constructed in multiple and complex ways must be analyzed as part of both a language of affirmation and a broader understanding of how identities are inscribed in and among various social, cultural, and historical formations. To engage issues regarding the construction of the self is to address questions of history, culture, community, language, gender, race, and class. It is to raise questions regarding what pedagogical practices will allow students to speak in dialogical contexts that affirm, interrogate, and extend their understandings of themselves and the global contexts in which they live. Such a position recognizes that students have several or multiple identities, but also affirms the importance of offering students a language that allows them

to reconstruct their moral and political energies in the service of creating a more just and equitable social order, one that undermines relations of hierarchy and domination.

Second, a politics of voice must offer pedagogical and political strategies that affirm the primacy of the social, intersubjective, and collective. To focus on voice is not meant simply to affirm the stories that students tell; it is not meant simply to glorify the possibility for narration. Such a position often degenerates into a form of narcissism, a cathartic experience that is reduced to naming anger without the benefit of theorizing in order to understand both its underlying causes and what it means to work collectively to transform the structures of domination responsible for oppressive social relations. Raising one's consciousness has increasingly become a pretext for legitimating hegemonic forms of separatism buttressed by self-serving appeals to the primacy of experience. What is often expressed in such appeals is an anti-intellectualism that retreats from any viable form of political engagement, especially one willing to address and transform diverse forms of oppression. The call simply to affirm one's voice has increasingly been reduced to a pedagogical process that is as reactionary as it is inward-looking. A more radical notion of voice should begin with what hooks calls a critical attention to theorizing experience as part of a broader politics of engagement. Referring specifically to feminist pedagogy, she argues that the discourse of confession and memory can be used to "shift the focus away from mere naming of one's experience . . . to talk about identity in relation to culture, history, politics" (110). For hooks, the telling of tales of victimization, the use of one's voice, is not enough; it is equally imperative that such experiences be the object of theoretical and critical analyses so that they can be connected to rather than severed from broader notions of solidarity, struggle, and politics.

Conclusion

In this essay I have attempted to introduce readers to some of the central assumptions that govern the discourses of modernism, postmodernism, and postmodern feminism. In doing so, I have rejected pitting these movements against each other and tried instead to see how they converge as part of a broader political project linked to the reconstruction of democratic public life. Similarly, I have attempted here to situate the issue of pedagogical practice within a wider discourse of political engagement. Pedagogy, in this case, is not defined simply as something that goes on in schools. On the contrary, it is posited as central to any political practice that takes up questions of how individuals learn, how knowledge is produced, and how subject positions are constructed. In this context, pedagogical practice refers to forms of cultural production that are inextricably historical and political. Pedagogy is, in part, a technology of power, language, and practice that produces and legitimates forms of moral and political regulation that construct and offer human beings particular views of themselves and the world. Such views are never innocent and are always implicated in the discourse and relations of ethics and power. To invoke the importance of pedagogy is to raise questions not simply about how students learn but also about how educators (in the broad sense of the term) construct the ideological and political positions from which they speak. At issue here is a discourse that both situates human beings within history and makes visible the limits of their ideologies and values. Such a position acknowledges the partiality of all discourses, so that the relationship between knowledge and power will always be open to dialogue and critical self-engagement. Pedagogy is about the intellectual, emotional, and ethical investments we make as part of our attempt to negotiate, accommodate, and transform the world in which we find ourselves. The purpose and vision that drive such a pedagogy must be based on a politics and view of authority that link teaching and learning to forms of self- and social empowerment, that argue for forms of community life that extend the principles of liberty, equality, and justice to the widest possible set of institutional and lived relations.

Pedagogy as defined within the traditions of modernism, postmodernism, and postmodern feminism offers educators an opportunity to develop a political project that embraces human interests that move beyond the particularistic politics of class, ethnicity, race, and gender. This is not a call to dismiss the postmodern emphasis on difference so much as it is an attempt to develop a radical democratic politics that stresses difference within unity. This effort means developing a public language that can transform a politics of assertion into one of democratic struggle. Central to such a politics and pedagogy is a notion of community developed around a shared conception of social justice, rights, and entitlement. Such a notion is especially necessary at a time in our history in which such concerns have been subordinated to the priorities of the market and used to legitimate the interests of the rich at the expense of the poor, the unemployed, and the homeless. A radical pedagogy and a transformative democratic politics must go hand in hand in constructing a vision in which liberalism's emphasis on individual freedom, postmodernism's concern with the particularistic, and feminism's concern with the politics of the everyday are coupled with democratic socialism's historic concern with solidarity and public life.

We live at a time in which the responsibilities of citizens transcend national borders. The old modernist notions of center and margin, home and exile, and familiar and strange are breaking apart. Geographic, cultural, and ethnic borders are giving way to shifting configurations of power, community, space, and time. Citizenship can no longer ground itself in forms of Eurocentrism and the language of colonialism. New spaces, relationships, and identities have to be created that allow us to move across borders, to engage difference and otherness as part of a discourse of justice, social engagement, and democratic struggle. Academics can no longer retreat into their classrooms or symposia as if these were the only public spheres available for engaging the power of ideas and the relations of power. Foucault's notion of the specific intellectual, who takes up struggles connected to particular issues and contexts, must be combined with

Gramsci's notion of the engaged intellectual, who connects his or her work to broader social concerns that deeply affect how people live, work, and survive.

But there is more at stake here than defining the role of the intellectual or the relationship of teaching to democratic struggle. The struggle against racism, class structures, and sexism needs to move away from being simply a language of critique, and redefine itself as part of a language of transformation and hope. This shift suggests that educators must combine with others engaged in public struggles in order to invent languages and provide spaces both in and out of schools that offer new opportunities for social movements to come together. By doing this we can rethink and reexperience democracy as a struggle over values, practices, social relations, and subject positions that enlarge the terrain of human capacities and possibilities as a basis for a compassionate social order. At issue here is the need to create a politics that contributes to the multiplication of sites of democratic struggles, sites that affirm specific struggles while recognizing the necessity to embrace broader issues that both enhance the life of the planet and extend the spirit of democracy to all societies.

Rejecting certain conservative features of modernism, the apolitical nature of some postmodern discourses, and the separatism characteristic of some versions of feminism, I have attempted in this essay to appropriate critically the most emancipatory features of these discourses in the interest of developing a postmodern feminist pedagogy. Of course, the list of principles I provide is far from complete, but it does offer the opportunity for educators to analyze how it might be possible to reconceive as pedagogical practice some of the insights that have emerged from the discourses analyzed in this essay. Far from being exhaustive, the principles offered are meant only to provide some "fleeting images" of a pedagogy that can address major issues: the importance of democracy as an ongoing struggle, the meaning of educating students to govern, and the imperative of creating pedagogical conditions in which political citizens can be educated within a politics of difference that supports rather than opposes the reconstruction of a radical democracy.

Notes

1. A version of this article was published in Giroux, *Postmodernism, Feminism, and Cultural Politics*, in 1991.
2. The debate over the periodization and meaning of modernism has a long history and is taken up quite brilliantly by Anderson. Of course, this also points to the unstable ground on which definitions of postmodernism have been developed. Representative analyses of the range of disciplines and writers who inhabit this slippery landscape known as postmodernism can be found in Foster; Huyssen; Kroker and Cook; Arac; Hebdige, *Hiding*; Hutcheon, *Politics*; Aronowitz and Giroux, *Postmodern*.
3. Dick Hebdige provides a sense of the range of meanings, contexts, and objects that can be associated with the postmodern: "the decor of a room, the design of a building, the diegesis of a film, the construction of a record, or a 'scratch' video, a TV commercial, or an arts documentary,

or the 'intertextual' relations between them, the layout of a page in a fashion magazine or critical journal, an anti-teleologial tendency within epistemology, the attack on the 'metaphysics of presence,' a general attenuation of feeling, the collective chagrin and morbid projections of a post-War generation of Baby Boomers confronting disillusioned middle age, the 'predicament' of reflexivity, a group of rhetorical tropes, a proliferation of surfaces, a new phase in commodity fetishism, a fascination for 'images,' codes and styles, a process of cultural, political or existential fragmentation and/or crisis, the 'de-centering' of the subject, an 'incredulity towards metanarratives,' the replacement of unitary power axes by a pluralism of power/discourse formations, the 'implosion,' the collapse of cultural hierarchies, the dread engendered by the threat of nuclear self-destruction, the decline of the University, the functioning and effects of the new miniaturized technologies, broad societal and economic shifts into a 'media,' 'consumer' or 'multinational' phase, a sense (depending on whom you read) of 'placelessness' or the abandonment of placelessness ('critical regionalism') or (even) a generalized substitution of spatial for temporal co-ordinates" ("Postmodernism" 78).

4. The now classic defense of modernity in the postmodern debate can be found in Habermas ("Modernity," *Discourse*). For more extensive analyses of modernity, see Berman, *Air*; Lunn; Bernstein; Frisby; Kolb; Connolly; Larsen. An interesting comparison of two very different views on modernity can be found in Berman, "Why Modernism"; and Richard.
5. A representative sample of postmodern feminist works includes Benhabib and Cornell; Diamond and Quinby; Flax, "Postmodernism"; Hutcheon, *Politics*; E. Kaplan; Morris; Nicholson.

Works Cited

Alcoff, L. "Cultural Feminism vs. Poststructuralism: The Identity Crisis in Feminist Theory." *Signs* 13.3 (1988): 405-36.

Anderson, P. "Modernity and Revolution." *New Left Review* 144 (1984): 96-113.

Appignanensi, L., and G. Bennington, eds. *Postmodernism: ICA Documents 4*. London: Institute of Contemporary Arts, 1986.

Arac, J., ed. *Postmodernism and Politics*. Minneapolis: U of Minnesota P, 1986.

Aronowitz, S. "Postmodernism and Politics." *Social Text* 18 (1987/88): 94-114.

______, and H. A. Giroux. "Schooling, Culture, and Literacy in the Age of Broken Dreams." *Harvard Educational Review* 58.2 (1988): 172-94.

______, and H. A. Giroux. *Postmodern Education: Politics, Culture, and Social Criticism*. Minneapolis: U of Minnesota P, 1991.

Barthes, R. *Critical Essays*. New York: Hill & Wang, 1972.

Bartky, S. L. "Foucault, Femininity, and the Modernization of Patriarchal Power." Diamond and Quinby. 61-86.

Baudrillard, J. "Modernity." *Canadian Journal of Political and Social Theory* 11.3 (1987): 63-72.

Benhabib, S., and D. Cornell. *Feminism as Critique*. Minneapolis: U of Minnesota P, 1987.

Berman, M. *All That Is Solid Melts into Air: The Experience of Modernity*. New York: Simon & Schuster, 1982.

______. "Why Modernism Still Matters." *Tikkun* 4.1 (1988): 11-14, 81-86.

Bernstein, R., ed. *Habermas and Modernity*. Cambridge: MIT Press, 1985.

Birke, L. *Women, Feminism, and Biology: The Feminist Challenge*. New York: Methuen, 1986.

Calinescu, M. *Five Faces of Modernity: Modernism, Avant-Garde, Decadence, Kitsch, Postmodernism*. Durham, NC: Duke UP, 1987.

Cherryholmes, C. *Power and Criticism: Poststructural Investigations in Education*. New York: Teachers College P, 1988.

Christian, B. "The Race for Theory." *Cultural Critique* 6 (1987): 51-64.

Clifford, J. *The Predicament of Culture: Twentieth Century Ethnography, Literature, and Art*. Cambridge: Harvard UP, 1988.

______, and G. Marcus, eds. *Writing Culture: The Poetics and Politics of Ethnography*. Berkeley: U of California P, 1986.

Collins, J. *Uncommon Cultures: Popular Culture and Post-Modernism*. New York: Routledge, 1989.

Connolly, W. *Political Theory and Modernity*. New York: Basil Blackwell, 1988.

Connor, S. *Postmodernist Culture: An Introduction to Theories of the Contemporary*. New York: Basil Blackwell, 1989.

Crimp, D. "On the Museum's Ruin." Foster. 43-56.

de Lauretis, T. *Alice Doesn't: Feminism, Semiotics, Cinema*. Bloomington: Indiana UP, 1984.

______. "Feminist Studies/Critical Studies: Issues, Terms, Contexts." De Lauretis, ed. *Feminist Studies/Critical Studies*. Bloomington: Indiana UP, 1986. 1-19.

______. *Technologies of Gender*. Bloomington: Indiana UP, 1987.

Derrida, J. *Of Grammatology*. Trans. G. C. Spivak. Baltimore: Johns Hopkins UP, 1976.

Dewey, J. *Democracy and Education*. New York: Macmillan, 1916.

Diamond, I., and L. Quinby. "American Feminism and the Language of Control." Diamond and Quinby, eds. *Feminism and Foucault: Reflections on Resistance*. Boston: Northeastern UP, 1988. 193-206.

Eagleton, T. "The Subject of Literature." *Cultural Critique* 2 (1985/86): 95-104.

Ebert, T. "The Romance of Patriarchy: Ideology, Subjectivity, and Postmodern Feminist Cultural Theory." *Cultural Critique* 10 (1988): 19-57.

Epstein, B. "Rethinking Social Movement Theory." *Socialist Review* 20.1 (1990): 35-65.

Flax, J. "Reply to Tress." *Signs* 14.1 (1988): 201-3.

______. "Postmodernism and Gender Relations in Feminist Theory." Malson et al. 51-73.

Foster, H. "Postmodernism: A Preface." Foster, ed. *The Anti-Aesthetic: Essays on Postmodern Culture*. Port Townsend, WA: Bay, 1983. ix-xvi.

Foucault, M. *Language, Counter-Memory, Practice: Selected Essays and Interviews*. Ed. D. Bouchard. Ithaca, NY: Cornell UP, 1977.

______. *Power and Knowledge: Selected Interviews and Other Writings*. Ed. G. Gordon. New York: Pantheon, 1977.

______. *Discipline and Punish: The Birth of the Prison*. New York: Vintage, 1979.

______. *The History of Sexuality*. Vol. I: *An Introduction*. New York: Vintage, 1980.

Fraser, N. "What Is Critical about Critical Theory? The Case of Habermas and Gender." *New German Critique* 12.2 (1985): 97-131.

______. *Unruly Practices*. Minneapolis: U of Minnesota P, 1989.

______, and L. Nicholson. "Social Criticism without Philosophy: An Encounter between Feminism and Postmodernism." Ross. 83-104.

Frisby, D. *Fragments of Modernity*. Cambridge: MIT Press, 1986.

Giddens, A. *The Consequences of Modernity*. Stanford, CA: Stanford UP, 1990.

Giroux, H. *Schooling and the Struggle for Public Life: Critical Pedagogy in the Modern Age*. Minneapolis: U of Minnesota P, 1988.

______, ed. *Postmodernism, Feminism, and Cultural Politics: Rediscovering Educational Boundaries*. Albany: State U of New York P, 1991.

______, and R. Simon, eds. *Popular Culture, Schooling, and Everyday Life*. South Hadley, MA: Bergin & Garvey, 1989.

Grossberg, L. "On Postmodernism and Articulation: An Interview with Stuart Hall." *Journal of Communication* 10.2 (1986): 45-60.

Groz, E. A., et al., eds. *Futur*fall: Excursions into Postmodernity*. Sydney: Power Institute of Fine Arts, 1986.

Grumet, M. *Bitter Milk: Women and Teaching*. Amherst: U of Massachusetts P, 1988.

Habermas, J. *Communication and the Evolution of Society*. Boston: Beacon, 1979.

______. "Modernity versus Postmodernity." *New German Critique* 8.1 (1981): 3-18.

______. "The Entwinement of Myth and Enlightenment." *New German Critique* 9.3 (1982): 13-30.

______. "Modernity—An Incomplete Project." Foster. 3-16.

______. *The Philosophical Discourse of Modernity*. Trans. F. Lawrence. Cambridge: MIT Press, 1987.

Hannam, M. "The Dream of Democracy." *Arena* 90 (1990): 109-16.

Haraway, D. "Situated Knowledges: The Science Question in Feminism and the Privilege of Partial Perspective." *Feminist Studies* 14.3 (1989): 575-99.

Harding, S. *The Science Question in Feminism*. Ithaca, NY: Cornell UP, 1986.

Hartsock, N. "Rethinking Modernism: Minority vs. Majority Theories." *Cultural Critique* 7 (1987): 187-206.

Hebdige, D. "Postmodernism and 'The Other Side.' " *Journal of Communication Inquiry* 10.2 (1986): 78-99.

______. *Hiding in the Light*. New York: Routledge, 1989.

Hicks, E. "Deterritorialization and Border Writing." Merrill. 47-58.

Hirsch, E. D., Jr. *Cultural Literacy: What Every American Needs to Know*. Boston: Houghton Mifflin, 1987.

hooks, b. *Talking Back*. Boston: South End, 1989.

Hutcheon, L. "Postmodern Problematic." Merrill. 1-10.

______. *The Politics of Postmodernism*. New York: Routledge, 1989.

Huyssen, A. *After the Great Divide*. Bloomington: Indiana UP, 1986.

Jagger, A. M. *Feminist Politics and Humanist Nature*. Totowa, NJ: Rowman & Allanheld, 1983.

Kaplan, C. "Deterritorializations: The Rewriting of Home and Exile in Western Feminist Discourse." *Cultural Critique* 6 (1987): 187-98.

Kaplan, E. A. "Introduction." Kaplan, ed. *Postmodernism and Its Discontents, Theories, Practices*. London: Verso, 1988.

Kearney, R. *The Wake of Imagination*. Minneapolis: U of Minnesota P, 1988.

Keller, E. F. *Gender and Science*. New Haven, CT: Yale UP, 1985.

Kellner, D. "Postmodernism as Social Theory: Some Challenges and Problems." *Theory, Culture and Society* 5.2/3 (1988): 239-69.

Kolb, D. *The Critique of Pure Modernity: Hegel, Heidegger, and After*. Chicago: U of Chicago P, 1986.

Kristeva, J. "Oscillation between Power and Denial." E. Marks and I. de Courtivron, eds. *New French Feminisms*. New York: Schocken, 1981. 165-67.

Kroker, A., and D. Cook. *The Postmodern Scene: Excremental Culture and Hyper-Aesthetics*. Montreal: New World Perspectives, 1986.

Lacan, J. *Speech and Language in Psychoanalysis*. Trans. A. Wilden. Baltimore: Johns Hopkins UP, 1968.

Laclau, E. "Politics and the Limits of Modernity." Ross. 63-82.

______. "Building a New Left: An Interview with Ernesto Laclau." *Strategies* 1.1 (1988): 10-28.

______, and C. Mouffe. *Hegemony and Socialist Strategy*. London: Verso, 1985.

Larsen, N. *Modernism and Hegemony: A Materialist Critique of Aesthetic Agencies*. Minneapolis: U of Minnesota P, 1990.

Lash, S., and J. Urry. *The End of Organized Capitalism*. Madison: U of Wisconsin P, 1987.

Lather, P. "Postmodernism and the Politics of Enlightenment." *Educational Foundations* 3.3 (1989): 7-28.

Lipsitz, G. *Time Passages: Collective Memory and American Popular Culture*. Minneapolis: U of Minnesota P, 1990.

Lunn, E. *Marxism and Modernism*. Berkeley: U of California P, 1982.

Lyotard, J. *The Postmodern Condition*. Minneapolis: U of Minnesota P, 1984.

Malson, M., et al. "Introduction." Malson et al., eds. *Feminist Theory in Practice and Process*. Chicago: U of Chicago P, 1989. 1-13.

McCarthy, T. "Introduction." Habermas 1987. vii-xvii.

McLaren, P., and R. Hammer. "Critical Pedagogy and the Postmodern Challenge: Toward a Critical Postmodernist Pedagogy of Liberation." *Educational Foundations* 3.3 (1989): 29-62.

McRobbie, A. "Postmodernism and Popular Culture." Appignanensi and Bennington. 54-58.

Merrill, R. "Toward Ethics/Aesthetics: A Post-Modern Position." Merrill, ed. *Ethics/Aesthetics: Post-Modern Positions*. Washington, DC: Maisonneuve, 1988.

Michnik, A. "Notes on the Revolution." *New York Times Magazine* (11 March 1990): 38-45.

Minh-ha, T. T. *Women, Native, Other: Writing Postcoloniality and Feminism*. Bloomington: Indiana UP, 1989.

Morris, M. *The Pirate's Fiancee: Feminism, Reading, Postmodernism*. London: Verso, 1988.

Mouffe, C. "Radical Democracy: Modern or Postmodern?" Ross. 31-45.

______. "Toward a Radical Democratic Citizenship." *Democratic Left* 17.2 (1989): 6-7.

Newman, C. *The Post-Modern Aura: The Age of Fiction in an Age of Inflation*. Evanston, IL: Northwestern UP, 1985.

______. "Revising Modernism, Representing Postmodernism." Appignanensi and Bennington. 32-51.

Nicholson, L. *Feminism/Postmodernism*. New York: Routledge, 1990.

Oreskes, M. "America's Politics Lose Way as Its Vision Changes World." *New York Times* (18 March 1990): 1, 16.

Owens, C. "The Discourse of Others: Feminists and Postmodernism." Foster. 57-82.

Peller, G. "Reason and the Mob: The Politics of Representation." *Tikkun* 2.3 (1987): 28-31, 92-95.

Penley, C. *The Future of an Illusion: Film, Feminism, and Psychoanalysis*. Minneapolis: U of Minnesota P, 1989.

Popkewitz, T. "Culture, Pedagogy, and Power: Issues in the Production of Values and Colonialization." *Journal of Education* 170.2 (1988): 77-90.

Poster, M. *Critical Theory and Poststructuralism*. Ithaca, NY: Cornell UP, 1989.

Richard, N. "Postmodernism and Periphery." *Third Text* 2 (1987/88): 5-12.

Rorty, R. "Habermas and Lyotard on Postmodernity." Bernstein. 161-76.

Rosaldo, R. *Culture & Truth: The Remaking of Social Analysis*. Boston: Beacon, 1989.

Ross, A., ed. *Universal Abandon? The Politics of Postmodernism*. Minneapolis: U of Minnesota P, 1988.

Roth, R. "The Colonial Experience and Its Postmodern Fate." *Salmagundi* 84 (1988): 248-65.

Ryan, K. *Politics and Culture: Working Hypotheses for a Post-Revolutionary Society*. Baltimore: Johns Hopkins UP, 1989.

Scott, J. W. *Gender and the Politics of History*. New York: Columbia UP, 1988.

Sculley, J. *Line Break: Poetry as Social Practice*. Seattle: Bay, 1988.

Shapiro, S. *Between Capitalism and Democracy*. Westport, CT: Bergin & Garvey, 1990.

Showalter, E. "Introduction: The Rise of Gender." Showalter, ed. *Speaking of Gender*. New York: Routledge, 1989. 1-13.

Simon, R. *Teaching against the Grain*. Westport, CT: Bergin & Garvey, 1992.

Spivak, G. C. *In Other Worlds: Essays in Cultural Politics*. New York: Methuen, 1987.

Thompson, E. P. "History Turns on a New Hinge." *The Nation* (29 January 1990): 117-22.

Tyler, S. *The Unspeakable: Discourse, Dialogue, and Rhetoric in the Postmodern World*. Madison: U of Wisconsin P, 1987.

Warren, M. *Nietzsche and Political Thought*. Cambridge: MIT Press, 1988.

Welch, S. D. *Communities of Resistance and Solidarity: A Feminist Theology of Liberation*. Maryknoll, NY: Orbis, 1985.

Chances of Being Kind: Rorty, Irony, and Teaching Modern Literature

Two tendencies marked Western cultural history in the late nineteenth and early twentieth centuries. First, thinkers and artists realized that, in W. B. Yeats's famous words, the center was no longer holding; the nihilism of Nietzsche, the psychoanalytic theory of Freud, and the horrors of World War I, to name only a few relevant developments of the period, led people to view religion, morality, and Enlightenment rationalism as relative and historically contingent values rather than unchanging absolutes. Second, and in response to this shift, many creative minds strove to reestablish a solid, universal intellectual footing for culture. Yeats's creation of a personal, visionary cosmology, the apotheosis of the machine in Italian futurism, and T. S. Eliot's evocation of the archetypal underpinnings of modern life, among many other modern artistic endeavors, illustrate this tendency.

These two aspects of early modern culture form the background of our understanding of contemporary thought. David Harvey, Ihab Hassan, and other critics understand the present age in Western culture as a time when thinkers and artists have abandoned the modern quest to restore lost universals and are consciously celebrating the very "anarchy" that frightened Yeats. Discussing the strong sense of contingency many contemporary intellectuals find at the heart of experience, Harvey writes: "[Postmodern thought] does not try to transcend it, counteract it, or even define the 'eternal and immutable' elements that might lie within it. Postmodernism swims, even wallows, in the fragmentary and the chaotic currents of change as if that is all there is" (44).

Richard Rorty examines the moral implications of this shift. Rather than indulging in nostalgia for a lost era in which absolute values were the accepted currency of Western moral thought, or resigning himself to await their "second coming"—as Alasdair MacIntyre does, for example, in *After Virtue*—Rorty asks how we can understand and discuss human actions and values in their absence. He maintains that theoretical forms of expression such as philosophy, theology, and sociology, as traditionally practiced, have failed to describe postmodern life adequately, because these disciplines have been unable or unwilling to give up the traditional Western predilection for interpreting the world in terms of absolute, universal principles. Rorty finds Nietzsche's stance particularly telling. Nietzsche consciously argues for the contingency of human thought, but bases his position in the idea of a will-to-power that to Rorty sounds suspiciously absolutist:

> As long as he is busy relativizing and historicizing his predecessors,

> Nietzsche is happy to redescribe them as webs of relations to historical events, social conditions, their own predecessors, and so on. . . . But at other moments, the moments when he is imagining a superman who will not be just a bundle of idiosyncratic reactions to past stimuli, but will be *pure* self-creation, pure spontaneity, he forgets all about his perspectivalism. When he starts explaining how to be wonderful and different and unlike anything that has ever existed, he talks about human selves as if they were reservoirs of something called "will to power." (106)

Rorty proposes that the most useful way to avoid this danger in responding to the cultural "anarchy" announced by modern thought is to look to modern literature. He believes that the best of modern literature—his paradigm is Marcel Proust—focuses on particular behavior as such, without seeking to "explain" it in "pure," universal terms. Such writing presents us with idiosyncratic and even repulsive characters, who, Rorty writes, "obviously share the finitude of the books in which they occur—we are not tempted to think that by adopting an attitude toward them we have adopted an attitude toward every *possible* sort of person" (107).

For Rorty modern literature serves an ethical end, not in the traditional sense, by depicting moral exemplars that illustrate a universally good (or bad) human nature, but by continually redescribing individual lives in terms that make readers aware on a case-by-case basis of the suffering caused by the ironic mismatch between people's everyday lives and the false universals they concoct or unthinkingly accept to understand those lives. According to Rorty, such ironic redescriptions fall into two broad categories. Some works—he mentions *Nineteen Eighty-Four* (1948) and *Animal Farm* (1946)—show us how social institutions either do not see or do not care how their own claims to absolute truth restrict other people. Other stories—*Lolita* (1955) and *Pale Fire* (1962) are his examples—"show how our attempts at autonomy, our private obsessions with the achievement of a certain sort of perfection, may make us oblivious to the pain and humiliation we are causing" (141).

Rorty is attracted to these types of stories because they demonstrate that what we share with people or literary characters who might at first seem totally different from us is not a common nature but a similar susceptibility to irony. For Rorty, modern irony understood in this postmodern situational sense is not a metaphysical absolute of the kind he rejects, because we cannot see each individual instance of it as a copy of some ideal and unchanging essence. He maintains instead that this irony results from two givens of twentieth-century life. We must live in a world where the generalizations invoked by cultural and political institutions (and in some cases by powerful individuals) have coercive force. We are also alive at a time when people have come to value self-consciousness, a faculty that makes us aware of the way in which each of our individual existences deviates from those generalizations, however powerful they may be.

Rorty's most compelling point is that such ironic self-consciousness can have a positive social dimension. Whereas nineteenth- and twentieth-century liberal thought based its ethical ideas on the metaphysical universals that in Rorty's view have lost their currency—"liberty," "equality," "dignity"—postmodern thought moves toward "liberal" ends by offering up descriptions of particular instances of suffering:

> Within a liberal metaphysical culture the disciplines which were charged with penetrating behind the many private appearances to the one general common reality—theology, science, philosophy—were the ones which were expected to bind human beings together, and thus to help eliminate cruelty. Within an ironist culture, by contrast, it is the disciplines which specialize in thick description of the private and idiosyncratic which are assigned this job. In particular, novels and ethnographies which sensitize one to the pain of those who do not speak our language must do the job which demonstrations of a common human nature were supposed to do. Solidarity has to be constructed out of little pieces, rather than found already waiting, in the form of an ur-language which all of us recognize when we hear it. (94)

In light of the modern insight that there is no universally true, Archimedean point that lies beyond the fray of specific, contingent human interactions, we can, in Rorty's view, still "construct solidarity" with others if we change our idea of what form such interaction takes. He maintains that in discussing and evaluating human behavior we need to speak less of the motivation for action and more of its occasions. While earlier thought attempted to explain behavior in final terms, postmodern thought seeks merely to describe particular ironic instances in terms of the real suffering they cause:

> The ironist thinks that the *only* redescriptions which serve liberal purposes are those which answer the question "what humiliates?" whereas the metaphysician . . . wants *our wish to be kind* to be bolstered by an argument, one which entails a self-redescription which . . . is something more than our shared ability to suffer humiliation. The liberal ironist just wants our *chances of being kind*, of avoiding the humiliation of others, to be expanded by redescription. She thinks that recognition of a common susceptibility to humiliation is the *only* social bond that is needed. (91)

Rorty is arguing that when faced with a real moral choice, whether we should help an infirm person across a busy street, for example, we do not have to stop and ask, "Why should I do this?" but can act instead on our immediate ability to understand the predicament of that person, who suffers in this instance because the design of city intersections and the flow of urban traffic do not take individual needs into account. In a similar way, Rorty claims that in thinking and talking about human behavior, we can also forgo the need to explain motivation in favor of an increased appreciation of the chances of understanding suffering.

An unsubtle example of the kind of irony Rorty writes about is the slogan "Arbeit Macht Frei" that the Nazis inscribed over the main gate at Auschwitz. He would contend that a work such as Elie Wiesel's *Night* (1960), which describes the life of a particular prisoner living in that environment, can make readers aware of the way in which the power to impose or at least to inscribe generalizations caused humiliation and suffering for particular individuals. To be sure, our appreciation of the disparity between the slogan's claim and the reality of Wiesel's life in Auschwitz does not "explain" the Holocaust or let us believe that it will not happen again. The story does allow, however, for the possibility that some readers can overcome—if only temporarily—the blindness to suffering that allows individuals to cause suffering for other people.

This they can do, in Rorty's view, not by interpreting the story as the account of a violation of human freedom and dignity, but by reconsidering a historical moment in human terms, as a visceral experience of how another human has suffered. Redescribing the world in this way offers a chance for kindness rather than intellectual or philosophical satisfaction. Wiesel's story, though not fiction, provides an example of the "thick description" that Rorty says can serve a moral purpose by allowing readers to make a connection with those who suffer. This consciousness in itself does not necessarily lead to the kind of political action that reduces human suffering, such as efforts to ensure that another Holocaust never occurs. Rorty's point, however, is that any such public action in which people do engage, and that some people may in fact describe by using universal ideas such as liberty, equality, and dignity, need not be understood only as the effect of a person's application of abstract universal values.

Formal Considerations

Rorty's theory raises the pedagogical questions of what it would mean to teach works of literature ironically, as occasions for kindness rather than as specific instances of universal models of human nature, and whether it is worthwhile to do so. I want to go about answering these questions in two ways, the first formal and the second practical. First, I intend to demonstrate how several works of modern literature invite and sustain the kind of interpretation Rorty proposes. Second, I intend to discuss how this approach can be of use to those of us who have the increasingly difficult job of teaching literary analysis, especially to beginning students. I have chosen to look at three "old chestnuts" of the modern canon: James Joyce's "Counterparts" (1914), Ernest Hemingway's "A Clean, Well-Lighted Place" (1933), and William Faulkner's "Dry September" (1931). I have selected these short stories first because they appear frequently in anthologies as representative modern works, and second because they feature characters who are particularly unattractive in traditional moral terms.

Farrington in "Counterparts" suffers and makes others suffer as a result of the mismatch between the everyday realities of his life as a poor Dublin clerk and his unrealistic idea of his own "perfection," which makes him think he can impose his will on the world. The narrator captures the full irony of Farrington's situation when he tells us that after a frustrating and humiliating day at his job, Farrington "felt strong enough to clear out the whole office single-handed. His body ached to do something, to rush out and revel in violence" (90). The violence in which we finally see him engage only demonstrates Farrington's lack of power: he loses at arm wrestling in a pub and beats his young son when he finally returns to his home.

Farrington is no more successful when he tries to take control of his situation by using his wits. When he cannot explain why he has not copied a necessary document on time, his employer explodes with anger and demands, "Do you think me an utter fool?" The narrator tells us that Farrington's response astounds himself no less than it does the other clerks in the office: "I don't think, sir . . . that that's a fair question to put to me" (91). This unpremeditated retort to his boss makes him a hero in the pubs after work, but his unexpected and brief moment in the limelight only confirms his isolation and powerlessness. To partake of the festivities, he must pawn his watch so he can stand his turn at buying rounds of drinks. As Farrington and his friends drift from bar to bar, he is constantly reminded that his triumph over his boss has not bestowed on him any real power or recognition: one man in the party orders expensive drinks Farrington cannot afford; a woman to whom he is attracted ignores him; a younger man defeats him at arm wrestling. His evening on the town leaves him with familiar feelings: "A very sullen-faced man stood at the corner of O'Connell Bridge waiting for the little Sandymount tram to take him home. He was full of smoldering anger and revengefulness. He felt humiliated and discontented; he did not even feel drunk; and he had only twopence in his pocket. He cursed everything" (96-97).

The narrative form that Joyce chooses for this story encourages us to see it as an occasion for kindness rather than as something we can explain in final, absolute terms. Joyce presents readers with the vivid details of a world whose background we never really understand any better than Farrington does. Joyce's description of Farrington's employer as a scrawny and overbearing man suggests that human arrogance might lie at the heart of Farrington's suffering at work. His emphasis on the men's need to release their pent-up tensions through drinking might be read as offering escapism through alcohol as an explanation of Farrington's conduct. In having Farrington return home to find his wife in church, Joyce may be proposing the destructive influence of institutional religion as the cause of Farrington's domestic problems.

Joyce upsets all these possible generalizations, however, by leaving his plot open and choosing a narrative form that focuses on a slice of Dublin life in all its tawdriness rather than on a detailed consideration of the formation or even the rise and fall of an individual Dubliner. Even when we consider the story in the context of *Dubliners*, it still is not clear how we are to move from an appreciation of the details of Farrington's life to passing moral judgment on them. Joyce does not directly manipulate our interpretation of the life he describes, in the manner of Honoré de Balzac and Charles Dickens, but he controls us in a different way by refusing to make our efforts to interpret Farrington too easy or too public. The ironic achievement of "Counterparts" and its characteristic modernism lie in Joyce's refusal to try to convince us explicitly—or even to let us explain—whether Farrington is right or wrong in any absolute sense. We can of course pass judgment about Farrington and his story, but we must import the terms of that assessment into our deliberations, because Joyce does not present or even imply them in the story itself. He structures the work more as an occasion for compassion than as an immediate means of analysis and explanation; finally all we can say is that Farrington's brute force causes suffering for others and for himself.

We find this same pattern in Hemingway's "A Clean, Well-Lighted Place." The old waiter, by espousing nihilism, highlights the disparity between his own emotions and intentions and the general terms with which he understands them. The narrator makes the waiter's philosophy quite clear: "What did he fear? It was not fear or dread. It was a nothing that he knew too well. It was all a nothing and a man was nothing too. It was only that and light was all it needed and a certain cleanness and order. Some lived in it and never felt it but he knew it all was nada y pues nada y nada y pues nada" (382-83). This outlook denies that there is meaning or function for any form of social interaction, such as church, marriage, and family, that might unite the older waiter to others and give him purpose. He gently rebukes his younger coworker for his unshaken faith in at least one of these institutions:

> "And you? You have no fear of going home before your usual hour?"
> "Are you trying to insult me?"
> "No, hombre, only to make a joke." (382)

The older waiter's "joke" is that the younger waiter's unquestioning confidence in his wife might be misplaced. Earlier he had pointed out to the younger man that an old deaf patron in the café who had previously attempted suicide "had a wife once too" (381).

The narrator also tells us that the old waiter empathizes, at a distance, with the suicidal deaf patron, who the waiter senses must have the same feelings of nothingness and purposelessness that he does. The old waiter suffers because the only way he can articulate this feeling of solidarity is in the unwittingly ironic terms of a generalization—nihilism—that undermines it. In this sense the situation of the waiter, who has concluded he can only sit helplessly by and contemplate the café patron's suicide at a distance, is more frightening than the condition of the patron who has attempted to take his own life.

Hemingway's choice of an open, unresolved plot leads his reader, like Joyce's, to experience a slice of modern existence that is frustrating and immobilizing and that, finally, Hemingway tries to put beyond discussion. The old man's position is best summed up in his parody of the Lord's Prayer ("Our nada who art in nada, nada be thy name" [383]), but these words are of little use to readers in evaluating the waiter's life, since they undercut any claims to universality their religious formula might seem to be making. It is hard to say something about *nada*; the story's readers are left to their own devices, and end up not unlike the story's protagonist: isolated, able to feel empathy, and engulfed in a sense of powerlessness. We can evaluate nihilism, but not on any terms provided by the story itself. All we can learn from the actual work is that any generalization we adopt to explain the waiter's beliefs might be as limiting as the one he uses as the basis of his interaction with the people around him. As in the Joyce story, we are called on to witness suffering rather than to explain or "resolve" it in any final or absolute terms.

Faulkner's "Dry September" offers the most extreme example of this seepage of a character's ironic situation into the story's narrative form. Minnie Cooper is an unmarried 40-year-old woman who suffers because her experience is at odds with the social vocabulary that her world provides for her to understand that experience. In the small Mississippi town where the story is set, social life centers on marriage and family, and Minnie has no way to establish her identity except by shopping for new dresses and acting as a kind of older "cousin" to the teenage daughters of her former school friends. Minnie differs from the other two protagonists considered here, however, in that her race gives her a modicum of power. She responds to her situation by using that power to gain some visibility. She charges that a black man in the town, Will Mayes, either attacked her or insulted her; Faulkner purposely leaves the details unclear.

The notoriety this incident brings to Minnie takes a heavy toll on her. In a movie theater where a friend has brought her several nights after her accusation of Mayes, the presence of young couples on dates causes Minnie to be overcome by a sudden attack of laughter, and she must be escorted home. Whether she suffers a nervous breakdown Faulkner leaves us to infer; the incident merely makes it clear that she gains no victory over irony through her accusation of Mayes.

The sections of the story presenting Minnie's stream of consciousness are interspersed with sections giving the reaction of several townspeople to the rumor of the attack. The men's hatred and violence, which we see extend also to their interactions with their wives, are ultimately no more successful than Minnie's accusation. The men act, attempt to assert themselves, and even kill Mayes, but their power gives them no more satisfaction than Minnie's affords her.

As readers, we do not gain this satisfaction either. The story's use of stream-of-consciousness narration from several perspectives, none of them particularly reliable, keeps us from knowing any hard facts about the events. Faulkner's narrator almost taunts us with our lack of certainty in the first paragraph of the work, which associates the limited perspective of the characters with the dry, hot weather the town is experiencing:

> Through the bloody September twilight, aftermath of sixty-two rainless days, it had gone like a fire in dry grass—the rumor, the story, whatever it was. Something about Miss Minnie Cooper and a Negro. Attacked, insulted, frightened: none of them, gathered in the barber shop on that Saturday evening where the ceiling fan stirred, without freshening it, the vitiated air, sending back upon them, in recurrent surges of stale pomade and lotion, their own stale breath and odors, knew exactly what had happened. (169)

Faulkner does attempt to provide a context in which we can make some sense of this confusion. The last sentences of the story describe McLendon, who has organized the murder of Mayes, looking out his screen door into the oppressively hot September night:

> He was sweating again already, and he stooped and hunted furiously for the shirt. At last he found it and wiped his body again, and, with his body pressed against the dusty screen, he stood panting. There was no movement, no sound, not even an insect. The dark world seemed to lie stricken beneath the cold moon and the lidless stars. (183)

Faulkner imposes a sense of closure on the sordid events he describes by extending his vantage point to focus on their larger, cosmic background; the story comments on its characters' unsuccessful efforts to control their lives by placing this failure within the larger scheme of things.

This seemingly widened perspective is the story's most frustrating irony, in that it promises precisely that final, absolute way of seeing and judging the characters that "Dry September" takes great pains not to provide. In this work, as in the other two stories I have considered—and, I would say, in most of modern fiction—there is no Archimedean point of view from which we can make absolute sense of the events and the moral issues the works present; there are only limited and relative perspectives through which we can see and judge characters and actions. These stories offer us the opportunity to redescribe rather than resolve their formal and thematic irony. They let us empathize with the characters we meet without letting us feel we are necessarily superior to them.

PRACTICAL CONSIDERATIONS

Those of us who teach literature to beginning students have all at some point heard students complain, sometimes sincerely, sometimes disingenuously, and always with frustration in their voices, that all literary interpretation is "just subjective" and therefore useless. We usually respond to this situation with the idea of intrinsic criticism, the belief that the process of reading and understanding fiction is more or less self-contained and "objective." Using this approach, and looking at the context created by the story itself—its imagery, plot, characters, setting, narrative style, and so on—we can say with something like objective certainty that "A Rose for Emily," for example, is about the decline of the traditional South, the restrictive place that society accorded to women, or even the destructive emotions we often find intertwined with love, and not in any immediate way about the dangers of alcoholism, the War of 1812, or the Christian myth of the fall and redemption of humankind.

Wayne Booth makes this argument when he proposes that in interpreting and teaching literature we should concern ourselves with the kind of irony he calls "stable": "Any written or spoken work of stable irony, I have assumed, is a structure of meanings, an order which rules out some readings as entirely fallacious, shows other readings to be partially so, and confirms others as more or less adequate" (242). Booth declares himself a partisan of this approach because he is disturbed by what he sees as the alternative, the unstable irony we find in absurdist philosophy and literature that holds "that since the universe (or at least the universe of discourse) is inherently absurd, all statements are subject to ironic undermining" (240-41). For Booth, this unsettling possibility puts in jeopardy not just the Literature 101 class, but the entire business of interpretation:

> Pursued to its logical extremes, such a view would lead, I suppose, to the abandonment of all books of interpretation (or perhaps of all books), the dismissal of all classes in literature (or indeed in any subject), the cessation of all criticism, and finally to complete silence—a completely silent response to match the increasing approximations to silence in the works themselves. (244)

Booth claims that a belief in stable irony is necessary for us to be able to interpret literature, especially modern literature, at all. On the surface, this approach to irony, though a bit extreme, seems logical and defensible; after all, "A Rose for Emily" is not about the War of 1812. The challenge of modern fiction, however, at least as it is represented by the stories considered here, is that these works are structured by ironies that we cannot interpret solely on the basis of intrinsic evidence. If we want to establish our difference from Farrington, the old waiter, Minnie, and McLendon, we have to move outside the stories. If we discuss the "themes" of these stories directly, we must assess the effects of poverty, alienation, and racism on the characters and actions we encounter. More indirectly, we have to ask whether the unresolved tension between these characters' intentions to act and their failures to achieve anything through their actions gives an acceptable and accurate picture of the modern world.

Especially in introductory-level courses, nothing keeps us from begging these questions entirely and sticking to areas—such as imagery, plot, character—where we can speak with "authority" and show students how to do the same. Or we can attempt to speak with "authority" about these issues, an effort that usually causes us to embrace simplifications and well-intentioned platitudes that for lack of time, interest, or "expertise" we leave undeveloped: "In the modern world people feel alienated." "Racism is bad."

Gary Handwerk argues that if we choose to leave the plane on which stable irony as Booth defines it is at work and abandon the authority that approach affords us, we can respond to literature with another kind of authority, which arises from the recognition that the process by which we create and understand irony is not under our individual control. Like Rorty, Handwerk sees this as an "ethical" approach to irony:

> Ethical irony begins with the recognition that this state [confronting irony] necessitates an expansion of the frame of reference, given that well-balanced alternatives can remain undecidable at the level of the text or utterance. Most characteristic of ethical irony, however, is the insistence that such expansion of context can only effectively occur through the interrogation of another subject. (2)

When, as I did above, I turn to other readers for corroboration of my interpretation of "Dry September," I cannot naively presume that they are any less stymied by irony than I am. This does not mean that we cannot come to some agreement about what the story is about—on what grounds we could condemn Minnie and McLendon, in this instance. What it does mean is that our assessment can never be an absolute or permanent statement whose validity I can justify in the same way I can "prove" that the story is not about the War of 1812. We can agree only on whether I have adequately redescribed the story's irony.

This is an "ethical" realization because it involves not just the fictional characters I encounter, but also my own nature as an agent passing judgment: "The ultimate force of ethical irony is thus to undermine the integrity of the subject it seemed to imply existed. It attacks the notion of the subject as equivalent to conscious intentionality or personal self-consciousness. To be in language is instead to be located in and by the social domain" (3). That we are "located in and by the social domain" means that we do not simply depend on the world beyond us to accept or reject an interpretation we have made on our own; as language-using beings what we can mean is determined by social and linguistic convention, and not simply by our own intentions. The disparity between personal experience and social reality, between what we intend to mean and what we can mean, is as much a condition of speaking, reading, and thinking as it is a literary situation to be interpreted.

Handwerk's "ethical" approach to irony differs from Booth's more traditional way of handling it in the same way that the attitude toward language of descriptive grammarians and lexicographers differs from that of their prescriptive counterparts. The latter view the grammar book and dictionary opaquely, as absolute arbiters of disputes; the former see them more transparently, as the contingent, conventional creations of specific people with specific points of view, works subject to change and amendment, whose authority derives from the overt or tacit consent of those who appeal to them.

Handwerk's answer to the frustrated beginning student would be that all interpretations are in fact subjective, but only if we define "subjectivity" as a shared condition of our speaking, rather than as a simple assertion of individual intention. Acknowledging this common and inescapable dependency on an "outside" world to confirm our individual intentions in reading and understanding is another way of saying that all of us, authors and readers, teachers and students, are caught in a web of ironies that we cannot hope to resolve in any final sense. All we can do is find creative and moving ways to redescribe them.

In this sense even beginning students of modern literature come to the classroom as "experts," or at least with considerable experience in the irony that informs it. An ironist pedagogy would build on this base and make it the peg on which students learn to hang the "close readings" they do of the intrinsic evidence the text presents them. Seen in light of Rorty's theory, the frustration they feel in seeking a final, "objective" interpretation of ironic stories such as the ones I consider here is itself a redescription of the irony those stories try to capture.

Educational critic and theorist Parker Palmer contends that the silence and resistance we often meet in our students results not from their stupidity or lack of motivation but from the fact that in the traditional classroom (and, I would add, in the traditional way of interpreting irony) they are told to be quiet, that their experience is irrelevant to the topics under discussion:

> The academy has been dominated by an objectivist image of knowing that holds the knower at arm's length from the known so that "subjective" biases will not distort our knowledge. This image of knowing is both reflected in and conveyed by our dominant mode of teaching, which, as Dewey said, turns education into a spectator sport. Students are kept in the grandstand so they can watch the pros play the knowledge game but not interfere with its "objectivity." (12)

Rorty is suggesting that students' experience does in fact count because literature does connect to everyday life. Palmer is suggesting that the teaching of literature, like all good instruction, can draw on this connection. To paraphrase Joseph Conrad's Marlow, the classroom, also, is one of the ironic places of postmodern culture. Rorty is telling us that this realization does not necessarily lead us to "mere anarchy," but can create occasions for students to articulate that part of their experience that allows them to make common cause with both modern literature and everyone else who reads and appreciates it in the postmodern age.

Works Cited

Booth, Wayne C. *A Rhetoric of Irony*. Chicago: U of Chicago P, 1974.

Faulkner, William. "Dry September." *Collected Stories of William Faulkner*. New York: Random House, 1950. 169-83.

Handwerk, Gary J. *Irony and Ethics in Narrative from Schlegel to Lacan*. New Haven, CT: Yale UP, 1985.

Harvey, David. *The Condition of Postmodernity*. London: Basil Blackwell, 1989.

Hemingway, Ernest. "A Clean, Well-Lighted Place." *The Short Stories of Ernest Hemingway*. New York: Scribners, 1938. 379-83.

Joyce, James. "Counterparts." *Dubliners*. 1914. New York: Penguin, 1967. 86-98.

Palmer, Parker. "Good Teaching, a Matter of Living the Mystery." *Change* 22.1 (1990): 11-16.

Rorty, Richard. *Contingency, Irony, and Solidarity*. Cambridge: Cambridge UP, 1989.

THE POLITICAL RESPONSIBILITY OF THE TEACHING OF LITERATURES

The title with which I begin is not of my own choosing: except for the *s* at the end of "literatures," this was the title of a session in which I was one of the speakers at the 1989 MLA meetings[1]—meetings where, not for the first time, and no doubt not for the last, an urge within our profession to estimate (or sometimes affirm) our relation to "the political" emerged in many sessions marked by what I read as an anxiety stronger than it has been for some while. That anxiety is, by and large, a self-lacerating one: an endless registration of the guilt of bourgeois intellectuals and teachers who fear that our political will and even our liberal goodwill might not be directly exercisable within the confines of the academy; who suspect our distance from some putative "real world" where "the political" exists but where we ourselves somehow don't; who all too easily imagine the very material of our enterprises to be always already marginal to "larger issues." That set of fears and apprehensions about our role appears to have a new intensity right now, when the profession of literatures can be perceived to be under attack from within: when, that is, literature as a topic for our teaching and writing seems to be losing a good deal of its privilege; when literatures are apparently under threat of being displaced by theory, by the promotion of other cultural texts such as film and television, and by the increasingly prevalent will to cultural studies; and when the handy and compact reading lists of the various European and American literary traditions are being revised to include the cultural productions of excluded minorities. And often enough, to make matters worse, these recent influences on the profession of literatures parade openly beneath the banner of "politics," constituting an unmistakable accusation against the way things have chronically been.

So to ask now specifically about the political responsibility of the teaching of literature is in a definite way to risk rubbing salt in the wounds, or at the very least increasing the anxieties. These I'm happy to risk—partly because it can surely be no bad thing to have any of the institutions we inhabit continually on their toes in relation to basic manners, assumptions, and epistemologies; but also in part because I've long been susceptible to my own kind of distress when faced with what we might call the flight from politics in whatever discipline or activity. That flight is most often taken by way of simple disavowal or a reactive dismissal of what I take to be an obvious condition of our profession, and it might be as well to begin by reaffirming that condition.

That is, there can be no question but that to teach literatures is to engage in a political act. It is an activity that, like any other teaching, takes place in the arena of political and social relations. Evidently the function of universities, colleges, and schools within the cultures we inhabit is crucial for the production and reproduction of social relations and power, and thus is already highly politicized even before one considers the action of the state upon the processes of education. Equally, it is an activity that takes as its object of study particular discourses that are and have chronically been of considerable moment in the realms of ideology and culture. These are clearly and obviously political matters, and one could readily add to them what might be considered the micropolitical relations subsisting between students and teachers, among students, among teachers, between teachers and administrators, and so on.

The precise political character of any particular act of teaching is obviously dependent upon many circumstances and variables: the place or institution where instruction is carried out, the nature of the students (their diversity in terms of class, race, gender, aptitude, motivation), the teacher him- or herself, the topic and aim of the teaching, and so on. But in all cases, the production and transmission of what we call (in shorthand) "knowledge" always comports a relation to the *polis* and to the *oikos*—in our contexts, a relation to the political economy of an apparently ever-expanding capitalist entity, to which our knowledge is always related, in which it is always implicated, and that defines and is defined by it. In this sense I don't think that a version of Pierre Bourdieu's well-known metaphor of "cultural capital" is an outrageous one to describe what it is that we aid in transmitting: if we agree that as teachers we are agents in the circulation and accumulation of particular forms of cultural capital, we move immediately toward a definition of teaching that begins to grasp teaching in its inescapably political aspects.[2]

Bourdieu in fact has a special term for what sort of capital we deal in: "educational capital." Educational capital can be said to be constituted most broadly in the endowments that agents receive from their familial and educational cultures, and it becomes part of those agents' cultural capital. Bourdieu's observation on the nature and the form of the capital we help to circulate locates it deeply in the complexities of a social life based on exchange, surplus value, and capital accumulation. While his use of Marxist economic terms here is probably still best considered metaphorical, it is nonetheless a useful attempt to dialecticize superstructural and base elements of social life (rather than seeing one as determining the other) and has the not inconsiderable virtue of foregrounding and analyzing some of the ways in which agents take social and political advantage of their largely class-bound cultural formations.

For Bourdieu it follows that teaching—a profession that usually inhibits its practitioners from holding economic capital but that tends to encourage their continuing accumulation of cultural capital—is part of the system of reproduction[3] for a society highly dependent upon its agents' abilities to hierarchize and discriminate by way of recognizing, reading, and "appreciating" various legitimated cultural marks and symptoms. In that sense, our teaching as such is irrefutably political: it is supposed to play a maieutic role in the transmission, preservation, and exploitation of cultural capital. Additionally, we teachers in the humanities have historically held special responsibilities in relation to cultural capital. The subject matter of traditional humanities departments—the culturally sanctioned texts of always factitious and usually ethnocentric traditions—can be thought of as an especially rarefied set of markers of social distinction and cultural discrimination. As forms of cultural capital, the literatures or particular literary texts we deal in are especially highly valued and almost unproblematically legitimated. If there were any doubt on that score, it would be enough to consider how often the selection of texts in humanities curricula has at its inception the question, What do our students need to have read in order to go out into the world and be *x*?—where *x* names some kind of more privileged set of social relations to which we imagine they will then have access.

To pose the activity of "the teaching of literatures" in this way is, of course, only one way to express what I take to be the obvious: that it is scarcely intelligent to try to disavow or repress the political implication of that work. But again, the precise nature of all this is contingent, depending upon what we understand by *literatures*. *Literature* is itself an immensely variable term, as we teachers know full well. Even if we've been avoiding or ignoring the debates of the past few years concerning "the canon," we can assess its variations just by recalling the simple empirical fact that we don't take to the classroom all the literature or even all the types of literature with which we are familiar. The politics of literature is in a way a function of this, its variability as a form of cultural capital. Part of our task in relation to it, then, is to be aware of and to investigate, and to have our students investigate, this variability of the forms of cultural capital: that is (and to carry on the metaphor), to investigate the relation between cultural capital and cultural value.

It is important to remember here that literature is not value in itself, not the concretization of value. As Marx reminds us in the economic realm, value is not a concrete term, but only an abstract mediation that enables the accumulation and circulation of capital. Indeed, for Marx value is fundamentally hidden, representable only as a function of commodity differentiation in the circuits of exchange. The demystification and calculation of that process in the realm of literatures—the way in which literatures come to be instantiations of value—ought perhaps be a major focus of our attention as teachers. Thus we might become involved not so much in the teaching of literatures, but in the teaching of the function and uses of literatures within the *polis* and the *oikos* where we find ourselves, the function and uses of literatures in the establishment of largely hidden affirmations and assumptions of cultural value.

But, as we have often been assured by those of our profession who love literatures, literatures function on many levels. A literary text can be understood in several senses, then: not only as an element of cultural capital itself, but also as a more familiar kind of commodity. That is, although "literature" as a term of cultural capital is necessarily circulated and exchanged (as in classrooms), and although it might be argued that a literary text might have its own kind of use value (as, say, when the professor reads mystery novels on the beach, as it were "in private"), equally importantly it is also a commodity in the everyday sense: we buy it and sell it, and we act as specific agents in and for the literature industry. At this level literature is a commodity that plugs our teaching directly into the industrial circuits of this capitalist economy in which we live. It seems to me self-evident that the place of the literary text in those circuits is intrinsically part of its significance, its meaning. Thus a consideration in the classroom of that meaning ought perhaps to be a crucial element in the teaching of literatures. For instance, I think that it is an enlightening exercise to ask students to investigate the economic details, of, for example, Penguin's publishing and pricing of the Penguin Classics series—texts for which the publishers do not have to pay the same royalties as they would have to pay for something like Nancy Reagan's memoirs; or to ask students to research why you can no longer buy Samuel Delany's science fiction from shopping-mall bookselling chains; or to ask them to consider the economics of the kinds of library (public, college, and so on) to which they have access (or don't); or, perhaps most tellingly, to ask where they themselves get the money to buy their classroom texts. I'm suggesting here, then, that part of the "political responsibility of the teaching of literatures" is to recognize that we do not simply read and teach texts but that we are involved with what I have called elsewhere commodity-texts.

This stress on the fact that the literary texts we study and teach are in fact commodity-texts and the stress on the investigation of the relation between the literal and the metaphorical constructions of literatures as forms of capital both seem to me to be intrinsic to what it might mean to teach literatures politically. Both literatures and teaching itself are also institutions in and around which particular social and economic relations are established, upheld, and indeed enforced. It thus makes sense to me to entertain the proposal that our first pedagogical task is to allow students to think those relations; to think what are the political, social, and economic contexts of literatures; to think the place of literary teaching itself; and to think the uses of literatures or the uses to which literatures and their teaching are put.

Politics

It might well seem that so far I have merely been stating the obvious, making my argument at an unnecessarily basic level, by underlining the necessarily political nature of our acts as teachers of literatures. And a while ago I would have thought so too. But it strikes me more and more that it is necessary to keep reminding ourselves of the centrality of the political to our work. And I say that even though the program in which I myself teach (though I won't say I often or eagerly teach "literatures" in it), the Literary and Cultural Studies Program at Carnegie Mellon, is supposedly (and in the end I would argue *is*, in fact) in the vanguard of progressive English departments—where matters of the politics of curriculum and pedagogy are foregrounded in everyday practice; where theory, history, and cultural texts of all varieties are taught with as much emphasis as literature itself; and where all those texts that we could or can teach in order to combat the reification of literature and the mystification of its value may take a turn in the classroom. But—to become anecdotal for a moment or two—even there we are affected by the continual debates about the place canonical texts should hold in a newly expanded and differently oriented curriculum. We have, for instance, recently had long disputes about how many Shakespeare courses we should offer in a given year—proponents of "as many as possible" arguing that it is ungodly to teach three gender studies courses but only one Shakespeare. We've heard African-American courses dismissed by lovers of literature as "unnecessary" and as "exoticism." We've had long debates about whether or not our graduate students should be trained in a traditional literary period. We've heard fears that a potential hiree trained in media studies would be unable to teach properly in an English department. And so on.

These are just anecdotal moments, of course, and seen through my own peculiar lenses. But they suggest to me that what is at stake here in a broader frame is the question that is implicit in the name of our program and others like it: "literary and cultural studies." That is, in many of the new programs of the sort that we have established, a major pedagogical and theoretical problem is what ought to be the relation between these two terms, the literary and the cultural, where what is still implicit is the idea that literature should be preserved as an especially privileged artifact of culture. In some ways it seems to me an unnecessary and even obfuscatory question, as to think culture is surely to think literature as a part or subset of culture (whereas the converse is by no means the case—as we know from the work and attitudes of many in our profession, to think literature is not necessarily to think culture at all).

Here I am, of course, treading very close to the edges of ongoing debates about canons (or perhaps a more descriptive term for canons, systems of norms) and the concomitant debates about values—debates whose only and somewhat insufficient virtue, in my view, is to underscore the inescapably political nature of what we do. Because of my distaste for these debates and my sense that they ought to be unnecessary, I do not intend quite to enter the lists. But it has been remarkable (and, indeed, distressing) to me that among the consequences of these debates has been the increasingly legitimated role of what I'd call a liberalist mediation. Briefly, that mediation thinks to counter the multifarious challenges to the systems of norms, and the charges against systems of values, by importing the notions of cultural context and/or historical contingency—in the hope, I'm sure, of ultimately maintaining the privilege of literatures and the privilege of class-bound values.

That is, the continued championing of literatures often articulates itself by way of a supposed concern for history and context. The "thick description" of histories and contexts becomes then the preparatory gesture before literature is once again installed at the center. The current fetishization of histories and contexts thus often ends by being merely a diversion from the real fetishization of the literary. The central importance of literatures is attested to anew by the tendrils that they can be shown to throw out into other aspects of society and culture. In most cases it is entirely clear that the project is still the hermeneutics of literatures, rather than what we might call the sociology of literatures and cultures. Histories and contexts are used merely to help update the view of literary texts, in much the same way some in our profession now deploy "theory" to cast new light on the text: new critical methods (which are presumed to represent progress and growth of a sort) will illuminate the text in a new way. (The whiff of the liberal ideology of enlightenment here gets more and more oppressive as it comes to seem more and more wrongheaded.)

The new liberal mediators seem to locate themselves willingly within a very special kind of contradiction that is perhaps well exemplified in E. D. Hirsch, Jr.'s contention that the consolidation of "cultural literacy" should be considered a necessary part of the continued progress and growth of industrial society. The contradiction lies in the fact that the ideology of endless capitalist progress and growth is articulated alongside a cultural ideology that has recourse to a fixed thesaurus and that thus authorizes itself to try to establish a kind of gold standard. In other words, the terms and the objects of cultural *values* are posed as it were chiasmatically with the terms and objects of capitalism's *value*. What gets hidden by this chiasmatic maneuver is once again the whole system of social relations that underpins both values and value. Social norms, and what Marx called the juridical relations among agents, are safeguarded in the installation of both values and value, and thus one goal of a politically responsible teaching of literatures would be to historicize the conflicts and contradictions that the system of literatures suppresses between its norms/canons and its value.

This is by no means the same operation as hermeneutically historicizing the literary text. Perhaps the point can be made by suggesting that we refloat the archaic verb *to historize*[4] to dub those procedures that tend to conceal their own special cultural capital interests in the aim of prolonging them; this would leave the word *historicize* to the investigation of exactly those cultural capital interests. At any rate, one inevitable measure is the immediate and unceremonious impeachment of what can probably be accurately described as the canonical *method*—and along with it a whole series of other politically significant, politically motivated elements and effects (the notion, implied or overt, of genius; popular culture/high culture distinctions; the systematic or professionalized suppression of students' own cultures and reading experiences; and so on). The refusal of the canonical method, its overthrow, needs to be complete. It is not merely a question of opening our study to more texts, to more kinds of texts (a move that is more often than not just a supplementing or a complementing of the canon—repressive tolerance in action), but rather of installing a whole different view of texts in their relation to the activity of social life, a whole different view of the uses to which texts are, have been, or could be put, and so on—even if (especially if) that means exposing the bank and its gold standard to a kind of ruinous run. Literatures, traditionally understood, could well supply instances of texts, but within our dealings with cultures no text can remain privileged over any other, and the ideological construct of "Literature" itself cannot be taken for granted.

PEDAGOGY

If my essay has started off at too basic a level and then has moved to the anecdotal, I've risked compounding my sins by shifting to the theoretical level. Some of the impetus for the latter comments has been derived from a variety of texts by pedagogical theorists and teachers, as well as from Bourdieu's sociology of taste and, more silently, from Alain Touraine's attempts to formulate a "sociology of action."[5] Some impetus, too, has been drawn from one of Gayatri Spivak's most impressive and suggestive essays—her work on Mahasweta Devi's short story "The Breast Giver." Although that essay deals with what Spivak proposes as a very specific situation—wherein Devi's "subaltern" literary text might be negotiated in a foreign (that is, First World) pedagogical situation, and in my terms is potentially made available for assimilation into the cultural capital of the North—I've found much of what Spivak says suggestive in thinking about the necessities and potentialities of teaching literature in a politically responsible way in any context at all. That is, I think that some of the propositions Spivak makes from her "teaching strategy" (241) for this text in that context are perhaps generalizable.

In the pedagogical situation, Spivak proposes to look at Devi's text from the point of view of the (cultural) historian and the (literary) critic/teacher. These two personae "must critically 'interrupt' each other, bring each other to crisis" in their different dealings with the text (241). One effect of this interruption, or of what I like to call the "interlection" between differing subject positions of readers, is to reconstellate the text and to help make explicit its use (actual or potential) in different contexts. Without underplaying the particularity of the text and context Spivak addresses, one might easily extrapolate from what she proposes the notion that any text at all, when it is brought into a classroom, is necessarily alienated (it is drawn into foreign arguments, "other" concerns, contexts, and arenas of discourse than the ones to which it ostensibly addresses itself). This process of alienation seems to me to be what happens to literary texts in any pedagogical situation; and indeed the recognition that any text is not at home in this sense is prerequisite to "understanding" it.

This necessary interruption/interlection of the text and the drawing out of its uses is a process that is akin to a kind of *durcharbeiten*, a working-through with and by the text. The psychoanalytic reference here is partially intended to point to the way in which a pedagogy involving interlection and a working-through of interruptions would necessarily make use of a notion of resistance. That is, the dialectics of subject positions brought to the fore or deployed in the practice of reading is itself productive of resistance: resistance to the text, resistance to the codes that inform it, and resistance to the subject positions themselves. This resistance I call *agency*,[6] and think of as the productive process in any form of subjectivity whereby the "subject" interrupts and interlects interpellations and social codes.

One purpose of resistance or of encouraging interruptive/interlective resistance to the text would be to inhibit us from giving privilege to any particular voices or groups as bearers of knowledge and shapers of history; instead it would enable us to return the text to students' lives. This entails an engagement of student voice (not only its responsibility or its ability to respond, but its suggestive and agential ability) and to student experience in a way that encourages students' understanding of the discursive systems of exploitation and domination that surround them. At the same time, it seems necessary to begin or rebegin the process of privileging student writing as creative act or interaction in relation to the cultures that produce texts.

At the same time, too, it seems to me that however difficult this may be, it is the teacher's responsibility to submit to a continual reworking of his or her authority in the classroom. It is no use to put authority into play merely in the shape of the text's codes and the explanatory codes of our culture. We have, that is, to recognize that our own authority as teachers is constituted in and by those very same and other codes. These, too, need to be interlected. This is akin to the radical reshaping or reworking of texts, insofar as we must count ourselves among those texts. The authority of our explanations of the cultures we deal with is necessarily coded, and students therefore necessarily "read" us.

In another essay Spivak has proposed that "the pedagogy of the humanities [be seen] as the arena of cultural explanations that question the explanations of culture" (117). Taking this seriously would immediately present the task of unmaking and remaking our own methodologies, our own explanations (of which the canonical argument is perhaps a hegemonic one at the moment and thus should be the least sheltered from attempts to "explain" it). The classroom can become an arena of interruptions, a dialectic of interlections that will work through and work toward the perpetual consideration of the uses to which texts can be and are put.

Complicity and Critique

All this is probably (definitely) somewhat wishful and even willful at this point. It is even too early to say that the canonical method is impeached; indeed, it daily gets further impetus and support from the crisis mentality that has overtaken the official purveyors and administrators (the conservators) of educational integrity, and we are surrounded by the melancholia of those who still want to talk about the literature they love and about the importance of their feelings in relation to what they fear will become a lost object. In that context (at some moments a laughable and pathetic one, at others a gravely serious one), the would-be politically responsible teacher is forced to make a strategic choice: a choice, broadly, between some form of complicity with the politics of values and value and an unquestioned role in the transmission of cultural capital on the one hand and, on the other hand, a refusal of such complicity, an ongoing and ruthless critique of the transmission of gold-standard culture. My own choice is this latter, as excessive and even loutish as it might appear in our day. I want to be able to conclude that we have a political responsibility *not* to teach literatures wherever literatures are deployed in a way that eradicates and elides the social relations in which we live and obfuscates the norms and values that are the instruments of those social relations. Perhaps we now have a political responsibility *not* to teach literatures in any context where literatures, teaching itself, and the teaching of literatures are understood as not political—that is to say, wherever our colleagues do not promote the questioning of the very notion of the system of "Literature"; wherever students are not made aware of the unearned income they garner when literatures are perceived as a preeminent part, and not simply a subset, of cultural and political production; wherever students are encouraged to think of loving literature as something more than the melancholic perversion that it is; wherever it is in fact considered irresponsible to historicize literatures as forms of cultural capital in the way sketched out above. Political responsibility is in our hands as teachers, and I see it as part of our responsibility right now to intensify the challenges that the profession is currently feeling and to decide whether we will be teachers of literatures or not.

Notes

1. The present text is a revised and expanded version of my talk at that session. I thank John Clifford for inviting me to speak there in the distinguished company of Richard Ohmann and Jane Tompkins. I also thank the audience, especially Louis Kampf, for their provocative questions.
2. See Bourdieu and Passeron, and Bourdieu, *Distinction* and "Aristocracy."
3. Bourdieu and Passeron's analysis of schooling as reproduction of existing class distinctions and forms of social life has been seen by many as somewhat flawed and inflexible. See, for a thorough critique, Giroux. My own view is that the variety of forms and provenances of everyday cultures is not accounted for in Bourdieu, and that processes of agential and collective resistance (potential or actual) to reproduction are largely ignored. At the same time, it's obviously difficult not to take seriously the socially and ideologically reproductive insistence of institutions such as schooling.
4. Of the *OED*'s three definitions of *historize*, the third seems most apt: "To act the historian."
5. Particularly, I have been drawing on Aronowitz and Giroux, Freire and Macedo, Scholes, and Sharp. See too Giroux et al. On Bourdieu, see note 2 above. Touraine's work is perhaps best approached through *Return*. Some of my formulations above depend on his; see especially pp. 53-55 on the issue of values and norms.
6. See *Discerning* for my argument about the production of agency from multifarious interpellations and subject positions.

Works Cited

Aronowitz, Stanley, and Henry Giroux. *Education under Siege: The Conservative, Liberal, and Radical Debate over Schooling*. South Hadley, MA: Bergin & Garvey, 1985.

Bourdieu, Pierre. "The Aristocracy of Culture." *Media, Culture and Society* 2 (1980): 237+.

______. *Distinction: A Social Critique of the Judgement of Taste*. Trans. Richard Nice. Cambridge: Harvard UP, 1984.

______, and Jean-Claude Passeron. *Reproduction in Education, Society and Culture*. Trans. Richard Nice. London: Sage, 1977.

Freire, Paulo, and Donaldo Macedo. *Literacy: Reading the Word and the World*. South Hadley, MA: Bergin & Garvey, 1986.

Giroux, Henry A. *Theory and Resistance in Education: A Pedagogy for the Opposition*. South Hadley, MA: Bergin & Garvey, 1983.

______, David Shumway, Paul Smith, and James Sosnoski. "The Need for Cultural Studies: Resisting Intellectuals and Oppositional Public Spheres." *Dalhousie Review* 64.2 (1984): 472-86.

Hirsch, E. D., Jr. *Cultural Literacy: What Every American Needs to Know*. Boston: Houghton Mifflin, 1987.

Scholes, Robert. *Textual Power: Literary Theory and the Teaching of English*. New Haven, CT: Yale UP, 1985.

Sharp, Rachel. *Knowledge, Ideology, and the Politics of Schooling: Towards a Marxist Analysis of Education*. New York: Routledge, 1980.

Smith, Paul. *Discerning the Subject*. Minneapolis: U of Minnesota P, 1988.

______. "Pedagogy and the Popular-Cultural-Commodity-Text." Henry A. Giroux and Roger Simon, eds. *Popular Culture, Schooling, and Everyday Life*. South Hadley, MA: Bergin & Garvey, 1989. 31-46.

Spivak, Gayatri Chakravorty. "Explanation and Culture: Marginalia" and "A Literary Representation of the Subaltern: A Woman's Text from the Third World." *In Other Worlds: Essays in Cultural Politics*. New York: Methuen, 1987. 103-17, 240-68.

Touraine, Alain. *Return of the Actor: An Essay in Sociology*. Trans. Myrna Godzich. Minneapolis: U of Minnesota P, 1988.

Literacy and Literature: Making or Consuming Culture?

Knowing is not a neutral activity; therefore, education is never neutral. As educators, we are politicians. (notes from a conversation with Paulo Freire, 1974)

Intellect molds the concept of a nation; what gives it emotional vitality is the community of its dreams. Our brothers are those whose childhood was ruled by rhythms of the same epics and legends as ours. . . . Reading and the theatre, for unsophisticated people, are sources for imaginary lives. (Malraux 50)

This essay locates the work of Brazilian philosopher-educator[1] Paulo Freire in relation to recent developments in epistemology and sociolinguistic pedagogical theory, presents a vision of educational reform that rests on Freire's concept of literacy, and relates his work to the teaching of literature.[2]

Freire came to the attention of North American scholars in the late 1960s as the designer and teacher of courses in which illiterate adults in the Third World learn to read and write amazingly quickly (see Brown). Becoming literate, for Freire, is inseparable from locating personal and communal histories in relation to the history and social practices of the dominant culture in which the learners live (see Freire, *Pedagogy of the Oppressed*). Recognition that Freire's work has implications beyond the Third World has come slowly, at least in part because he challenges the traditional epistemological assumption that established bodies of knowledge are value neutral, apolitical, and ahistorical. Nevertheless, the past decade has seen increasing interest in his theory and method, as mainstream epistemological assumptions have been challenged by others, and as it has become clear that even—or especially—citizens of developed nations need to learn to read not just texts but the world out of which the texts arise. That is, they desperately need what Freire calls "literacy," the power to make sense of their lives in relation to cultural institutions and orthodoxies, or what Clifford Geertz has described as the power of "connecting action to its sense rather than behavior to its determinants" (178).

Freire sees literacy as a key to breaking a cultural code that was a mystery to the illiterate, economically and socially marginal adults with whom he worked, and as a means of enabling them to achieve cultural as well as linguistic competence. Texts of the culture's established literary canon represent a more sophisticated version of that same code. For Freire, the first step toward literacy is speech, which initiates the process of acculturation—a process that continues with the development of reading and writing. The full development of literacy includes reflection on the myths and structures of the culture. Thus literacy, which begins with speech, continues and becomes reflective and critical through the study of texts, including those of the literary canon. It is Freire's distinctive concept of literacy that makes his work especially relevant to the contemporary discussion about the social and political implications of "canonized" texts. This essay presents Freire's model of educational reform against the background of his distinctive understanding of literacy, and explores its special relevance to the teaching of literature and to the present debate about the canon.

Paulo Freire: Epistemological Foundation of Educational and Social Reform

In recent years two parallel discussions of education have been going on, one in the context of curricular reform and the other in the context of epistemological theory. Social and educational critics have called for the reform of higher education in the United States. Roughly speaking, critics fall into two groups—those who fault content and those who critique skills. Of those who focus their criticism primarily on content, some call for renewed adherence to the "traditional" texts of the Western canon, whereas others call for expanding the canon to include new voices or for abandoning it altogether and creating a new multicultural canon. Those critics who have seen skill development as the center of educational reform call for courses that emphasize critical thinking, analysis, and writing. Often, though certainly not always, the debate looks toward academic changes for a solution. Little is said either about the world in which the schools exist or about the theory of knowing that informs the way we have organized knowledge and conceived of learning and teaching.

While social critics have debated educational reform, scholars working in many different disciplines have challenged the empiricist epistemology that has dominated Western philosophy and science since the seventeenth century, and have articulated some "new" epistemologies.[3] Although there are important differences among them, Freire, Geertz, Thomas Kuhn, Richard Rorty, and many others have formulated accounts of knowing that differ from empiricism and share some central concepts. Rorty has identified the most telling tenet in arguing that knowledge is intersubjectively constructed rather than being a reflection of reality in the mind of the knower. We shall call these new accounts "constructionist" theories of knowledge.[4]

Freire's history and commitments as social critic, educator, and philosopher enable him to bring together the strands of social criticism and epistemological reform. At the heart of his work are his vivid insights into the role of language in structuring, creating, and sustaining social institutions, in orienting human action, and in constructing specifically human knowledge. His version of constructionist epistemology has pointed out the fundamentally teleological character of knowledge: all knowledge either reinforces existing concepts, practices, and institutions or reshapes them. An epistemological theory that enables people to understand this fact is empowering. Based on this theoretical insight, Freire has developed a pedagogical method that relies on the fact that because knowledge is a symbolic and usually linguistic construct, students can come, through structured reflection on language use, to identify the social interests and orientations represented in it. They can also begin to consider the degree to which their interests overlap with those implied by socially sanctioned patterns of discourse that dominate their cultures.

From Freire's perspective, in which different educational practices reflect different conceptions of knowledge, current debates about educational reform reveal commitments to opposing epistemologies. Every educational situation puts a theory of knowing into practice; as Freire comments in *Cultural Action for Freedom*, "All educational practice implies a theoretical stance on the educator's part" (5). Because his vision of educational reform is based on a new epistemology, it differs radically from proposals that assume the truth of the traditional post-seventeenth-century empiricist account of knowledge. Freire insists that the key to designing programs similar to his is the theory of knowledge that informs them. Thus we must grasp the differences between the new and older accounts of knowledge in order to make sense of Freire's view of education.

The single most striking difference between these two theories of knowledge may be the change in our understanding of what people do when they know something. For Freire and other constructionists, the specifically human way of relating to the world is knowing, and the most fundamental meaning of the verb *to know* is "to give meaning."

In Freire's epistemology, all specifically human experience of reality is mediated through symbols, primarily language (*Action* 6).[5] Language is the means by and through which a group creates a system of meanings, a cultural world. *World* and *reality* are not synonymous: *world* refers to those aspects of reality that have been given objective meaning by being interpreted and represented in a system of symbols. Freire's term "thought-language" indicates the human capacity to symbolize and thus to construct a world of meanings. Thought-language, though innate, "can only be realized in social settings" (Berthoff xiv). By expressing experience in linguistic symbols, people objectify it and distance themselves from it in order to make it knowable in the sense of being communicable, recognizable by themselves and others. This process construes as objectively real those aspects of reality that we have identified in relation to our interests. To crystallize experience in language is to participate in the most fundamental human act: as Freire observes in *Pedagogy of the Oppressed*, "To exist, humanly, is to *name* the world, to change it" (76).

A clear sign of the difference between constructionist and traditional epistemology has been the emergence of a new metaphor comparing knowledge to conversation rather than to vision. Geertz, among others (such as Jürgen Habermas and Rorty), has pointed out the significance of this change of metaphor: "What we are seeing[6] is not just another redrawing of the conceptual map . . . but an alteration of the principles of mapping. Something is happening to the way we think about the way we think" (166). The older metaphor implies a direct relation between the knower and the known, whereas the newer epistemology denies that knowing is "an unmediated relation to something non-human" (Rorty 5). Freire does not deny that there is a reality whose existence is independent of individual volition or activity; but for him, knowing, the human way of relating to this reality, is mediated by culturally established symbols, which, like lenses, bring certain features of reality into focus and leave others undefined.

If knowing is more like conversing than like seeing, then it is a social activity rather than a solitary one.[7] This idea must be taken both in the sense already noted—that thought-language, the distinctively human capacity for constructing meaning, can be actualized only in social settings—and in the sense that language directs attention to selected features of reality, those that are relevant to social interests. Freire does not hold that reality is created by human consciousness, a view that he calls "subjectivism"; rather, he says, by symbolizing experiences and communicating the corresponding meanings, people collectively establish knowable features of reality. Neither does he or any other constructionist espouse objectivism, the view that knowledge is a reflection of things as they are presumed to be, independent of human interpretation. Rather, "objective knowledge" is the meaning given to those features of reality that emerge in answer to the questions that we put to it, which are functions of our interests, our social and conceptual frameworks, and our technological sophistication at any given time. Thus knowing is not a two-term relation between the knower and the given but a three-term relation between people in dialogue about a knowable object. Intersubjective agreement, established in language within the system of meanings that constitutes our culture, is knowledge.

This position does not imply that all statements are equally true; what we call "truth" can still be distinguished from what we call "error" or "falsehood," just as subjective and objective features can be told apart. For example, the number of objects counted in a room by an intelligent microscopic organism would surely differ from the number that a person would count. Differences in scale and physical sensitivity lead to different constructions of reality, but once perspective and method are defined, some counts will be right and others wrong; some claims meet the predominant definition of "truth" and others do not. Meanings dismissed by some people at one time have come to be accepted after social structures have evolved, theoretical frameworks changed, or techniques of observation refined. Fantasy and opinion remain distinguishable from knowledge, which is the correlate of objective features that are recognizable by multiple subjects adopting a common perspective, discourse, and method of inquiry. Knowledge, then, is historical, changing, and partial, conditioned by past meanings but constantly transformed by new methods, concepts, and modes of observation and analysis.

The "conversation" metaphor suggests that because human behavior responds to interpretations of events, all meaning has political and social implications. To claim that knowledge is neutral and value free is to claim that we can formulate meaning that represents "facts" uncolored by any perspective, independent of their relations to any goal or theory. However, as Freire points out, the fact that thinking is always teleological means that it is always affected by assumptions about what is relevant in relation to a projected goal.

Many ways of structuring knowledge remain unexplored because no one cares to explore them. The aspects of reality that are of greatest interest to humankind are the most widely construed as "objective." Social factors inform the construction of certain bodies of knowledge rather than of others. Established bodies of knowledge reflect the pressing questions of dominant groups as well as the limits that material, social, and conceptual conditions impose on the construction of knowledge. Regardless of how or whether it is applied, all knowledge supports and reveals some group's interests and values. Those concerns are, of course, revealed in the discourses that describe human experience and tell the histories of the multiple, overlapping communities and subcommunities (such as nations, neighborhoods, families, professional circles, religions) in which we live.

Literacy and Criticism

Literacy, as Freire uses the term, is not merely the skill of matching sounds with letters, or even the ability to connect socially established meanings with words. Literacy requires an understanding of the connection between the linguistic power exercised in "naming" (that is, in giving socially sanctioned meaning) and social interests. Since meaning governs action, the definition of social reality in socially sanctioned language dictates practices that the uncritical thinker takes for granted as "natural." The literate, then, understand the purposes embedded in the language chosen to express and communicate experience and thought. Groups powerful enough to "name the world" have great influence because the language that expresses their worldviews and interests becomes the lens through which others perceive social elements; this language creates and reinforces an interpretation of reality that is generally assumed to represent "things as they are."

Freire understands literacy as fundamentally a lifelong "political project" in which men and women "constitute and reconstitute their relationship with the wider society" (Giroux 7). This understanding grew out of his work in Brazil with people who, being technically illiterate, existed outside the dominant culture and could not find themselves in its story. Usually those whose interests were represented by the dominant culture believed that illiterates had chosen or at least were responsible for their status as outsiders. Neither group attributed the illiterate peasants' situation to historical events.[8] But as Brazilian peasants learned to read and write, they also learned to analyze language in relation to interests; they discovered that the label "outsider" concealed on the one hand the historical connection between peasant conditions and work, and on the other an economy and culture designed to maintain and protect the benefits of a privileged class. As people become more literate, they become less "innocent," more aware that meanings are rooted in history and culture, and thus more able to exercise "criticism," which makes explicit the purposes that are embedded in a particular discourse and reveals the links among language use, cultural patterns, and historical interests and situations.

Freire could agree with Michel Foucault's view that the real political task in contemporary societies is to unmask the assumed neutrality of cultural institutions; Freire sees such criticism as having two objectives. One objective, as Foucault suggests, is to show how patterns of discourse hide power relations by naturalizing cultural institutions; the other, as Anne Berthoff writes, is heuristic, optimistic, and empowering:

> *Criticism* for Freire always means interpreting one's interpretations, reconsidering contexts, developing definitions, tolerating ambiguities, so that we can learn from the attempt to resolve them. And it means the most careful attention to naming the world. Any "discourse" has embedded in it at some level the history of its purposes, but Freire continually reminds us, as well, of its heuristic (generative) character: we can ask "What if . . . ?" and "How would it be if . . . ?" By thus representing the power of envisagement, language provides the model of social transformation. (xix)

Freire's usual word for this process is *conscientização*.[9] Education that fosters *conscientização* begins with reflection on the names that we have chosen to give our experiences. By comparing our own and others' interpretations of experience, we begin to discover the harmonies and incongruities between interpretations, which represent different interests in the language used to articulate experience. This process moves from recognition of the way a personal past influences language use toward an understanding of how individual lives are connected. In the context of this recognition, Freire refers to reading as a "political act." To read a text is to be able to rewrite it; that is, to construct or reconstruct its meaning as the record of the experience of a particular group that is concerned with particular problems and that moves toward specific goals within the limits of its conceptual and methodological frameworks. The right of all people to participate explicitly and consciously in constructing the common social world derives from the common human vocation of speech: reading and writing are both extensions of speaking, which is the paradigm of human knowing.[10]

Freire conceives of illiteracy, on the other hand, as not merely the inability to read and write but as all "forms of political and ideological ignorance that function as a refusal to know the limits and political consequences of one's view of the world" (Giroux 5). Illiteracy reflects an acritical attitude toward knowledge (whether established by a dominant group or by subcommunities) and toward the world; this attitude Freire describes as "alienation." Without attention to the most fundamental level of thought—the choice of linguistic symbols—thinking is "critical" only with respect to a very narrow range of abstractly logical issues, and such thinking rarely leads to an understanding of either self or society. This is why Freire refers to such thought as a form of illiteracy, or sometimes as "de-moralized thought,"[11] sanitized of all relation to the social world.

An illuminating comparison can be made between Freire's conception of illiteracy and Roland Barthes's conception of myth. Barthes defines myth as "depoliticized speech that denies its roots in history" (230). By shaping people's perceptions and behavior to conform to the status quo, myth gives such human constructions as history and culture the appearance of natural objects. By treating names as labels rather than as interpretations of reality, we are acting as if the institutions named had the quality of inevitability. Mythic speech masks the relation of intention and agency to institutions, the ways in which language and actions are related to history and interests. To the naive thinker, the world appears as what Pierre Furter terms "a massive presence to which I can but adapt" rather than "as a scope, a domain which takes shape as I act upon it" (quoted in Freire, *Pedagogy of the Oppressed* 81).

Freire and others influenced by him have argued that reflection on language use is the primary means of transforming naive thinking into critical thinking. Those who do not deliberately participate in giving meaning to their experiences of the social world allow the world to be named by others from a perspective generated by possibly alien interests. Articulating our experience of the world we share with others is a first step toward helping to shape that world.

This is why Freire equates educating for literacy, for "critical consciousness," with "cultural action for freedom" (the title of his 1971 monograph): educational reform is inseparable from social reform. This connection is precisely what is implicitly denied by epistemologies that focus on logical truth and empirical determinants of acts rather than beginning an account of knowledge with reflection on the social source of the meanings that subsequently are logically related. Educational practices and methods governed by such an epistemology encourage the learner not to participate consciously in giving meaning to the world, but rather to accept already established meaning as a given. For this reason, students often experience education as requiring memorization and social conformity rather than as encouraging analytic and creative thinking and responsible social action.

Setting aside the large and important question of the social function of educational institutions in the United States at present, there is much that individual teachers can do to encourage literacy. Different teaching styles reflect different concepts of knowledge and hence have different political implications, encourage different behaviors, and foster different conceptions of society and institutions. The way in which students relate to knowledge reflects the way in which teachers present knowledge and structure the learning process. Regardless of the teacher's conscious intention, the epistemology that informs a pedagogy encourages students to behave either as "subjects" (that is, as agents consciously participating in creating culture) or as "objects" (whose role as knowers and potential shapers of culture is sacrificed to the transmission of cultural artifacts shaped by others). Change is collaborative; the educator, no matter how aware, cannot simply lead the learners: "No one conscientizes anyone else" (Freire, *Politics* 125).

Respect for students as participants in the ongoing work of creating and shaping culture leads to genuine exchanges between teachers and students concerning the topic of study (the "text"), in which all individuals seriously examine their own interpretations and seek to understand the factors that influence various interpretations by analyzing the language that expresses these readings. Ultimately this process leads to a reconsideration of the text informed by a new awareness of how personal and cultural perspectives implicit in language motivated the initial interpretation. In this process, teachers as well as students are learners; as Freire reminds us, "We can learn a great deal from the very students we teach" (*Politics* 177).

When, through discussion and reflection, students examine their initial interpretation of a text, some surprising things happen. Their capacity to create knowledge, rather than merely to remember it, is affirmed. Hence whatever is said about the text will be in dialogue with the code established by the students; other interpretations will not be impositions, but responses in a conversation about the text. Once students think and share their thoughts, all others, including the teacher, must rethink their own previously given or accepted meanings.

This process simultaneously produces self-knowledge and knowledge of the world. By way of example, in a recent class discussing education I asked some students what they considered to be positive features of college. Most of them mentioned freedom. When pressed, they defined freedom in very different ways. One understood it as an absence of parental demands, another as cultural nonconformity, and a third as a wide variety of choices. Eventually, all could recognize the factors that conditioned their own notions of freedom and see how these notions were rooted in a personal past, but the influence of their shared culture was also evident in the general association of college with some form of freedom as a dominant cultural value. Such an effort to understand one's own history in relation to the dominant values of one's community is precisely the goal of criticism.

Educators have long seen that the traditional academic curriculum is alien to the experiences of many minority students, but have less readily acknowledged that many—perhaps most—white middle-class students likewise cannot recognize their experiences in the texts taught in school and feel themselves silenced in the classroom, both in relation to the texts and by the dominant pedagogical style of lecturing.

For students to come alive in school, schools must be committed to reexamining and practicing the values of justice, inclusivity, and respect for individual participation in public life.

Freire offers no blueprint for education. Pedagogical method is not a matter of technique, and thus it cannot be copied: he writes in *Pedagogy in Process* that "experiments cannot be transplanted; they must be reinvented" (9). The foundation on which to build educational programs similar to his is epistemology. There are pedagogical principles that follow from Freire's constructionist epistemology, as to him "every thematic investigation which deepens historical awareness is . . . really educational, while all authentic education investigates thinking" (*Pedagogy of the Oppressed* 101). By reflecting on the symbols—conceptual, historical, technical, logical, personal, and ethical—that influence the meanings we give to experience and that condition our thinking, we add a critical dimension to that thinking.

Naming transforms experience into language, thereby creating what Freire calls a "code." In order to achieve "decodification"—his word for interpreting language to discover the social interests embedded in it—education must encourage criticism. That is, it must enable students to distinguish culture from nature, to understand language as a system of signs rather than as a list of labels, and to examine texts as records of historically situated thinking.

Literacy and Literature

Perhaps one reason Freire feels the need to stress that literacy has sociopolitical importance, in addition to its technical utility, lies in the linguistic context of his thought. In Portuguese, the language Freire habitually writes in, the root for "literacy" is connected to the alphabet rather than, as in English, to letters. Thus an illiterate is *analfabeto*, illiteracy is *analfabetismo*, to teach someone to read and write is *alfabetizar*, and a literate person is *alfabetizado*. The Portuguese words, based on the first two letters of the Greek alphabet, suggest very clearly the technical side of reading and writing, whereas the Latin-derived English root also evokes broader concepts such as "letter" (epistle), "letters" (learning), and "literature."[12]

In addition, our term *literacy* has expanded its usage in expressions such as "mathematics literacy," "computer literacy," and, more recently, "cultural literacy." In general, our society recognizes that to be literate, people must not only decipher words but also make sense of texts, including not only "literature" and other written expressions of culture but also nonprint media such as photography, cinema, and video. In order to have a chance of performing these interpretive tasks, the reader must have access to a broad cultural competence. Even literacy in both the technical and the Freirean senses will not suffice. In our society, at least, the slow, four-year process of a broadly based "liberal arts" college education offers potential readers one good opportunity among others to achieve the cultural competence needed to make sense of texts and contexts as well as the opportunity to acquire the sense of personal authority needed to challenge and participate in changing dominant cultural assumptions. Thus what we might call "literature literacy" is a path to cultural empowerment as well as to personal *conscientização* or critical awareness.

The approach to reading, of course, will vary in different societies. While Freire's work is deeply marked by the colonial-anticolonial opposition and by his particular Third World experience of socioeconomic domination, in the United States the same progress from literacy to cultural analysis and empowerment is no doubt made more accessible to students through approaches involving gender and race. Students able to use any one of these approaches to understanding text and culture are likely, sooner or later, to be able to assimilate and make use of the others.

Freire's work with adult illiterates gives him less opportunity to distinguish the functions of literature than the functions of literacy. His consideration of literature is generally limited to works, particularly poems, of manifest revolutionary content. Literature of all sorts, however, readily invites the type of reflection and critical thinking that Freire advocates. Although reading literature requires far more sophistication than most students at first expect, at least they are apt to approach literature perceiving a sameness between the words and actions of the people portrayed in literature and those of the people who can be observed in life.[13]

Because, like any other culturally privileged product, literature produces and reproduces culture, it has had great pedagogical importance in the traditional American curriculum. On one level, like all canonical cultural expressions, literature helps enculturate the young with the values that, for better or worse, society deems useful. But at the same time, reading such texts is a valuable exercise in the intersubjective creation of meaning, as it is hard to be unaware that such reading is an act of interpretation on which different readers bring different backgrounds and perspectives to bear. In the literature class, it is less likely that any individual, even an authoritarian-minded teacher, will convincingly claim total access to truth than in some other disciplines, particularly in the natural and many social sciences.

Furthermore, it is evident that the literary text is not itself reality, but rather an author's interpretation of certain aspects of it, whereas the less accessible texts of, say, nuclear physics may more readily appear to meet traditional criteria for objective truth. Thus literature makes explicit the presence of a layer of interpretation between us and reality. Other disciplines appear to study the earth, society, human psychology, and the like, though they may actually examine individuals' ideas of those things; but in literature we study an undeniably human creation. Even the more traditional type of literature class includes dialogue in which individuals reveal and challenge different interpretations of an author's interpretation of reality. In literature, perhaps more than in any other discipline, it quickly becomes clear that, as Stanley Fish has said, "interpretation is the only game in town" (355).

It is no doubt the prominence of interpretation in literary criticism that has, over the past couple of decades, put that discipline, along with such affiliated fields as philosophy, at the leading edge of intellectual speculation in our society. It is also in part the vitality of literary criticism that has drawn the social sciences—with anthropology, which makes cultural differences explicit, in the lead—away from traditional scientific models toward the modes of thought and discourse of the humanities. From an older perspective, it was proverbially said that literature was the safest domain in which to practice interpretation, given that a wrong reading by the theologian, physician, or attorney can condemn someone to death or damnation. Literary critics have usually eschewed such concrete responsibilities; as Fish writes, "At the heart of the institution is the wish to deny that its activities have any consequences," and critics' "greatest fear is that [they] be found guilty of having interpreted" (355). But now, in the ten years since Fish's book appeared, the reading, interpretation, and teaching of literature have become more prominently linked not only to other fields of knowledge but also to "real life," including issues such as personal ethics, world politics, intergroup prejudice, and the interplay of literacy and power.

By serving as a model of the conversation that, according to the constructionist epistemology, creates meaning, the literature class can help the learner to become literate in the Freirean sense. Reading literature happens to be a socially acceptable exercise, one even promoted by conservative educators.[14] Yet every literary text is also potentially subversive, in that—whether consciously or not—it nourishes critical skills and reveals concrete aspects of culture that lend themselves to the practice of criticism. "Decodification," in the Freirean and deconstructive sense, reveals a text's presences and absences, its relation to a culture, and the degree to which it reproduces that culture.

As a result of this exercise, students may be expected to perceive that if they can decode the literary text that mediates between us and human experience, they can perform the same operation on any other sort of text. Thus an individual who is able to decode literature also has the preparation to do so in reading the media, political discourse, and even scientific texts. Indeed, the content of the text matters less once one has learned to recognize and make allowances for the mythical screen of language. If the literary canon is itself interpreted as a manifestation of certain traditions and power structures, its components can actually be useful as a point of reference to which we can compare sets of texts emanating from other cultural centers. As Peter McLaren writes in his review of *Literacy*:

> Works of literature cannot be detached from their social origins. What Freire and Macedo take seriously, and prescriptivists do not, is the means by which history has granted certain texts canonical status and excluded the local cultural canons of subjugated groups. In other words, history is often written by the powerful, and the literary texts most likely to be found on a list of

> prescribed works are those which rarely threaten the social and economic stability of the established order. . . . The issue . . . is not necessarily to add oral literatures, minority literatures, and other noncanonical works to the canon, but to study canonical and noncanonical works comparatively, with an eye to the historical and ideological reasons why some works are canonized and others are not and [to] the interests such works promote within power and knowledge junctures constructed in wider institutional and social contexts. (224-25, 227)

Discussion of the canon inevitably brings up the topic of "cultural literacy." Despite the current controversy over the topic, the acquisition of "cultural literacy" is something that educators of all persuasions should be able to embrace, provided that it is understood as the process of appreciating and comparing how human experience has been named by different communities. Learners of all backgrounds can profit from having access to the tradition of high culture as represented by the canon, not necessarily so that they can become or act "cultured" but so that they can understand and evaluate the canon and the culture that produced it. Learners and educators alike need to see that the canon and the resulting curriculum are culturally determined and therefore, like culture, subject to change and challenge. As Rorty points out, "To pick a core curriculum is . . . to pick a community—or, better, to decide what sort of community one would like to see come into being" (12).

What then is pernicious is not cultural literacy as such, but the presentation of a single strand of cultural texts as an ahistorical measure of all human experience in such a way as to promote what Freire calls "massification" (*Politics* 87), by which "ways of thinking become as standardized as ways of dressing and tastes in food" (88). To the restrictive brand of cultural literacy, one can apply the statement that Freire makes about condescending texts for the illiterate (characterized by sentences like "The wing is of the bird"): "By relying on words that transmit an ideology of accommodation, such literacy work reinforces the 'culture of silence' that dominates most people. This kind of literacy can never be an instrument for transforming the real world" (*Politics* 9). Or as Stanley Aronowitz and Henry Giroux write of E. D. Hirsch, Jr.'s universalized concept of literacy: "Not only is the notion of multiple literacies (the concept of cultural difference) ignored in this formulation, but those who are considered 'illiterate' bear the burden of forms of moral and social regulation that often deny their histories, voices, and sufferings" (193).

Multiple cultural literacies are necessary precisely to stimulate comparative and critical thought. Thus the literacy that representatives of the dominant culture would acquire if they became more familiar with minority culture and literature would be useful in moving our society toward true dialogue. Such dialogue and mutual understanding by groups within society would do more to achieve the national harmony desired by Hirsch than would the restriction of cultural literacy to familiarity with a single tradition linked to power and prestige.

Certainly it is not inappropriate to extend, as we have done, Freire's discussion of literacy to the area of literature. The study of literature is closely related to the study of language and composition: as readers develop skill at interpreting others' and their own use of symbols, they become more aware as writers of their relation to their potential reader. Given that there is no reading of literature without literacy, it is hard to imagine literacy, in our society, without the ability to read literature, as well as related genres such as film, advertising, or the news media.

As our society has become more diverse, the need for interpretation of texts and communication of ideas about texts has become more pressing. Material change and demographic evolutions will continue to put increasing pressure on institutions. It has become apparent that as more students enter college without sharing the dominant worldview, the university community is less likely to accept as given the value of canonical works. The ongoing diversification of faculties and student bodies has already enriched the choice of texts examined and also the conversation about texts, both canonical and noncanonical.

In conclusion, many educators—including those influenced by Freire—have seen that, distressingly, neither mass media nor public education necessarily aims at fostering literacy or criticism in the Freirean sense. We must therefore urgently ask whether our society desires critical thinkers or thinkers whose capacity for critique is narrowly focused. Courses that embody Freire's epistemology accept the risk of making explicit students' responsibility to evaluate the learning they are offered and to participate in shaping culture rather than merely in consuming it. At the heart of his pedagogical method lies "the idea that naming the world becomes a model for changing the world" (Berthoff xiv). This approach offers a way to counter the pervasive influence of myth in a mass-mediated culture, in public discourse, and in education. The question Freire poses is still *the* question for educators: Are we agents of cultural transformation or transmitters of data? In either case, intellectuals cannot escape their own responsibility: our acts are not neutral, and "as educators, we are politicians."

Notes

1. The terms *education* and *pedagogy*, derived as they are from classical roots meaning "to lead," may seem inappropriate in representing the work of an "educator" who does not believe that people can be led to knowledge, but rather that they are accompanied and empowered in the learning process. Even *teacher* implies a one-way flow of knowledge incompatible with the Freirean perspective; *to learn* is a more compatible term, as long as the "teacher" remains a learner. Freire generally uses the term "teacher-learner" to emphasize this point. Ideally, Freirean ideas are expressed as the script of a conversation recording interacting points of view, as in his recent "talking book" with Ira Shor (*A Pedagogy for Liberation: Dialogues on Transforming Education*) and "spoken book" with Antonio Faundez (*Learning to Question: A Pedagogy of*

Liberation). The classroom situation, in which individuals may question and explicate their own and others' use of language, is inherently more educational than any treatise on education.

2. The primary author of the section headed "Paulo Freire" is Linda Shaw Finlay; Nathaniel Smith is primary author of the section "Literacy and Literature." We are grateful to Lynette McGrath for reading several drafts of this essay and making a large number of very helpful suggestions, and to the *College Literature* readers for their useful insights, which we have taken into account as much as space permitted.
3. The roots of this critique lie in Continental philosophers such as Martin Heidegger, and in the analytic tradition as represented by Ludwig Wittgenstein, but the explicit formulation of a new epistemology is the product of many late-twentieth-century thinkers from various disciplines.
4. By calling these epistemologies "constructionist" we are following the lead of Lynn Hoffman, who differentiates constructionist and constructivist epistemologies. Although the two are similar, constructivist epistemological theory is rooted in a body of scientific, particularly biological, theory—developed by Humberto Maturana and Francisco Varela and used by cybernetician Heinz von Foerster and linguist Ernst von Glasersfeld—that suggests that the brain may "not process images of the world the way a camera does but, rather, computes them like music on compact discs" (Hoffman 2). In the light of these scientific developments, von Glasersfeld has drawn on the work of Vico, Kant, Wittgenstein, and Jean Piaget to develop a philosophical position that he terms "radical constructivism." By calling the theory that this essay presents "constructionism," we are identifying Freire's work with that of thinkers who "place far more emphasis on social interpretation and [the] intersubjective influence of language, family and culture, and much less on the operations of the nervous system" (Hoffman 2).
5. Freire is aware, of course, that people have unmediated experience—awareness of smells, movement, and so on—but insists that sensations that are *known* (as opposed to sensed) are mediated through language.
6. *Sic*! The old metaphor is not easy to eradicate from our speech.
7. This is not, of course, to deny that knowing has receptive and individual dimensions. Freire himself stresses the need for reflection, which is basically a solitary activity.
8. One might compare Brazil's treatment of the illiterate to our society's treatment of the homeless. The latter are literate to the extent that they attribute their condition to politicosocial causes, in opposition to a dominant current in our public life that has held that the homeless have chosen their homelessness, or at least are capable of ending it.
9. *Conscientização* can translate as "conscientization," or "learning to perceive social, political, and economic contradictions, and to take action against the oppressive elements of reality" (Freire, *Pedagogy of the Oppressed* 19n1, translator's note). It is worth noting that, in line with Freire's communitarian epistemology, this favored term of his comes from the Latin roots meaning "knowing" and "together." One aspect of literacy can be returning to the original meanings hidden within words, beneath the coverings that successive cultures have heaped upon them. As the literal meanings of the Latin *conscientia*—"joint knowledge" and "common knowledge"—coexisted with the more absolute-seeming meanings "knowledge" and "moral sense," so our word *intelligence*, ultimately derived from the Latin *intelligentia*, is underlain by the ideas of "together" (*inter-*) and gathering, collecting, or choosing (*leg-*, the root that also denotes the act of reading). Thus in adopting the position that knowledge has a communal origin, we return to the Latin origins of English words denoting knowledge and meaning.
10. Speech—which is social, historical, and intersubjective, and which validates experience as ostensibly objective—contains, on a rudimentary level, all the elements of more developed forms of constructing human knowledge.
11. Freire used this phrase in a speech given at Cornell University in December 1983.
12. In Latin, the plural *litterae* already had the broader meaning of "writing, document, epistle."
13. This apparent sameness, however, is a trap that can lead readers to see literature as an imitation of reality and prevent them from seeking out the structures in which the lives they lead and the literary narratives they read are embedded. It is therefore important for students to recognize

that all texts equally are cultural products and that literary texts have no inherent superiority to any other sort of text.

14. In our society, that is. The connection between reading and power is brought out explicitly by those societies that have restricted access to literacy for a majority of people, in extreme cases including even the written form of the dominant sacred texts. For a remarkable American observation of this phenomenon under the slaveholding subculture, see the connection between literacy and freedom made in Frederick Douglass's autobiography. In the second version, the young Douglass's master says: "If you teach that nigger . . . how to read the bible, there will be no keeping him" (146). As it turned out, Douglass did learn to read and was not "kept," entering American public discourse with a vengeance.

Works Cited

Aronowitz, Stanley, and Henry A. Giroux. "Schooling, Culture, and Literacy in the Age of Broken Dreams: A Review of Bloom and Hirsch." Rev. of Allan Bloom, *The Closing of the American Mind: How Higher Education Has Failed Democracy and Impoverished the Souls of Today's Students*, and E. D. Hirsch, Jr., *Cultural Literacy: What Every American Needs to Know*. *Harvard Educational Review* 58 (1988): 172-94.

Barthes, Roland. *Mythologies*. Paris: Seuil, 1957.

Berthoff, Anne E. "Foreword." Freire and Macedo. xi-xxiii.

Brown, Cynthia. *Literacy in 30 Hours: Paulo Freire's Process in Northeast Brazil*. Chicago: Alternate Schools Network, 1975.

Douglass, Frederick. *My Bondage and My Freedom*. 1855. New York: Arno, 1968.

Fish, Stanley. *Is There a Text in This Class? The Authority of Interpretative Communities*. Cambridge: Harvard UP, 1980.

Foucault, Michel. *The Order of Things: An Archaeology of the Human Sciences*. New York: Pantheon, 1971.

Freire, Paulo. *Cultural Action for Freedom*. Harvard Educational Review Monograph Series 1. Cambridge: Harvard Educational Review, 1971.

______. *Pedagogy in Process*. Trans. Carman St. John Hunter. New York: Seabury, 1978.

______. *Pedagogy of the Oppressed*. Trans. Myra Bergman Ramos. New York: Seabury, 1973.

______. *The Politics of Education*. Trans. Donaldo Macedo. South Hadley, MA: Bergin & Garvey, 1985.

______, and Donaldo Macedo. *Literacy: Reading the Word and the World*. South Hadley, MA: Bergin & Garvey, 1987.

Geertz, Clifford. "Blurred Genres: The Refiguration of Social Thought." *American Scholar* 49.2 (1980): 165-79.

Giroux, Henry. "Introduction." Freire and Macedo. 1-27.

Hoffman, Lynn. "Constructing Realities: An Art of Lenses." *Family Process* 29.1 (1990): 1-12.

Malraux, André. *The Temptation of the West*. New York: Vintage, 1961.

McLaren, Peter L. "Culture or Canon? Critical Pedagogy and the Politics of Literacy." Rev. of Paulo Freire and Donaldo Macedo, *Literacy: Reading the Word and the World*. *Harvard Educational Review* 58 (1988): 214-34.

Rorty, Richard M. "Hermeneutics, General Studies, and Teaching." *Synergos: Selected Papers from the Synergos Seminars* 2 (Fall 1982): 1-15.

(POST)MODERN CRITICAL THEORY AND THE ARTICULATIONS OF CRITICAL PEDAGOGIES

Since the early 1970s, there has been much talk in American universities about the need to change literary studies, especially the study and teaching of English. These discussions have been prompted by the impact of the works of those European philosophers, intellectual historians, anthropologists, and literary critics collectively known as structuralists and (post)structuralists. Initially there appeared a strong resistance in the United States to these thinkers, not only because their ideas were so unfamiliar but because they delivered them in a language unintelligible to the average American academic. Words and phrases such as *aporia, mise-en-abyme, interpellation, pleasure, dissemination, articulation*, and *the subject* were part of a language so opaque that it appeared to parody the very idea of communication.[1]

The most basic reaction was to claim that what these thinkers offered was fake and fraudulent, nothing more than old ideas couched in arcane jargon. For example, the humanists (as traditional literary scholars were called by their opponents, who themselves came to be named theorists) argued that *the subject* was merely a fancy term for *the individual* and that the theorists were trading on a false newness by applying an unfamiliar term to a well-known idea. For their part, the theorists took the humanists' equation of the subject with the individual as a sign of the latter's philosophical naïveté. Left-leaning theorists argued that resistance to the idea of "the subject" was not just philosophical simplicity, but rather part of a hidden political agenda, a result of an unwillingness to give up the notion of the free, enterprising, independent "individual." For politically active critics and English professors, in fact, the question of "the subject" eventually became the rallying point for showing how the traditional literature curriculum—like that of the humanities in general—prompts students to view themselves as free individuals, while blocking any inquiry into the status of this freedom.

To outsiders, of course, all this sounds rather insignificant; the choice between *subject* and *individual* may seem like mere quibbling. Most people see education (that is, liberal education) as a matter of turning out skillful, well-rounded, and independent-minded students. Theorists, however, argue that what is seen as the goal of liberal education—the production of the well-rounded person—is in fact the cornerstone of contemporary capitalism. In their view, capitalism works by "producing" (what Louis Althusser calls "interpellating") individuals in such a way that they think of themselves as the controllers of their actions, as the masters of their destinies, as the source of social values—in short, as "sovereign subjects." Theorists maintain that capitalism needs people who are unaware that they are constituted by existing social arrangements (for instance, by class, race, gender relations) and who instead see themselves as being the way they are "naturally."

The conflict between humanists and theorists, therefore, revolves around the understanding of the human person. Theorists argue that students who have been produced by liberal education to think of themselves as free subjects will then "freely" subject themselves to the economic needs of the capitalist system and sell themselves, as the popular phrase goes, to the highest bidder. From their point of view, far from "educating" well-rounded, free individuals, liberal education is actually constructing one-dimensional subjects to fit the economic needs of the ruling classes. In this process, English departments therefore work as the agents of the capitalist economic system: they teach students to read literary works (the classics) in terms of their moral values and with attention to their stylistic features, thus evading questions about their ideological and political functions. Accordingly, in order to change English departments, a new set of questions should be raised about such fundamental issues as "the subject" (the student as a structure of cultural codings that have political implications and consequences), reading lists (the established canon of "acceptable" and "relevant" readings), and the act of reading itself.

The debate over new modes of reading and dismantling the established canon has led ultimately to a larger battle over the curriculum. In this war, which has in the past decade or so divided English departments nationwide into traditionalists and theorists, the real institutional power has been held, more or less, by liberals who occupy the political "center"—those who, for the sake of advancing their careers, opportunistically adopt new theories to do the same old thing under new names. Although sympathizing mainly with the traditionalists and with humanist conventions, liberals have had to acquire the theorists' vocabulary, if only to update their skills and maintain their marketability. This liberal group, which constitutes the numerical majority and in a sense "runs" the universities by involvement in committee work and in the established system of awards/rewards, has grown more comfortable with theory in recent years, but is still unwilling to abandon the basic tenets of established humanities studies.

The result has been a curious rewriting of the literary studies curriculum in American universities. The curriculum has indeed "changed" in a certain sense: not only graduate students in English but even undergraduates are being taught "theory" today. Some departments and programs have even gone so far as to change their names (for example, from Department of English to Department of Textual Studies). However—and this is what disturbs many politically committed professors—in spite of this "change," everything remains the same: the basic ideology of the curriculum remains as it was, and in spite of the possibilities for change offered by "theory," English department faculties continue to recycle the old values and practices by means of new theoretical strategies.

The most visible recent examples of the use of a "new" curriculum to contain change are to be found at elite private universities such as Duke and Carnegie Mellon, which have tried to enhance their academic prestige by revamping their traditional programs. Carnegie Mellon's program is called Literary and Cultural Studies. Duke's well-publicized move to transform its literary studies programs illustrates how the curriculum can be "changed" without changing the basic structure of English studies, and at the same time, how the idea of change can be used to conduct a public-relations blitz. In 1987 Duke was the subject of a three-page feature article in the *Chronicle of Higher Education* titled "A Constellation of Recently Hired Professors Illuminate the English Department at Duke." In the article, Frank Lentricchia, one of the academic stars at Duke, pointedly acknowledges the widespread expectation that if the consequences are taken seriously, curricular change can be painful and disruptive to institutions. But he nevertheless claims with pride that Duke has miraculously escaped paying the price for significant change. Lentricchia is quoted as saying that in his department, where what is supposedly a revolution in English studies is taking place, there "ain't any [bloodshed]" (Heller 12). That is not surprising, given that upon closer inspection it becomes clear that the changes at Duke are liberal "reforms" aimed at saving the free subject of capitalism (by preserving the dominant "structures" of knowledges).

It is significant that the recently hired chairman of Duke's "changed" English department, Stanley Fish, is a leading American exponent of the theoretical approach to literary studies called "reader-response criticism." According to this theory, the reader does not merely, as in the traditional view, passively extract from the text the meaning the author has put into it or the text's own (objectively verifiable) meaning, but in fact puts into the text what he or she then regards as meaning. This theory has been enthusiastically received in the American academy because it gives new legitimacy to the traditional idea of the free, enterprising individual and endorses the popular notion of participation without ever forcing questions about the political and social consequences of what one is participating in. To "disparticipate," from this theory's point of view, is seen as being "inactive" and not as rejecting the "entrepreneurial" practices that are actually celebrated in the guise of a theory of reading. Rather than asking, What are we reading for? or What's being legitimated in our reading? Fish is merely interested in finding out what operations are involved in the act of reading and how what might look like a "foundation" for "meaning" is itself actually the effect of prior readings/meanings.

Similarly, Duke's so-called revolutionary curriculum purports to undermine the traditional notion of the canon by altering the relationship among major authors, minor authors, and authors completely beyond the pale. On this issue, the *Chronicle* emphasizes that another new member of the Duke faculty is working not on classic American authors such as Herman Melville, but on the popular fiction of Louis L'Amour, as if the "replacement" by a popular-culture author of a high-culture author means in fact the "displacement" of the idea of the canon itself. All it actually suggests is either that the canon, as the dominant pattern of literary knowledges, is being reformed to include previously excluded authors or that another (in this case, a popular-culture) canon is being formed to parallel the traditional one.

Instead of adopting Duke's expensive approach of hiring star professors, Carnegie Mellon has focused on producing a rather fully worked-out plan foregrounding the new theoretical languages and ideas. This plan's principal advocate, the former English Department chair Gary Waller, has dubbed it—with evident satisfaction—"the first post-structuralist literary curriculum" in North America (6). What this means, however, is that students at Carnegie Mellon will be "exposed to" a wide range of ideas drawn from the various (post)modern theoretical strategies (Ferdinand de Saussure and linguistics, Umberto Eco and semiotics, Jacques Lacan and psychoanalysis, Luce Irigaray and feminism, Jacques Derrida and deconstruction, and so forth) side by side with conventional survey courses and courses on such "literary" figures as Shakespeare and company. Again, then, as at Duke, what is being offered is an updated and adjusted curriculum that includes new knowledge (theory) within the existing institutional frame, a curriculum that professionalizes theory and thus robs it of its political edge in order to ensure that business in the renovated academy will continue along the same old lines.

This "reformism"—changing some insignificant features in order to relegitimate the dominant structure—can be seen in many new curriculum plans. At Syracuse, for example, the "new" English curriculum reintroduces a politically oppressive form of eclectic pluralism simply by providing three levels of study: the political, the historical, and the theoretical.[2] Once again (as in the traditional curriculum), the notion is that a liberal education should produce a well-rounded individual, one who knows—in a *balanced* way—history, theory, and politics as the tropes of contemporary discourses on knowledge. What better way to do so than to expose students to many modes of knowing? The more diverse your knowledge, the better educated you are.

Syracuse's new curriculum is similar to many other "new" curricula in that it is part of a concerted political effort by conservatives to contain change by recycling traditional educational ideas and practices through updating "literary studies" as the study of "rhetoric." This revival of the concept of "rhetoric" (through the deployment of the strategies developed in the writings of Derrida, Paul de Man, and their annotators and followers) is basically "formalist": its main concern is with *how* discourses are produced and received, without any concern with *why* they are there to begin with. Some more "relevant" forms of "rhetorical studies," following the later writings of Michel Foucault, attempt to overcome the reactionary aspect of rhetoric by posing "ethical" (but not political) questions about the ways that a particular text or discourse is "legitimated" in a given moment.

Yet there is a vast difference between examining how certain ideas get legitimated and asking radical questions about their "legitimacy." In fact, by distracting the attention of students to the study of the processes of legitimation, the study of "rhetoric" actually represents all existing discourses as automatically legitimate by virtue of their very existence and thus by implication as "equal." A rhetorician—in the name of the (liberal ideal of) freedom of objective inquiry—can be as much interested in the rhetoric of the Ku Klux Klan as in the rhetoric of imprisoned black South Africans: for the rhetorician all social phenomena are occasions for cognitive inquiries. There are no priorities, because priorities are assumed, in liberal ethics, to be motivated politically (nonobjectively). But the very erasure of priorities is actually a form of giving priority to the already "prior"—of perpetuating, in the name of equality, the inequality of the already established and powerful. This, of course, fits right into the dominant picture of what the academy is and should continue to be: a place where all inquiries are "objective" and "equally" urgent.

Advocates of theory who envision the radical reconstitution of the student as a "subject of study" have found their study trivialized. The liberal faculty majority, while marching today under the banner of fundamental educational innovation in almost every American university and college English department, has actually contrived merely to trade one set of studies (authors, texts, canons) for another, purposely leaving intact the overall institutional system for constructing student-citizens as bourgeois subjects and willing servants of the status quo. Marx once wrote, "It is clear that the arm of criticism cannot replace the criticism of arms. Material force can only be overthrown by material force: but *theory itself becomes a material force when it has seized the masses*" (251). The question for radical pedagogy, then, is how to make "theory" a material force; in other words, how to oppose both the traditional humanistic curriculum, which attempts merely to "enlighten" the student, and the now flourishing conservative (post)modern curriculum, which also attempts to "enlighten" the student, but in a "new" and "different" way.

Both traditional pedagogy and the "new" conservative (post)modern pedagogy are versions of what might be called the "pedagogy of pleasure," an educational program that takes the student for a "free," enterprising individual and tries merely to enhance (make more "pleasurable") that supposed autonomy. By contrast, radical pedagogy is a pedagogy of enablement, one that attempts to turn theory not into yet another professional topic, but into a "material force." To do this, one has to raise questions that are missing not only from the traditional curriculum but also from the "new" ones; for instance, the question of what kind of student these various programs attempt to produce: a "knowledgeable," "enlightened," "well-rounded" person, or a critical subject who knows that knowledge is a social product with political consequences and is therefore willing to "intervene" in the way knowledge is produced, not only in the classroom, but in all other sites of culture.

Radical pedagogy teaches the student to see that his or her understanding of all of culture's texts, from philosophical treatises to popular television shows, is a result of her or his situatedness in a complex network of gender, class, and race relations, and that reading (and meaning) change, depending on whether the reader is male or female, Hispanic or white American, working class or upper class. Such students can then begin to make the necessary connections between how they read *Great Expectations* and how they "read" Nicaragua and the changes in Eastern Europe, between the supposed "aesthetic beauty" of a Shakespeare sonnet and the purely "pragmatic" question of the plight of single mothers in the ghettos of New York City. In radical pedagogy, not only are the boundaries between texts dissolved, as conservative (post)-modernism advocates, but also the lines between knowledges (literature, economics, sociology, urban planning, and so on) are broken down. In this way a new transdisciplinary form of knowing emerges. The question, then, is not that of forming an alternative canon, but that of how any particular canon is used. One can use either Shakespeare or Dickens (as the traditional curriculum does) or Saussure and Derrida (as the "new" curriculum does) in order to legitimate the dominant social system. The minimal radical alternative is to "read" the dominant social system and its texts against itself by finding, in the folds, seams, and fault lines of its ideologies, spaces in which to oppose oppressive modes of social and economic domination. Anything less than this will be a trivialization of educational "change."

Critical Pedagogy

As we enter the 1990s, this struggle over pedagogical practices and the curriculum can no longer be dismissed—as some have wanted it to be—as merely a matter of petty squabbles among academic factions, because it has produced far-reaching effects, among them the institutional reconfigurations mentioned above. These institutional changes result, as C. J. Worth has suggested, from the "new kinds of coherence" produced by the impact of theory (29). Even more significant, it has resulted in the formation of a new field of intellectual and academic inquiry that we shall refer to as Critical Pedagogy.

Before the onslaught of theory, notions of the good college or university teacher tended to rely heavily either on an analysis of the qualities of the teacher in question (that is, on the humanist notion of the "essentialized" individual) or on the presumed "quality" of the institution of higher learning to which the teacher is attached (that is, on uninterrogated assumptions about institutional rankings: a teacher at Harvard is presumptively better than a teacher at Outerville State College). Yet in recent years, under the impact of (post)modern theory, a sizable body of work in Critical Pedagogy has been produced that pressures received valuations. For instance, it not only problematizes the concept of the "individual" but also inquires into the operations of educational institutions in the production of the power/knowledge relations of culture. Further, it shows that the "prestige" of an institution (which is equated with the quality of the institution's pedagogy) is in fact the complex effect of political and economic (not simply knowledge) relations.

The scope of interest in this new field of inquiry can be indicated in brief by calling attention to an assortment of developments. First is the existence of professional groups such as GRIP (Group for Research into the Institutionalization and Professionalization of Literary Studies, a kind of American version of the French GREPH, Group for Educational Research in Philosophy), which carries on investigations of these issues through conferences it sponsors and through its publication *Critical Exchange*. Then there is the frequent appearance of special issues or parts of issues of major journals devoted to pedagogical concerns—one example is the winter 1990 issue of *South Atlantic Quarterly* on "The Politics of Liberal Education"; another is the substantial portion of the February 1990 issue of the *Women's Review of Books* called "Women's Studies Enters the 1990s: A Special Section on Feminism in (and out of) the Classroom." Not only critical and scholarly but also strictly professional journals (such as the MLA's *Profession*) pay attention to such matters. Further, interest is spreading from research institutions into other levels of academia, including community colleges and high schools; for instance, the National Council of Teachers of English is sponsoring a book to be titled *Practicing Theory in Introductory College Literature Courses*, which will try to reach not only college teachers but high school teachers as well. Finally, a number of university presses have begun to publish so many books on these questions that they have come to constitute something like a series. For example, the University of Illinois Press has published or will publish the following: Cary Nelson, ed., *Theory in the Classroom* (1986); Bruce Henricksen and Thaïs Morgan, eds., *Reorientations: Critical Theories and Pedagogies* (1990); Susan Gabriel and Isaiah Smithson, eds., *Gender in the Classroom* (1990); and Donald Morton and Mas'ud Zavarzadeh, eds., *Theory/Pedagogy/Politics: Texts for Change* (1991).

The burgeoning of this new field of inquiry—how it came into being and what differing and contesting approaches are taken to it—can be traced in a set of texts published in the past decade or two in critical and scholarly journals supported by the most widely respected academic presses in the United States.

One prominent strand of Critical Pedagogy has defined itself within a deconstructive framework. An early moment of this effort in the United States is described in Christopher Fynsk's essay "A Decelebration of Philosophy," which reviews the book *Qui a peur de la philosophie?* produced by GREPH, with which Derrida is associated. The book's title (Who's Afraid of Philosophy?) was evidently chosen to hint at the anxiety shown by those who occupy positions of privilege and power about the de-author-izing and decentering possibilities of speculative thought, which by definition moves beyond and disrupts culture's established "common sense." As Fynsk indicates, the whole point of GREPH's project was to understand—in response to specific historical conditions—the relation of knowledge-practices to structures of power: their project was "a critique of the French philosophical institution . . . as a response to a more or less systematic project of isolation and even suppression of the discipline of philosophy [in French educational institutions]" that had gained new impetus from various legislative reforms. It was GREPH's goal to "defend" philosophy's current place in the lycée (the "classe de philosophie") while instituting "a systematic critique of that position and a demand for its transformation" (Fynsk 80). In other words, the GREPH project raises the possibility of a "defense" of philosophy that is not a "celebration" of it as it stands but a "decelebration" (or critique) of it that aims at its transformation. Fynsk's essay was followed—in the pages of *diacritics*—by a number of texts that began not only further to articulate the issues but to situate them with increasing specificity in relation to the American academy; these texts include James Siegel's "Academic Work: The View from Cornell" and Derrida's response to Siegel, "The Principle of Reason: The University in the Eyes of its Pupils."

The deconstructive—broadly (post)structuralist—line of Critical Pedagogy was expanded and institutionally consolidated by the appearance of an issue of *Yale French Studies* edited by Barbara Johnson titled "The Pedagogical Imperative: Teaching as a Literary Genre" (1982). This collection (which includes a few contributions by European thinkers such as Derrida and Jean-François Lyotard, but a great number by American critics such as de Man, Shoshana Felman, Neil Herz, Steven Ungar, Jane Gallop, Joan de Jean, and Johnson herself) constitutes a modest "Who's Who" of (post)structuralist critical practice in America. Johnson characterizes these essays not only as dramatizing "the problematics of teaching," but also as providing teachers (the writers of the essays and those they address) with the opportunity "to reflect on the nature of their profession and to examine the dynamics of their own language—indeed of language itself—in relation both to the play of power and to the process of understanding" (iii). The deconstructive and grammatological import of the project is further indicated in the special stress placed on "literarity": Johnson says she does "not mean to estheticize pedagogy into a form of art, but rather to attempt to analyze how and what the literarity of literature itself 'teaches' " (iii). Following an exemplary deconstructive analysis of "The Rime of the Ancient Mariner" in her introduction, Johnson concludes that what literarity teaches is in fact "the agony of teaching": in other words, teaching is the moment of confronting the aporia in the text and learning the lesson of the fundamental undecidability of meaning.

Furthermore, in Johnson's assertion that there is "always a 'written' dimension to the learning process" (which is an implicit invocation of the Derridean notion of Writing, with a capital, as the agency of *différance* and self-division—the lack of that very "identity" that is the ground of humanist pedagogy), we can begin to glimpse the trajectory of what was shortly to come in Gregory Ulmer's well-known study, *Applied Grammatology: Post(e)-Pedagogy from Jacques Derrida to Joseph Beuys* (1985), and in his more recent *Teletheory: Grammatology in the Age of Video* (1989). Together these texts represent the fullest statement to date of deconstructive Critical Pedagogy, which he calls "applied grammatology" and treats as a species of anecdote ("mystery") as the site of theorizing. For Ulmer, "anecdote" plays the same pedagogical role that Johnson attributes to "literarity": they are both places in which one "learns" not a "positive," "certain," "decidable" knowledge but a new relationship (of Lacanian "ignorance") to the "real." The practical results of Ulmer's kind of pedagogical project can be seen in the textbook he wrote with Robert Scholes and Nancy R. Comley, *Text Book: An Introduction to Literary Language* (1988).

The traditional humanist response to the pressure of theory—particularly of (post)-structuralist theory—is articulated in the line of new pedagogy exemplified in the issue of *Critical Inquiry* published later in book form as *Canons*, edited by Robert von Hallberg (1984). The genealogy of this line of thought (its connection, for instance, to the practices of I. A. Richards, Erich Auerbach, and even Foucault) is traced, in part, in Paul Bové's *Intellectuals in Power: A Genealogy of Critical Humanism* (1986). In the Hallberg collection, the mainstream academy is supposed to be making an effort to come to grips with the pressures of contemporary thought on its own "standard," "normative," "self-evidently meaningful" pedagogical and curricular practices. However, in the very act of making the effort, the project underwrites itself once again with the same presuppositions that have always informed traditional practices: eschewing the theoretical consistency and rigor of the Johnson collection, this one is frankly eclectic, its essays reflecting what Hallberg calls "the range of current thinking about canon-formation" (iii).

To return to the distinctions introduced above, whereas the Johnson collection represents the interests of "the theorists" (who stress the value of speculative thought, the importance of theoretical rigor, the inseparability of theory from practice, the limitations of "common sense," and so on), the Hallberg collection represents the interests of "the humanists" (who assume that theory is a metalanguage occupying a space distant from, and barely related to, their concerns: the importance of "practical" and not "speculative" thought, the celebration of "common sense," and so on).

The distance between the two collections, between their preoccupations and theoretical commitments, is evident in the different, if somewhat overlapping, conceptual series designated by each editor as fundamental to the project. Johnson sees her collection as concerned with "authority, seduction, judgment, resistance, desire, mystification, narrative, ignorance, and the relations between the sexes" (iii), whereas Hallberg sees his as concerned with " 'politics,' 'economy,' 'social,' 'authority,' 'power' " (iii). The difference is, in part, that the first discursive/conceptual series contains a reflexiveness (by which, for instance, "authority" is problematized through such notions as "desire" and "seduction") that is absent in the second series. According to Hallberg, the *Canons* collection as a whole investigates three broad questions: "how artists determine canons by selecting certain styles and masters to emulate; how poet-critics and academic critics, through the institutions of literary study, construct canons; and how institutionalized canons effectively govern literary study and instruction" (iii-iv).

One must note that the discourses of this "overview" have nothing to do with (post)-modern theory and hardly give any evidence of reflexive thought; instead, they draw heavily on the traditional category of the "individual," essentialize the human subject in a commonsensical fashion, and thus situate the Hallberg project as an effort by the traditional mainstream—which needs to show that it can indeed "look at itself and its practices" when pressured to do so—to respond to the challenge of theory. When Hallberg remarks that "the formation of canons is a measure of the strength of institutions devoted to the study of art" (iii), this is a hint that his volume—whatever the "critical" intentions of some of its contributors—is basically a "celebratory" rather than a "*de*-celebratory" project (to abandon "canons" would require abandoning the very premises of "essentialism," "eclecticism," and so on, on which the collection is based). The remark also implies that the volume represents business as usual in the academy, where criticism rather than critique is the only intelligible and acceptable mode of operation. Furthermore, although Hallberg tries to locate the collection in an oppositional political space by noting that today's "intellectuals" (he is presumably referring to himself and his contributors) recognize their "adversarial role" "by consensus," he conflates "intellectuals" with "academics" and in any case goes on to trivialize their supposed opposition by suggesting that it is motivated simply by the fact that they are not getting their "share" of the wealth of the economy. In Hallberg's view, then, intellectuals/academics merely constitute one more "interest group" (even if an upper-middle-class professional rather than a blue-collar one) like all the other interest groups, which take as their social goal the attempt to get their fair slice of the American pie.

Although the (post)structuralist and traditionalist perspectives have largely dominated the domain of Critical Pedagogy, others have begun to pressure both positions. For instance, the risk that focusing on the question of the canon may itself be a kind of "business as usual," a way of trivializing the issues, has recently been pointed out by Hazel Carby, who writes that "debates about the canon are misleading debates" (36), if they really come down—as they have done in the recent controversies over changes at Stanford and Duke—only to an argument about which texts should or should not be included in reading lists. The "hotly contested debates" about the canon are "absurd," she argues, because they "avoid the deeper problem" by forcing even people interested in "radical change" "to act as if inclusions of the texts they favor" would take care of the problems of inequality (37). Carby demonstrates that both traditionalist Critical Pedagogy, which focuses on the surface questions of (canonical) inclusion/exclusion, and (post)structuralist Critical Pedagogy, which is preoccupied with "representation," "texts," and "textuality," are failing to reach the most significant levels of inquiry in pedagogical and curricular practices.

Although Carby's observations must themselves be further investigated, her remarks nevertheless hint at the complicity in these two presumably opposed forms of Critical Pedagogy that dominate the academic arena and collaborate to occlude more socially and politically productive modes of analysis. If (post)structuralist theory has introduced a dimension of self-reflexiveness lacking in humanist practices, it has nevertheless defined this self-reflexiveness more in textual, discursive, and significatory than in political terms. The implication to be drawn from remarks like Carby's is that we have reached a new stage in the debate over these issues, at which the simplicities of a narrative that pits the "humanists" against the "theorists" must be pressured to reveal the overlapping political interests of the "humanists" with the dominant group of "theorists," that is, (post)structuralists: these groups, once thought of as at war with each other, are actually working together today to maintain the academic status quo.[3] By the 1990s, in other words, (post)structuralist theory has been thoroughly absorbed by the academy; nevertheless, the language of *différance* doesn't seem to have made any difference in academic practices.[4]

From this perspective, what is urgently needed is a New Critical Pedagogy that reveals the merely localizing and re-formist (not trans-formist) character of both traditional pedagogical and (post)structuralist pedagogical practice. The former pedagogy defends the concept of the autonomous and sovereign "individual" as its basic premise, sees signification as the effect of the "individual," and conducts politics "as usual." The latter pedagogy, though it displaces the notion of the "individual" in favor of the concept of the "subject" and sees the "individual" as the effect of signification, nevertheless limits politics by situating it as a purely textualist and significatory activity, the aim of which is basically the supposedly "oppositional" act of delaying the connection of the signifier to the signified. What even the latter presumably "political" approach ignores is a politics that aims at questions of the access of disenfranchised groups to culture's bank of power/knowledge/resources: this is the "deeper problem" (the structural, not merely significatory, character of oppressive and exploitative social relations) to which writers such as Carby refer. Recently published texts that begin to probe this "deeper problem" tend to come from British academics, who show a stronger awareness of inequalities in access to power and resources (that is, of the problems of class structure) than do their American counterparts; for example, Peter Widdowson, ed., *Re-reading English* (1982); Janet Batsleer et al., *Rewriting English: Cultural Politics of Gender and Class* (1985); and Frances Barker et al., eds., *Literature, Politics and Theory: Essays from the Essex Conferences 1976-84* (1986).

The foregoing analysis raises a pressing question: If these competing and contesting understandings of teaching are indeed—as we claim—really decisively different, then how do they all form parts of something called Critical Pedagogy? This question has to be explored in terms of the different understandings of the word *critical* involved in the practices of each group. Contemporary humanists still tend to regard their pedagogy as "critical" in the sense that it involves "criticism," or the evaluation and judgment of the merits of various works of art and of those who teach them. That is, they still use *the critical* in the sense exemplified in such works as F. R. Leavis's famous book *Revaluations* (1947). For the other two groups, the term *critical* relates to the practice called "critique," which, unlike criticism, must be understood as the investigation of the enabling conditions for production of meaning in culture. If this is the common ground of the latter two kinds of Critical Pedagogy, then what separates them? What is the difference between (post)structuralist "critique" and oppositional "critique"? How does the latter respond to the former's preoccupation with the significatory, the textual, the discursive? These are some of the issues that must be addressed in the project of articulating a radically transformative *Critical* Pedagogy.[5]

Notes

1. The first section of this essay appeared in a slightly different form in *In These Times* (28 October-3 November 1987: 18-19). We wish to thank the editors for permission to use that material here.
2. See Cohan et al. This document was offered to anyone interested in it in a notice in the winter 1988 issue (20.4: 18) of the *MLA Newsletter*, which summarizes the Cohan text in this manner: "What emerges is a portrait of one department's attempt to redefine the English curriculum as textual studies and cultural critique."
3. For further articulations of these issues, see Morton, "Texts of Limits," and Zavarzadeh, "Theory as Resistance."
4. For a sustained inquiry into this issue, see Morton, "The Politics of the Margin."
5. For extended investigations of these questions, see Morton and Zavarzadeh, *Theory/Pedagogy/Politics*.

Works Cited

Althusser, Louis. "Ideology and Ideological State Apparatuses." *Lenin and Philosophy and Other Essays*. New York: Monthly Review P, 1971. 127-86.

Barker, Frances, et al., eds. *Literature, Politics and Theory: Essays from the Essex Conferences 1976-84*. London: Methuen, 1986.

Batsleer, Janet, et al. *Rewriting English: Cultural Politics of Gender and Class*. London: Methuen, 1985.

Bové, Paul. *Intellectuals in Power: A Genealogy of Critical Humanism*. New York: Columbia UP, 1986.

Carby, Hazel. "The Canon: Civil War and Reconstruction." *Michigan Quarterly Review* 28.1 (Winter 1989): 35-43.

Cohan, Steven, et al. "Not a Good Idea: A New Curriculum at Syracuse." Syracuse: Syracuse U Department of English, 1988.

Derrida, Jacques. "The Principle of Reason: The University in the Eyes of Its Pupils." Trans. Catherine Porter and Edward P. Morris. *diacritics* 13.3 (Fall 1983): 3-20.

Fynsk, Christopher. "A Decelebration of Philosophy." *diacritics* 8.2 (Summer 1978): 80-90.

Hallberg, Robert von, ed. *Canons*. Chicago: U of Chicago P, 1984.

Heller, Scott. "A Constellation of Recently Hired Professors Illuminate the English Department at Duke." *Chronicle of Higher Education* (27 May 1987): 12-14.

Johnson, Barbara, ed. *The Pedagogical Imperative: Teaching as a Literary Genre*. New Haven, CT: Yale UP, 1982.

Marx, Karl. *Early Writings*. Trans. R. Livingston and G. Benton. New York: Vintage, 1975.

Morton, Donald. "The Politics of the Margin: Theory, Pleasure, and the Postmodern *Conférance*." *American Journal of Semiotics* 5.1 (1987): 95-114.

______. "Texts of Limits, the Limits of Texts, and the Containment of Politics in Contemporary Critical Theory." *diacritics* (forthcoming).

Morton, Donald, and Mas'ud Zavarzadeh. *Theory/Pedagogy/Politics: Texts for Change*. Urbana: U of Illinois P, 1991.

Scholes, Robert, et al. *Text Book: An Introduction to Literary Language*. New York: St. Martin's, 1988.

Siegel, James. "Academic Work: The View from Cornell." *diacritics* 11.1 (Spring 1981): 68-83.

Ulmer, Gregory L. *Applied Grammatology: Post(e)-Pedagogy from Jacques Derrida to Joseph Beuys*. Baltimore: Johns Hopkins UP, 1985.

______. *Teletheory: Grammatology in the Age of Video*. New York: Routledge, 1989.

Waller, Gary. "Working within the Paradigm Shift: Poststructuralism and the College Curriculum." *ADE Bulletin* 81 (Fall 1985): 6-12.

Widdowson, Peter, ed. *Rereading English*. London: Methuen, 1982.

Worth, C. J. "Our Departments Today: New Kinds of Coherence?" *MMLA Bulletin* (Spring 1980): 29+.

Zavarzadeh, Mas'ud. "Theory as Resistance." *Rethinking Marxism* 2.1 (Spring 1989): 50-70.

Robert Miklitsch SIX

The Politics of Teaching ~~Literature~~: The "Paedagogical Effect"

> This problem [the general question of language] can and must be related to the modern way of considering educational doctrine and practice, according to which the relationship between teacher and pupil is active and reciprocal so that every teacher is always a pupil and every pupil a teacher. (Gramsci 349-50)

> As for the technique that needs to be developed for all such operations [for transforming the radio into an apparatus of communication], it must follow the prime objective of turning the audience not only into pupils but into teachers. (Brecht 52)

What is the difference between the politics of teaching and the teaching of politics? Assuming there is a difference (a genuine question, for some), does it reduce to the difference between teaching and politics? In other words, is teaching irreducible to politics (and vice versa), or is teaching always already, as some argue, an instance of politics?

There is a certain vertiginous self-reflexivity to such questions. Which is not to say they are merely rhetorical; indeed, I will return to these questions below. Given the topic, however, it will be obvious by now that the above interrogative structure elides one of the terms of the topic: "Literature."[1]

> A Brechtian maxim: do not build on the good old days, but the bad new ones. (Benjamin 219)

> [Molly and Case's] room might have been the one in Chiba where he'd first seen Armitage. He went to the window, in the morning, almost expecting to see Tokyo Bay. There was another hotel across the street. It was still raining. A few letter-writers had taken refuge in doorways, their old voiceprinters wrapped in sheets of clear plastic, evidence that the written word still enjoyed a certain prestige here. (Gibson 88)

The above "erasure" would seem to suggest that Literature today is marginal or peripheral, and in the conclusion to *The Noise of Culture* (1988), William Paulson argues as much:

> What I am trying to propose . . . is a way of understanding the reading and teaching of literature, *not* in a society in which such reading and teaching appear [*sic*] to be an essential aspect of society's continual self-reproduction, but rather in a civilization where such teaching and reading are not essential or no longer appear to be. . . . At this juncture our strongest move may be to suppose that literary studies *are* something marginal, to argue from the assumption that they are indeed no more than a source of perturbations on the edge of a cultural system that gives the appearance of being able to get along without them. (155)

I am sympathetic to Paulson's point of view, but his stress on appearances—subordinate as it is—blunts, if it does not altogether sabotage, his argument. It may also betray a residual nostalgia for the "good old days," for Literature with a capital L. Indeed, Paulson's rhetoric intimates, *à la* Nietzsche, that we might perish if we knew the Truth about Literature: that its sociocultural centrality is (was?) mostly illusory. Hence the, for me, uncanny appearance in the above passage of the presumably consoling logic of Truth-and-Appearances. Hence also the not-quite-subliminal pathos.

Yet one does not have to get apocalyptic about the future of Literature (LITERATURE IS DEAD!) to wonder about the individual and institutional anxiety about the question of its marginality.[2] However, in order to understand this anxiety, it is necessary, it seems to me, to investigate the historicity of the concept of Literature. In *Marxism and Literature* (1977), for instance, Raymond Williams explains that the concept of "literature" did not emerge in its modern form until the eighteenth century and "was not fully developed until the nineteenth" ("Literature" 46). Moreover, "literature"—as "a category of use and condition rather than of production" (that is to say, of reading rather than writing)—"specified a particular social distinction" ("Literature," 47).

But if it is "relatively difficult to see 'literature' as a concept," it is even more difficult to see "literature" as a class concept, a concept *for* a class—that is, a concept used by a particular class to construct its ideological hegemony: "[The] forms of the concepts of *literature* and *criticism* are, in the perspective of historical social development, forms of a class specialization and control of a general social practice, and of a class limitation of the questions which it might raise" (Williams, "Literature" 49).[3] Literature, of course, is not simply a class concept, nor for that matter one of race or gender, ethnicity or sexuality. Inasmuch as it is associated with the "relatively uniform and specializing technology of print" ("Literature" 53), it is a historical category as well. Which does not, as Williams notes, "diminish its importance" ("Literature" 53). In fact, the concept of "literature" is important precisely because of its historicity, because it tells us so much about history, and not only literary history, but history "as such," our history.

And yet, with the emergence of the new technologies and the consequent "information revolution"—to return to the subject of William Paulson's book—it would appear we are entering a new postprint phase where Literature will no longer constitute the central medium for the cultural reproduction of society. In other words, if, in Williams's terms, the new technologies are now emergent, not to say dominant, Literature and its "means of production" ("the particular technology of print" ["Literature" 54]) are, or will soon be, residual. The institutional consequences of this event should be equally apparent: English departments should not restrict themselves to Literature, even where Literature has been redefined—according to a liberal-pluralist logic—to include popular, multicultural, and/or postcolonial literatures.[4]

It may well be that Literature has served its usefulness as a concept and even, perhaps, as a discipline. Cultural studies may not be the answer (either as a discipline or, in particular, as a concept),[5] but one thing is clear: history is ultimately about change, and the dominant hegemonic moment of English Literature—real or otherwise—is over. Such a claim has, it seems to me, profound implications for "The Politics of Teaching Literature," implications that teachers of literature are going to have to address if we are going to resist the present powerful current of nostalgia ("the good old days") in the name of the future and the forces of change.

The Politics of Teaching

> And your education? Is not that also social, and determined by the social conditions under which you educate, by the intervention of society, direct or indirect, by means of schools, etc.? (Marx and Engels 100)

> The work of teaching and organizing the others fell naturally upon the pigs, who were generally recognized as the cleverest of the animals. (Orwell 25)

> We should begin, then, with political questions. (Kampf and Lauter 7)

My emphasis in this section will be on "the politics of teaching" or, as I want for strategic reasons to rephrase it, the "politics of pedagogy."[6]

Today, according to a disciplinary logic that Michel Foucault has reconstructed in all its micrological discursivity,[7] the teacher-student relation frequently displays a "master"-"slave" structure, where the student is positioned as a child, a child *to be educated* (i.e., "socialized"). Education in this sense is an apparatus of or a vehicle for social reproduction, and the aim of a "normal education" (as in "normal science") is to school students in the interests and ideology of the "ruling class."[8] Though scholastic reproduction—even and perhaps especially in the most totalitarian circumstances—is never and can never be complete (there are always pockets of resistance, of struggle and contestation),[9] there is I think more than a grain of truth to the educative-reproductive thesis. In other words, the above pedagogical paradigm remains the dominant one.

I rehearse these familiar arguments about education-as-social-reproduction and the master-slave model of pedagogy in order to frame the following, openly autobiographical remarks about the politics of teaching and what I want to call, recollecting Noam Chomsky via James Merod, the responsibility of the teacher.[10] Part of this responsibility devolves, I want to argue, to the proposition that teachers must begin from the pedagogic subject-position to which they have been assigned.[11] If the latter position is not necessarily one of mastery (in either sense of the word), it nonetheless remains one of authority. In other words, to attempt absolutely to renounce the pedagogic subject-position—from whatever motivation, liberal or otherwise—is not only to accede to a "bad" egalitarian logic, it is to evade our responsibility as teachers. And that responsibility—which, needless to say, is an implicitly political one—involves recognizing those structures (social, cultural, economic, and so on) that both enable *and* constrain our activities.

Let me relate an anecdote. A couple of years ago I was scheduled to teach a course at Tufts, primarily for "freshmen," titled "Politics and Writing."[12] Now, with such "seminar" courses, I typically arrange the seats in a circle so as to encourage intimacy and facilitate discussion, but the room to which we had been assigned, I found out the first day of class, was not amenable to such an arrangement, as the desks were *nailed* to the floor. Moreover, at the front of the room, there was a raised platform and, upon the platform, a lectern from which I was supposed to preach—I mean, teach. Faced with this explicitly disciplinary *mise-en-scène*, I elected to teach from the back of the class.

It will come as no surprise that although my gesture did have a certain effectivity (mostly short-lived), the class ultimately was not a successful one, at least according to my "subjective" standards, and I'm starting to think it had something to do with my decision to teach from the back of the class or, as some might say, ass backwards. And yet, causal and other possible explanations aside (perhaps I performed poorly; perhaps it was just a bad class, a bad time, etc.), this specific class—precisely because of its unique *architexture*—afforded me an opportunity to think about certain things that I might not otherwise have thought about, in particular what I have called the pedagogic subject-position as it relates to the physical space of the classroom.

In retrospect, I now realize that although I did effect a palpable change in the spatial relations of the room, I did not sufficiently articulate my reasons for doing so. In Brechtian terminology, I failed to *demonstrate* the point of my gesture, with the net result that the gist of my gesture, the *gestus*, was almost immediately neutralized.[13] I'm not suggesting that given the quasi-fixed configuration of the room, I should have resigned myself to its potentially negative pedagogic implications. What I am suggesting—and I don't make any claims for novelty here—is that it is not enough simply to reverse a dominant-inflected structure. Indeed, a reversal of sorts having been effected, it might have been more useful to switch back to the "original" arrangement, all the while re-marking (perhaps with some help from Foucault) the disciplinary nature of the classroom as it is conventionally arranged.

My response to and reading of the above scenario are not, needless to say, the only ones. I could, for example, have found another classroom or, better yet, another, different space. When possible, I have in fact done so. My point, however, is that it is not always possible to do so, that sometimes there are structural limits to situations, and that this is precisely when the question of strategy comes into play.

While all of this architextural analysis may seem much ado about nothing, too many teachers and theorists of teaching neglect, it seems to me, this aspect of the educative process. As I have tried to illustrate, the materiality of the classroom is ineluctably a practical *and* theoretical affair. In other words, the classroom is one of the contexts—a *material*, not negligible one—within which both the discourse of knowledge and the student-teacher relation is constructed.

Having touched on the question of, generally speaking, context, I would now like to address the subject of text(s). But before I broach the question of the general political economy of the American student as it intersects with *Animal Farm* (1945), I want to describe in some detail my pedagogic approach to the text with which I chose to begin the aforementioned "Politics and Writing" course. Though the course in fact began with a discussion of what exactly we all meant by the word *politics* (I also asked students to narrate on paper what they thought was their most political act), the first book I assigned was a quasi-canonical one: *The Communist Manifesto* (1848). Given this choice, a difficult pedagogical problem immediately posed itself: How does one go about teaching this particular text, a text that for many students is not only intellectually demanding (all that Hegelian jargon!) but ideologically suspect.

True to Hegel and Marx, the best approach to the *Manifesto* was, I felt, a dialectical one. In other words, I felt it was necessary to bring out—if possible, Socratically—its "positive" and "negative" moments. To accomplish this, to make Marx and Engels's treatise materialize as the prescient *and* historically determined text it is, I endeavored to situate it in its historical-intellectual context (e.g., the "revolutionary" 1840s and post-Hegelianism). But if it was crucial to see the *Manifesto* as a work that simultaneously "reflects" and "transcends" its historical preconditions, it was also crucial, I felt, to situate it within a larger, explicitly critical, context.

To this end, I assigned A. J. P. Taylor's introduction to the Penguin edition of the *Manifesto*, an eminently readable and witty preface to what is at times a rather ponderous and tendentious text (7-47). Taylor's donnish *esprit*, however, tends to negate whatever force, rhetorical or otherwise, the *Manifesto* possesses. Hence, as a "positive," dialectical foil to Taylor, and because it is committed to democracy but critical of both American capitalism and Soviet-style "socialism" (so-called actually existing socialism), I also assigned "The Democratic Essence," the second chapter of Michael Harrington's neglected *Socialism* (1972).[14] Together, Taylor and Harrington would, I felt, effectively legitimate the *Manifesto* as a text to be read and reread like any other "classic."

I might add that as an audiovisual coda of sorts, I also screened *Red Nightmare* (1952), a Defense Department "docudrama" directed by one George Waggner and narrated by none other than Jack Webb of *Dragnet* fame. Suffice to say, I hoped this film would cast a retrospectively comic light on the anticommunist rhetoric of the fifties even as it pointed up the decidedly unfunny causes and consequences of such Cold War propaganda (i.e., Soviet expansionism and McCarthyism).

Despite the screening of *Red Nightmare*, the *Manifesto* set the tone for the course, a tone that I would characterize, not unfavorably, as an explicitly *ideological* one (i.e., left but not "communist"). Yet despite my efforts to present Marx and Engels's work in as dialectical a light as possible, the students were extremely skeptical about its critique of capitalism, not to mention its proletarian-inspired vision of a future state of classlessness. Of course, with recent events in the Soviet Union and Eastern Europe as well as China still reverberating across the world stage in all their revolutionary and counterrevolutionary repercussions, not to be skeptical about the claims of classical Marxism is to be hopelessly naive. Indeed, one might argue that one of our tasks as teachers is to encourage a "healthy" skepticism on the part of our students. The irony is that the kind of skepticism I encountered was more reactive than radical.

As Nietzsche says, do not misunderstand me. I am not saying that my students' response was merely reactive (which would be to represent it as a form of "false consciousness"). Nor am I saying that their skepticism was not radical simply because they did not share my point of view, a point of view that—as I have said—was explicitly ideological. In fact, one might argue that in *their* extreme skepticism, *their* openly ideological posture (what I would characterize as, at best, right-centrist and, at worst, "anticommunist" *à la* Ronald Reagan), these students were vigorously contesting my authorial subject-position—as in some sense, to some degree, they were. And that inasmuch as my posture was also openly polemical, they were "right" to do so.

None of these explanations, however, speaks satisfactorily to my experience of teaching the *Manifesto*. Which is only to say that they do not sufficiently explain the force and complexity of my students' response. But at this point I need to recontextualize what has become a rather speculative reading in order to problematize that response.

The *Manifesto*, Taylor/Harrington read, I decided—according to that dialectical imperative an instance of which I sketched earlier—to assign *Animal Farm*. Though I will not attempt to reconstruct my approach to this text, I do want to try to convey, albeit briefly and impressionistically, my sense of teaching Orwell after Marx and Engels. What struck me most about student response to *Animal Farm* was its relatively uncritical character: after having been forced to read the "bible" of Communism, they were more than willing to engage in some real suspension of disbelief. Overnight, extreme skepticism turned to anxiety-free enthusiasm. (*Now, this is a classic!*) Orwell's fable spoke deeply and directly to their beliefs—about Power, about Intelligence, about Totalitarianism. About, that is, Human Nature.

Again, I must bracket a number of absolutely crucial issues here (i.e., the formal qualities of *Animal Farm*, the difference between reading fiction and reading nonfiction, and so on) in order to isolate one: the subject-position, or general political economy, of the American student. Bluntly, I was unable to interest students in a reading of *Animal Farm* that was as critical as their reading of the *Manifesto*. It didn't matter, finally, that Orwell was something of a "chauvinist pig" (pun intended)[15] or that his dogmatically binary characterization of, say, pigs and horses—of, that is, intelligence and, *a fortiori*, stupidity and, still more, power and powerlessness, dominance and subalternity[16]—was less than persuasive from any considered point of view. Unlike Marx and Engels (who were pathologically interested in what I call Other-interest), Orwell understood "man" and his "nature," a "nature" that is determined, *essentially*, by self-interest. Human Nature is Human Nature, and damn the critics.[17]

The conclusions that follow from such a premise go something like this: Communism doesn't work because of its fundamental miscomprehension of Human Nature; Communism inevitably reduces to Totalitarianism (*Look at Stalin! Look at Napoleon!*); Capitalism is not only the American Way, it's the best way. Though this may be to generalize to the point of caricature my students' political-economic subject-position (even Socrates turns into a strawman in my hands, says Nietzsche), one problem with the above argument is that it misconceives capitalism, which, at least in its contemporary, welfare-state form, no longer corresponds to the object of Marx's critique and cannot therefore be diametrically opposed to communism. More to the point, if Marx was all wrong about communism, in particular its dialectical-historical inevitability, his insight about "human nature"—that it is, like communism and capitalism, historical, not natural—remains.

All of which brings me to the following questions: How can we empower students to interrogate not only their teachers' but their own beliefs? In other words, what can we do—as teachers—to encourage them to think, and to think long and hard, about those things they hold dearest to their hearts? *Is* it possible somehow to teach students to read themselves as carefully as they read the text that is their teachers' politics?

The Teaching of Politics

We want education that teaches us our true history and our role in the present-day society. ("What We Want, What We Believe," Black Panther Party Platform and Program [1966])

I don't see how teachers and departments and university faculties can make intelligent professional choices without consciously making them political choices. (Ohmann 304)

The traditionalism inherent in our project may make the list seem to some an obstacle to desired change. But wise change comes from competence, and that is what our list really addresses. (Hirsch 137)

In this final section I want to take up not only the question of "the teaching of politics" but what I want to call "political literacy." By the latter I mean what used to be called "civic education," the *process* of being schooled in the discourse of democracy as well as in the active exercise of citizenship, with its duties and practices, institutions and responsibilities. If on the subject of the political-as-"paedagogical" Brecht has been an important influence[18] (in addition to the recent work of, in particular, Henry Giroux), my sense of "political literacy" is a function of the recent dramatic and, occasionally, melodramatic debate about the concept of "cultural literacy," especially as that concept derives from the work of E. D. Hirsch, Jr.

Though it is dangerous to let the opposition define the terms and terrain of a problematic, what I intend by the term *political literacy* is not unlike what the author of *Cultural Literacy* calls "cultural politics," the aims of which are, according to Hirsch, "fundamentally different from those of teaching literacy":

> A chief goal of cultural politics is to change the content and values of culture. But the principal aim of schooling is to promote literacy as an enabling competence. Although our public schools have a duty to teach widely accepted cultural values, they have a duty *not* to take political stands on matters that are subjects of continuing debate. Only a descriptive list accords with these fundamental goals of universal education. (137)

Hirsch is right about one thing: the principal aim of "political literacy" or "cultural politics" is not merely "competence" but transformation, *social transformation*.[19] Hirsch is right as well, in a negative-theological way, about another thing: "political literacy" implies that both educators and institutions have a duty not only "to teach widely accepted cultural values" but different, less widely accepted, even dissenting ones.

Moreover (more important, that is), educators and institutions have a duty "to take political stands on matters that are subjects of continuing debate" (137). *Pace* Hirsch, teachers cannot and should not reify the undecidability of "continuing debate," which can all too easily become, in Hegel's terms, a bad infinity. It follows from this that every debate must be repeatedly punctuated, whether individually or collectively, although—and this can't be emphasized enough—the potentially infinite "textuality" of the dialectical imperative necessitates that each and every *decision* must be negotiated anew.

Of course, a transformative as opposed to what Giroux calls a "transmission pedagogy" also has a duty *not* to be dogmatic or, for Hirsch, "prescriptive." The "paedagogical" imperative, as I have insisted throughout this essay, is a dialectical one. If it recognizes, explicitly, the primacy of the political in any and every act of pedagogy, such a recognition does not rest on an assumption of their equivalence. (The "unequal sign," like Derrida's concept of *sous rature*, can be put to good use here: the political ≠ the pedagogical.) Thus, if—compared with a fundamentalist pedagogics such as Hirsch's—Graff's notion of a conflictual vis-à-vis a consensual pedagogy is a step in the "right" direction, from another, "paedagogical" perspective, his valorization of "cultural conversation" ("the cultural text"-as-"the context of teaching") is necessary but not sufficient (258). It is necessary because it situates Hirsch's ostensibly neutral but extremely interested notion of competence within a wider, more material field of forces and interests. It is not sufficient because it is not sufficiently political. That is to say, it is neither decisive nor transformative.

In order to sharpen the distinction I have been drawing between "*cultural* literacy" (or "*cultural* politics") and "*political* literacy," I want to return to Hirsch's text. In "The Decline of Teaching Cultural Literacy" (a title that recollects, slavishly, the rise-and-fall-of-the-Roman-Empire trope), Hirsch argues that his notion of "universal education" or what he elsewhere calls his "traditionalism" ("a descriptive list . . . necessarily emphasize[s] traditional materials, because widely shared information is not likely to be new" [137])[20] is neither an overt nor a covert affirmation of the "status quo." The claim that "universal cultural literacy" reinforces the dominant hegemony is paradoxical, according to Hirsch, "because in fact the traditional forms of literate culture are precisely the most effective instruments for political and social change" (22). Read this way (with the grain, as it were), "competence" is *the* medium of and for transformation.

To develop this argument—that "all political discourse at the national level must use the stable forms of the national language and its associated culture"—Hirsch cites a number of passages from the *Black Panther*, "a radical and revolutionary newspaper if ever this country had one" (22). This is an extremely clever rhetorical device on Hirsch's part, and true to the device, the passages are representative, not to say paradigmatic. However, the ideological *frisson* aside, Hirsch's reading of these rhetorically *and* politically rich passages illustrates the poverty of his theory—a conservative and counterrevolutionary theory if ever there was one.

Take, for example, this claim: "The *Panther* was highly conservative in its language and cultural assumptions, as it had to be in order to communicate effectively" (22). Yet if the following language is "highly conservative" (in the narrowest, formalist sense), its "cultural assumptions" are anything but:

> The present period reveals the criminal growth of bourgeois democracy since the betrayal of those who died that this nation might live 'free and indivisible.' It exposes through the trial of the Chicago Seven, and its law and order edicts, its desperate turn toward the establishment of a police state. (17 January 1970) (22)

What is interesting about this passage, for me, is the conflict between what one might call the language of nationalism (" 'free and indivisible' ") and the international language of Marxism ("bourgeois democracy").[21] In other words, a counterdiscourse, a discourse counter to the official discourse of late "state" capitalism, is sedimented in and can be constructed around the word "bourgeois" and its "*associated* culture" (italics mine), a culture whose history and language, whose language of history—the *Black Panther* is specifically drawing on.[22]

The construction of such a counterdiscourse—significant as it is—is not, however, sufficient, politically speaking, inasmuch as it is predicated on Hirsch's own premises about "cultural competence." Politics is never simply a matter of reading or discourse, just as empowerment is never simply a matter of competence. Just because you have mastered your ABCs, not to mention the appendix to *Cultural Literacy*, does not mean that racists will stop being racists, sexists sexists, and so on. Prejudice and *its* disabling effects cannot be countered wholly by communication, especially when communication is understood reductively, as it is in Hirsch, in terms of "effectivity." Indeed, in Hirsch's hands communication comes to seem yet another, belated version of instrumental rationality: cultural Taylorism, post-Fordist literacy for the underprivileged.

From a different, not unrelated perspective, Hirsch's "traditionalist" reading of the above passage from the *Panther* elides absolutely the historical specificity of the BPP's indictment of "this nation" and its "criminal campaign," especially as that campaign and its "law and order edicts" crystallized around "the trial of the Chicago Seven."[23] This act of idealization or dematerialization—the fact that Hirsch does not provide any context for the *Panther* passage (except to remark, repeatedly, the radicality of its "sentiment")—exposes the ahistoricism of his method. On the other hand, for Hirsch to have invoked, even cursorily, the history of the Black Panthers and that larger history within which their discourse must be situated if it is to be at all politically intelligible would have been to *educate* readers in the kind of "literate knowledge" that his model is expressly designed to suppress.[24]

Finally, the *Panther*'s "radical sentiment," its cultural *politics*, cannot, however incoherent, be separated from its supposedly "conservative language." As Marx would say, it is cut out of whole cloth. In this sense, Hirsch's analytic distinction between "sentiment" and "language"—a distinction that is no longer, it seems to me, a critical one—is not neutral but political. That is to say, Hirsch's nonreading is not so much a misreading as a pointedly political act.

After suggesting that "the writers for *The Black Panther* had clearly received a rigorous traditional education in American history, in the Declaration of Independence, the Pledge of Allegiance to the Flag, the Gettysburg Address, and the Bible," Hirsch adds that the *Panther* writers "also received rigorous traditional instruction in reading, writing, and spelling" (23). His conclusion:

> I have not found a single misspelled word in the many pages of radical sentiment I have examined in that newspaper. Radicalism in politics, but conservatism in literate knowledge and spelling: to be a conservative in the *means* of communication is the road to effectiveness in modern life, in whatever direction one wishes to be effective. (23)

In the last part of this passage, he sounds less like a critic than like a Rotarian Polonius. The peroration and its "wise"—that is, palpably condescending—tone aside, it is hard to imagine a more perfect illustration of how *not* to read: after having read "many pages" of the *Panther*, Hirsch is struck not by its politics but by its grammar ("I have not found a single misspelled word.").

One can only conclude that if Hirsch's reading of the Panther is an instance, as it well should be, of the kind of rigorousness and traditionalism that American "public schools" are desperately in need of, then it is clear that rigor and tradition—not to say grammar—are not, by themselves, enough. (I have not found a single misspelled word in the many pages of conservative sentiment.) From what I have said, it should be equally clear that the kind of conservative education in "literate knowledge" and, in particular, "American history" that Hirsch's pedagogic model privileges is not only narrowly conceived, dangerously so, but as ideologically interested as the "cultural politics" that is the manifest object of *his* polemic. Which is to say that "cultural literacy"—at least as Hirsch formulates it—is, in the final analysis, a form of political illiteracy.

In the space that remains I want to return to some of the claims and concerns of this essay in order to advance—against the above language of critique—what Giroux calls a "language of possibility." Bluntly, I want to present a positive instance of what I mean by "political literacy." To do so, however, I need to reengage the rhetoric of critique in order to examine the problem of print versus visual culture as it is played out in Giroux's *Teachers as Intellectuals* (1988).

In "Mass Culture and the Rise of the New Illiteracy: Implications for Reading," a chapter that both begins and ends with an epigraph from Brecht,[25] Giroux argues that not "visual" but "print technology" is "emancipatory at the present time" (81). Unlike "reading," which, historically speaking, "created a class-specific audience because of the technical and critical skills needed to use it" ("reading," for Giroux, is synonymous with "print culture"), visual culture has "all but eliminated any reliance upon a class-specific audience to use its technology or to understand its messages" (80). One would think that this democratic effect would be a good thing, especially for a class-sensitive critic like Giroux, but according to him, the very concept of "mass culture"—tied as it is to the emergence of the electronic media as "the most dominant form of communication"—"suggests not only the importance of quantity but also the reduction of thought and experience to the level of mere spectatorship" (80).

But precisely because "the written word is governed by the logic of conciseness, clarity, and cogency" (rather than the "logic" of emotion, diffusion, and fragmentation associated, for Giroux, with the image or the spectacle), the technology of print media "necessitates a form of rationality that *contains* room for critical thinking and analysis" (80; italics mine). Moreover, it is—at least compared with the mass media, which are "centrally controlled by the ruling interests" (81)—"inexpensive to produce and consume." In any event, the left "simply does not have access to the visual culture," as the latter's "modes of communication are much too important to the corporate interests to be democratized" (81). The "sociopolitical" bottom line: the visual media—in particular television—present "much greater possibilities for manipulation and social control" than the print media. Put another, epigrammatic way: "The visual media are presently demagogue of one-way communication" (81).

Giroux, it seems to me, has been reading too much Adorno and Enzensberger. If, as Williams says, concepts are problems, then concepts such as the "culture industry" and the "industrialization of consciousness" are especially problematic, as they lend themselves all too easily to monolithic characterizations of the mass media in general and the visual media in particular.[26] Giroux is not unaware of this "Orwellian" perspective, which can lead in turn to what he calls "technological fatalism." As he himself says: "The electronic media, as well as print culture, are not a causal agent as much as a mediating force in the reproduction of consciousness" ("Mass Culture" 79). However, despite such caveats (phrases such as "reproduction of consciousness," with their functionalist inflection, are of course equally problematic), Giroux's rationalist rhetoric of containment falls prey to precisely the kind of "technological determinism" and "cultural pessimism" that he warns against at the beginning of his essay (Williams, "Culture" 129).[27] For instance, to argue, as Giroux does, that the "left simply does not have access to the visual culture" is to leave that culture, uncontested, to the right.

To a "properly" dialectical argument such as the latter—which represents, for Giroux, "a noble but misguided position"—he submits instead the solace of a unilateral cultural politics:

> The electronic media are in the hands of the corporate trust, and it would take a redistribution of power and wealth to place them at the public's disposal. This is an important task, but it must be preceded by a change in the collective consciousness and accompanied by the development of an ongoing political struggle. ("Mass Culture" 83)

But in a society where literacy is increasingly more an audiovisual than a "verbal" matter, what is the future of a cultural politics that renounces outright, in the name of a revolutionary historical strategy, the emancipatory potential of the mass media (in both "visual" and "print" guises)?

If the recent presidential election, not to mention the rise of the Moral Majority, does not offer sufficiently convincing proof that the visual media are indispensable to any hegemony, counter or otherwise, then the work of Raymond Williams—from *Preface to Film* (1954) to, say, *Television: Technology and Cultural Form* (1974)—can and should be read as an extended cautionary tale to the effect that the electronic modes of communication are too important not to be democratized.[28] For critics like Williams, the task of the left is not to abandon but to find ways to gain access to visual culture. Furthermore (to take up another of Giroux's theses), though print technology in some cases may be less expensive to produce and consume than its visual counterpart, the argument that it is more "logical" than the "tactile" technology of the image ("Print culture . . . is not as obtrusive as the visual culture; it lacks the 'tactile' qualities of the latter" ["Mass Culture" 80]) is, pure and simple, specious. Print is neither more "rational" nor more "intentional" than visual culture. (Is, say, *USA Today* more progressive than *The MacNeil/Lehrer NewsHour?*) In the final analysis, the dominative or liberatory force of print or visual technology depends, in Giroux's own terms, on "use," not "potential."

Given Giroux's conjunctural thesis about the liberatory potential of print culture, it is not surprising that his analysis of the construction of citizenship in Hollywood films and television programming in *Schooling and the Struggle for Public Life* (1988) is located squarely within the parameters of the critique of the "ideology of the new nationalism and chauvinism" ("Celluloid Patriotism" 23). If his theoretical understanding of ideology is not, as he himself argues, the "orthodox, classical Marxist" one (ideology as economic last instance or "false consciousness"), his critical practice is decidedly Western-Marxist or, more pejoratively, Frankfurtian. Thus, although his general discussion of, for example, "the new anti-communism" in *Rambo* (1982), *Rocky IV* (1985), *White Nights* (1985), *Red Dawn* (1984), *Invasion U.S.A.* (1985), and *Moscow on the Hudson* (1984) is instructive on the "progressive ideological contradictions" at work in such films, his reading is not really persuasive because it privileges uncritically—that is to say, reflexively—the language of critique.[29] And despite his own insistence on the "latent possibilities, needs and hopes" that often constitute the subtext of "reactionary" films, his reading is compelled to privilege the language of critique because it privileges certain films rather than others: *Rambo* rather than *Missing* (1982), *Red Dawn* rather than *Under Fire* (1983), *Rocky IV* rather than *Salvador* (1986).[30]

If films such as *Missing, Under Fire*, and *Salvador* are more evocative of the "history of Hollywood itself" than of their professed historical subject or "political provenance,"[31] they nonetheless mobilize considerably different subject-positions than the above, manifestly "conservative" films. To be indifferent to *this* difference is to be dumb to the politicality of art in general and film in particular. To be fair to Giroux, in his most recent work—for example, "Popular Culture as a Pedagogy of Pleasure and Meaning" (written with Roger Simon)—he offers a "positive" but not uncritical reading of *Dirty Dancing* (1987).[32] Unlike his analyses of *Rambo, Rocky IV*, and so on, which are marked by a certain "critical"—that is, modernist—self-distance, Giroux's reading of *Dirty Dancing* re-marks his "white working-class" investment in the film even as it lays bare those "semantic" elements that conflict with and contradict it.[33] In fact, partly because of the element of transference (the critical impulse is, as we have seen, a given), Giroux's reading of *Dirty Dancing* as a "popular cultural" text is more dialectical, and therefore more persuasive, than his remarks on "Hollywood films and television programming." More important, it suggests a real reconsideration on his part not only of the role of the visual media in contemporary culture but *its* potential for "critical thinking and social action" ("Mass Culture" 84).

Given my critique of, among other things, English studies, Hirsch's notion of "cultural literacy," and Giroux's valorization of "print culture," I want to conclude by briefly describing the first part of a course I recently taught titled "Differences" as a "positive" instance of what I mean by "political literacy." The texts for this, the first section of the course—which was subtitled "Reading Race-as-Difference"—were *The Autobiography of Malcolm X* (1963), Martin Luther King, Jr.'s "Black Power" (1967), Cornel West's "The Paradox of the Afro-American Rebellion" (1984), and Spike Lee's *Do the Right Thing* (1989). As it will I hope have become obvious, I chose these texts in this particular order because they enacted that dialectical imperative that, I have been arguing, is crucial to the "paedagogical effect." In crudely Hegelian terms (crude Hegel, that is): if Malcolm X's autobiography is the thesis to which King's essay is the antithesis, West's article represents one historical-theoretical synthesis. More simply, if "Black Power" is a response of sorts to Malcolm X and his successors, "The Paradox of the Afro-American Rebellion" constitutes one organic-intellectual attempt to historically situate and theoretically mediate the two.

And yet, insofar as West's article privileges King at the expense of Malcolm X (and rather reflexively at that, at least as I read it),[34] the above discursive set also tends toward a certain closure. Given this constrained dialectic, the advantage of *Do the Right Thing* is that it not only *cinematically* puts into play both King's and Malcolm X's positions but, insofar as it privileges the latter (again, as I read it),[35] contests West's reading of the "logic" of the civil rights movement. Spike Lee's film is not, of course, without its totalizations: for instance, despite the fact that certain members of the neighborhood have acted collectively to avenge Radio Raheem's death, an act that can be read as a symbolic confirmation of Malcolm X's politics of violence-as-"intelligence," nothing seems to have changed at the end of the film. And yet, if the latter act is read as a catharsis devoid of any larger political meaning, the film's conclusion—in particular, the final ludic-musical shot (a parody, arguably, of the classic Hollywood ending)—appears as a spiked, ironic reflection on the present impasse of "the Afro-American rebellion," a historical "aporia" to which neither Malcolm X nor King is the answer. From this perspective, *Do the Right Thing*, which is clearly both a product of and meditation on the racially regressive Reagan eighties, poses the politically fraught question: Where, exactly, do we go from here?

Though my construction of the "race question" is obviously only one among many, such a construction illustrates—to take up the points with which I began this conclusion—that "TV and film should be taught within English courses" (a potentially "positive" effect of cultural studies [see McCabe]); that literacy is as much a political as a "cultural" issue (Is it really possible to divorce Spike Lee's film from that cultural politics from which it derives so much of its power and relevance?); and that "print" and "visual culture" *can* "complement each other" "at the present time" (indeed, they may even productively, dialectically interrupt each other). The reconstructive principle at the heart of the above construction—a principle that can and should be extended to include other discourses of rights, such as the gay and woman questions[36]—also illustrates the power of the language of possibility, what Giroux and Simon call "the affirmation of difference" and "the difference of affirmation": both "the possibility of a social imaginary for which a politics of democratic difference offers up forms of resistance in which it becomes possible to rewrite, rework, recreate, and reestablish new discourses and cultural spaces that revitalize rather than degrade public life" *and* the possibility of "claiming one's experience as a legitimate ground for developing one's own voice, place, and sense of history" (Giroux and Simon 13).

If the teaching of politics that is both different from yet implicated in the politics of teaching is going to mean anything today and in the future, it is going to have to come to terms with these different needs and discourses, languages and desires: the possibility of resistance and the irreducible, equally critical demand for affirmation.

Notes

1. *Literature*—in the uppercase—refers in this essay to that general, dominant-hegemonic conception of "the literary" that still circulates in most departments of English. Literature, in this sense, is something like "work" as opposed to "text"; for this distinction, see Barthes (155-64). This is *not*, however, to endorse the Barthesian concept of the Text.

   I have put Literature "under erasure" in order to mark the historical contingency of this particular concept-metaphor.
2. For the "speed readers," a caveat courtesy of James Carey: "To abandon the effects tradition does not . . . require turning up the academic temperature to Fahrenheit 451 and indulging in wholesale book burning. No one, except the congenitally out of touch, suggests . . . we can afford to stop reading the 'classics' in the effects literature" (93).
3. I bracket here the question of the historicity of the concept of "criticism." I would only add that "theory," though a historical category and activity as well, is tied to the epistemic deconstruction of both "literature" and "criticism."
4. For an early, and prescient, critique of what Graff (6-9, 249-50) calls the "field-coverage principle," see Richard Ohmann (224-28).

5. With respect to American institutionalization of cultural studies (which moment now appears to be on us), the recent controversial conference at Illinois is a case in point; for a report of the proceedings, see Scott Heller (A10-11).
6. I emphasize the word *pedagogy* because its etymological history is particularly instructive in this context. *Pedagogy* derives from *paidagōgos*, which derives in turn from *paidos* ("child") and *agein* ("to lead"). For the Greeks and Romans of antiquity, it referred—according to *Webster's*—to "a slave who attended the children of his master and conducted them to school, often also acting as a tutor." The irony, at least loosely speaking, is that the "original" master-slave relation has now been reversed.
7. See Foucault.
8. A paradigmatic passage from *The Communist Manifesto*: "The Communists have not invented the intervention of society in education: they do but seek to alter the character of that intervention, and to rescue education from the influence of the ruling class" (Marx and Engels 100).
9. For a résumé and critique of the discourse of education-as-social reproduction, see Aronowitz and Giroux (69-114).
10. See Merod (54-56) and Chomsky (323-66).
11. Paul Smith is instructive on this point: "In order to learn to resist a text or texts students need to come up against resistance from it and, by extension, from teachers. Teachers . . . not only cannot abrogate their responsibility to their own voices and their own cultural experience and knowledge; they are obliged to present those elements as needing to be taken into account by students" (42).
12. "Politics and Writing" is the title of one among a number of different sections ("Differences," "Conformity and Rebellion," etc.) that structure the second half of the two-semester writing requirement at Tufts. Tufts is a small, expensive "liberal arts" college located in Medford, a working-class suburb northwest of Boston.
13. For Brecht's sense of *gestus* ("gest"), see, for instance, "On Gestic Music": "The social gest is the gest relevant to society, the gest that allows conclusions to be drawn about the social circumstances" (105).
14. For Harrington, the years between 1848 and 1850 mark "the period of Marx's anti-democratic temptation" (49), a period that is "a classic source for the Bolshevik, and then the Stalinist, version of Marxism" (56). Need I add that, according to the dialectical imperative I have outlined here, Harrington's quasi-continuist democratic reading of Marx must also be put into critical circulation? For a countercritique of Harrington, see Cohen.
15. See, for example, Orwell's characterization of Mollie, "the foolish, pretty white mare" with her sugar and ribbons: "The stupidest questions of all were asked by Mollie. . . . The very first question she asked Snowball was: 'Will there be sugar after the Rebellion?' " (26). See also the scene in Jones's house when she is found primping in the mirror (31), the scene after the counterrevolution when she is found hiding in the stall (49), and her final ignominious defection to Foxwood (51-52).
16. I'm thinking of Orwell's naturalism, which is evident not only in the epigraph to this section ("The Politics of Teaching"), but in the following atypical passage: "With [the pigs'] superior knowledge it was natural that they should assume leadership" (35).
17. One can, I think, construct a critique of Orwell's humanism by mobilizing what I take to be the anti-anti-"Man" passages in *Animal Farm*: "There comrades, is the answer to all our problems. It is summed up in a single word—Man" (19).
18. For my understanding of what Brecht calls "the paedagogical effect," see Brecht (31-32). Though my sense of the "pedaedagogical imperative" has a specifically Brectian inflection, see also Felman.
19. On education-as-"social transformation," see Shor and Freire (177-87).
20. Given the increasingly attenuated sense of history associated with postmodernity, one might argue that the exact opposite is true: more people know (more) about Madonna than about, say, Julius Caesar. Put another way, the logic of "fashion" or, say, shock of the new, tied as it is to the

consumptive, deterritorializing flow of capital, has—at least since the advent of the historical avant-garde—*accelerated*.

21. Though the phrase "free and indivisible" appears to be a citation (Hirsch alludes later to the Pledge of Allegiance), it is in fact a conflation.
22. The Panthers' Marxist-Leninist, as well as Maoist, orientations are both well known and well documented. I cite an article that appeared in the *Black Panther* on the same date as Hirsch's citation (17 January 1970): "The Black Panther documents step by step the actions taken by, and programs instituted by the Black Panther Party in its unstoppable drive to serve the people; and documents before the whole world the repression and murders committed by Amerikkka's corrupt monopoly capital in its dastardly attempts to stop this move to institute people's power" (Foner 8). See also Foner (xvii-xix). Lest I be accused of wholeheartedly endorsing the Panthers' position, I should add that their sexism and homophobia are also well documented.
23. It is important to observe—inasmuch as it is irrelevant, apparently, to Hirsch's argument—that J. Edgar Hoover repeatedly issued directives to his Counterintelligence Program personnel to move against not only the BPP in general but the "distributors of the [Black Panther] Party newspaper, *The Black Panther*" (Churchhill and Vander Will 68).
24. For an account of that larger history within which the history of the BPP must be situated—I am of course referring to the sixties—see Gitlin, in particular "The Bogey of Race" (348-51). For an account of the *Black Panther*, see Peck (esp. 65-66, 76-77, 130-31, 223-25).
25. "Secure yourselves Knowledge, you who are frozen! You are starving, grab hold of a book: It's a weapon. You must take over leadership" (Giroux, "Mass Culture" 74 and 85). Though Brecht did not approve of, for example, G. W. Pabst's production of *The Threepenny Opera* (1931), he was not adverse—at least early on—to "visual culture"; on the contrary, he recognized its revolutionary potential. See, for instance, "The Film, the Novel and Epic Theatre (From *The Threepenny Lawsuit*)" (47-51). "Literature needs the film not only indirectly but also directly. That decisive extension of its social duties which follows from the transformation of art into a paedagogical discipline entails the multiplying or the repeated changing of the means of representation" (48). I might add that the heading for the part of the essay in which this passage appears is tellingly sarcastic: "Art Can Do without the Cinema."
26. Giroux tends to conflate the visual and the mass media when in fact the former is only one, albeit the dominant, part of the latter.
27. The linked notions of "technological determinism" and "cultural pessimism" are Williams's (see "Culture and Technology" 129). As for Giroux's language of containment, one might cite the conclusion to "Mass Culture": "Print technology contains the immediate promise of turning people into social agents who can manipulate and use the book, newspaper and other forms of print communication to their own advantage. It contains the emancipation" (85).
28. As Williams argues: "Whether the theory and practice [of television] can be changed will depend not on the fixed properties of the medium nor on the necessary character of its institutions, but on a continually renewable social action and struggle" (*Television* 134).
29. Paul Smith's "Popular-Cultural-Commodity-Text"—which comprises a frankly "condemnatory" reading of *Heartbreak Ridge* (1986) and *Lethal Weapon* (1987)—displays a similar negativity. However, unlike Giroux's "Celluloid Partiotism," its critique is more explicitly positioned against the recent "celebratory tendency" in the left/popular-cultural criticism and is therefore mobilized by a different, more nuanced rhetorical strategy. As will be obvious from, among other things, the conclusion to this essay, my polemical emphasis is different from both Giroux's and Smith's.
30. Though I cannot recommend its understanding of *cinematic* language, *Camera Politica* provides a more dialectical reading of the "discourse of anti-Communism" than Giroux. See Ryan and Kellner (194-216).
31. See Smith (46n12).
32. See Giroux and Simon (1-29). For a more critical approach, see Aronowitz (197-217).
33. Giroux notes that although the dichotomous construction of "reason and passion" in *Dirty Dancing* lines up along class lines (bourgeoisie-as-head, proletariat-as-body), Baby's introduction to the proletarian pleasures of "dirty dancing" (embodied in the person of Johnny Castle, the dance

instructor at Kellerman's Resort) evokes his own adolescent initiation into the differently inscribed "body politic" of black working-class dances (Giroux and Simon 19-20).

34. I cannot develop my reading of West's important article here. For his critique of Malcolm X, see pp. 51-52.
35. I would only note that Mookie's garbage-can throwing not only ignites the arguably self-defensive violence of the crowd but that this act of violence is consonant with the politics of Malcolm X, who has—as it were—the last word (note the epigraph).
36. Accordingly, the other sections of "Differences" address these "new social movements" as well as the "class question": "Coming Out: The Gay Question" (e.g., James Baldwin's *Giovanni's Room* [1956]), "Feminism, Fantasy, and Science Fiction" (e.g., Joanna Russ's *The Female Man* [1975]), and "Class Dance: Pictures of the American Proletariat" (e.g., Mike Nichols's *Working Girl* [1988]).

Works Cited

Aronowitz, Stanley. "Working Class Identity and Celluloid Fantasies." Giroux and Simon. 197-217.

Aronowitz, Stanley, and Henry Giroux. "Resistance in Radical Theories of Schooling." *Education under Siege: The Conservative, Liberal, and Radical Debate over Schooling*. South Hadley, MA: Bergin & Garvey, 1985.

Barthes, Roland. "From Work to Text." *Image/Music/Text*. Trans. Stephen Heath. New York: Hill & Wang, 1977. 155-64.

Benjamin, Walter. "Conversations with Brecht." *Reflections*. 1978. Trans. Edmund Jephcott. New York: Schocken, 1986.

Brecht, Bertolt. *Brecht on Theatre*. 1964. Trans. John Willet. London: Methuen, 1987.

Carey, James. "Overcoming Resistance to Cultural Studies." *Communication as Culture: Essays on Media and Society*. Boston: Unwin Hyman, 1989.

Chomsky, Noam. "The Responsibility of Intellectuals." *American Power and the New Mandarins*. New York: Vintage, 1969.

Churchhill, Ward, and Jim Vander Will. *Agents of Repression: The FBI's Secret Wars against the Black Panther Party and the American Indian Movement*. Boston: South End, 1988.

Cohen, Jean L. *Class and Civil Society: The Limits of Marxian-Critical Theory*. Amherst: U of Massachusetts P, 1982.

Felman, Shoshana. "Psychoanalysis and Education: Teaching Terminable and Interminable." Barbara Johnson, ed. *The Pedagogical Imperative: Teaching as a Literary Genre*. Spec. issue of *Yale French Studies* 63 (1982).

Foner, Philip S., ed. *The Black Panthers Speak*. Philadelphia: Lippincott, 1970.

Foucault, Michel. *Discipline and Punish: The Birth of the Prison*. 1978. Trans. Alan Sheridan. New York: Vintage, 1979.

Gibson, William. *Neuromancer*. New York: Ace, 1984.

Giroux, Henry. "Celluloid Patriotism in Hollywood Films and Television Programming." *Schooling and the Struggle for Public Life: Critical Pedagogy in the Modern Age*. Minneapolis: U of Minnesota P, 1988. 23-28.

______. "Mass Culture and the Rise of the New Illiteracy: Implications for Reading." *Teachers as Intellectuals: Toward a Critical Pedagogy of Learning*. South Hadley, MA: Bergin & Garvey, 1988. 74-85.

______, and Roger Simon. "Popular Culture as a Pedagogy of Pleasure and Meaning." Giroux and Simon, eds. *Popular Culture, Schooling, and Everyday Life*. South Hadley, MA: Bergin & Garvey, 1989. 1-29

Gitlin, Todd. *The Sixties: Days of Hope, Days of Rage*. New York: Bantam, 1987.

Graff, Gerald. *Professing Literature: An Institutional History*. 1987. Chicago: U of Chicago P, 1989.

Gramsci, Antonio. "The Study of Philosophy." *The Prison Notebooks*. Ed. and trans. Quintin Hoare and Geoffrey Nowell Smith. New York: International, 1971. 323-77.

Harrington, Michael. "The Democratic Essence." *Socialism*. 1972. New York: Bantam, 1973. 41-64.

Heller, Scott. "Protest at Cultural-Studies Meeting Sparked by Debate over New Field." *Chronicle of Higher Education* 36.3 (2 May 1990).

Hirsch, E. D., Jr. *Cultural Literacy: What Every American Needs to Know*. Boston: Houghton Mifflin, 1987.

Kampf, Louis, and Paul Lauter. Introduction. Kampf and Lauter, eds. *The Politics of Literature: Dissenting Essays on the Teaching of English*. New York: Vintage, 1972.

Marx, Karl, and Friedrich Engels. *The Communist Manifesto*. Trans. Samuel Moore. Harmondsworth: Penguin, 1987.

McCabe, Colin. "Class of '68: Elements of an Intellectual Autobiography 1967-81." *Tracking the Signifier: Theoretical Essays*. Minneapolis: U of Minnesota P, 1984. 1-32.

Merod, James. *The Political Responsibility of the Critic*. 1987. Ithaca: Cornell UP, 1989.

Ohmann, Richard. *English in America: A Radical View of the Profession*. New York: Oxford UP, 1976.

Orwell, George. *Animal Farm*. New York: New American Library, 1946.

Paulson, William. *The Noise of Culture: Literary Texts in a World of Information*. Ithaca: Cornell UP, 1988.

Peck, Abe. *Uncovering the Sixties: The Life and Times of the Underground Press*. New York: Pantheon, 1985.

Ryan, Michael, and Douglas Kellner. "Vietnam and the New Militarism." *Camera Politica: The Politics and Ideology of Contemporary Hollywood Film*. Bloomington: Indiana UP, 1988. 194-216.

Shor, Ira, and Paulo Freire. "The Dream of Social Transformation: How Do We Begin?" *A Pedagogy for Liberation: Dialogues on Transforming Education*. South Hadley, MA: Bergin & Garvey, 1987.

Smith, Paul. "Pedagogy and the Popular-Cultural-Commodity-Text." Giroux and Simon. 31-46.

Taylor, A. J. P. Introduction. *The Communist Manifesto*. 7-47.

West, Cornel. "The Paradox of the Afro-American Rebellion." Sohnya Sayres, ed. *The Sixties, without Apology*. Minneapolis: U of Minnesota P, 1984.

Williams, Raymond. *Television: Technology and Cultural Form*. New York: Schocken, 1975.

______. "Culture and Technology." *The Year 2000*. New York: Pantheon, 1983. 128-52.

______. "Literature." *Marxism and Literature*. 1977. Oxford: Oxford UP, 1985. 45-54.

Discipline and Resistance: The Subjects of Writing and the Discourses of Instruction

> When they make these intercultural, hybrid demands, the natives are both challenging the boundaries of discourse and subtly changing its terms by setting up another specifically colonial space of power/knowledge. And they do this under the eye of authority, through the production of "partial" knowledges and positionalities. . . . Such objects of knowledges make the signifiers of authority enigmatic in a way that is "less than one and double." They change their conditions of recognition while maintaining their visibility: they introduce a lack that is then represented as a doubling or mimicry. (Bhabha, "Signs" 161)

In the following pages I will argue that because liberal American culture situates the classroom in a hierarchical organization that is like colonization, the progressive ambitions of a poststructuralist pedagogy may shatter—or rigidify—in the resultant hall of mirrors. Authority and resistance double one another—and student resistance may appear not as a critical practice, but as a lack or even a refusal of theory's progressive authority. American students, like the subjects of British colonization, produce partial knowledges that "make the signifiers of authority enigmatic." Therefore the new pedagogy needs to address this complication by examining the enigmas of classroom subjectivities.

Poststructuralism has argued against empiricism that knowledge is a function of texts, and that our discourse produces the objects of study rather than transparently reporting facts. A growing number of critics, from the theoretically oriented Gregory Ulmer in *Post(e)-Pedagogy* through the advocacy of Robert Scholes in *Textual Power* to Vincent Leitch, Gayatri Spivak, Geoffrey Hartman, Sharon Crowley, and others in Douglas Atkins and Michael Johnson's *Writing and Reading Differently*, and increasing numbers of theorists in rhetoric and composition, such as Patricia Bizzell and David Bartholomae, have become convinced that we should put poststructuralist textual studies into practice in the classroom. Such pedagogy needs to include a theorizing of the people who participate as classroom subjects. There is nothing in Derridean theory to suggest that the relationships of individuals should escape deconstruction, but the way institutions operate tends to limit deconstructive activities to the safety of what's in print. Without addressing the positionality of students and teachers, a new emphasis on the text is not necessarily progressive. Like the old objectivities, it may in fact be accompanied by an increasing disenfranchisement of the agents of reading and writing—students and teachers. What I would like to argue is that an ongoing reflexivity about the powers exercised by the hierarchical order of education can loosen the hold of that order.

If teaching practices limit the discourses of instruction to textual discipline rather than including those cultural discourses that contend to produce the subjects of the class, theorists are in danger of subverting the access to power that might be the result of a postmodern pedagogy. Will the instructor facilitate cultural literacy or interrogate the processes of determining literacy? It is not a straightforward matter to question or resist the authority of discourse and institution. How might postmodern pedagogy approach student resistance when it takes the form of resistance to theory? Occupying the position of seeming authority, how might the teacher interrogate his or her own relationship to power and knowledge?

Power in the classroom is commonly construed as the opposition of teacher and students, with teachers practicing something like imperialism and students practicing mimicry or resistance. The teacher, that is, seems to occupy the position of authority. And that positioning of authority is probably an important component of the way students learn to read and write, though its effects may not be easily predictable. Like the racial difference that Abdul JanMohamed has called "the Manichean allegory" of British colonialism (61), "difference" as a category in pedagogy serves to regulate and essentialize the discourse of the classroom. "Difference" establishes a hierarchy of teacher over student, but also creates hierarchical distinctions among students, who, at the very moment that their individual differences are noted, appear as known subjects. The very gesture that asks that we respect differences goes on to designate categories to organize and limit the knowledge of classroom subjects: race, class, gender, ethnic origin, learning style, language, or local culture. These categories of difference assume the status of realities outside classroom inquiry—facts—and pedagogy therefore seems powerless to affect them. But by resisting the singular authority given the subject of pedagogy, teachers can open up the classroom to differences and to critical thinking.

Any pedagogy that eliminates the classroom "text" from its questioning repeats the colonizing gesture. Critical problematizing should therefore interrogate the authority relations that seem at once so stereotypical and so natural. However, neither teachers nor students will find this easy. The hierarchical ordering of all pedagogical discourse by examinations, grades, and other institutional procedures for certification makes critical approaches difficult and opposition not necessarily effective. For instance, in *Learning to Labor* Paul Willis has written about how the opposition of working-class lads to school was the very mechanism that effectively formed them as working-class subjects.

Homi Bhabha's work on colonization may help us to examine these pedagogical relationships. Just as the structure of the colonial situation demands that the colonized mimic the colonizer, the classroom situates students in a mirror relationship to authority that is enforced by structures largely determined outside the classroom. Bhabha argues that the colonized function to reflect—and so, in a narcissistic doubling, to create—the identity of the colonizer. The difference that is marked in the very act of mimicry delineates at once the totality of the colonizer and the otherness of the colonized, not an identity but "less than one and double." Following Bhabha's lead, one should look for student differences in student doubling of instructional authority. How does students' conformity to an economic, political, and social power they imagine to be operating in the university both produce and distort the image of education? How can instructors effectively resist the negative effects of this authority?

Of course, Bhabha's analysis of colonial mimicry could be criticized for its political passivity with respect to the operations of imperialism—and a similar analysis of pedagogy is vulnerable to a similar objection. However, simple opposition to the authority of institutions and disciplines positions students so they are simply reproducing imaginary power relationships. How might productive resistance be characterized? How do we recognize the forms of difference at work? If students and teachers alike are functions of the discourses of instruction, where are the cracks in the social reproduction, and where are the borders or limits where antagonism might be located?

These power relations show up in obvious ways in student writing, but may also be hidden within subtexts that produce lacks that appear as ignorance. Let us consider, for example, the case of a North Dakota student, asked a couple of years ago by his composition instructor to write a paragraph making a case for a belief to which he had strong personal commitment. What the student wrote didn't please his instructor much—it was neither concrete nor specifically personal. It was, however, written at a moment when the contradiction between the violent social and economic upheaval experienced by rural families and the middle-class ethic of individual responsibility had become pressing. Here is what he said:

> I believe in failure. I think that there are two kinds of failure, partial and complete. Partial failure is when you have accomplished part of your goal, but didn't reach the point you expected to. Complete failure is failure to attain any part of your goal. Your amount of failure depends on the goal you set and the standards of yourself and others. What is a failure to one person may not be to another person, depending on their own personal goals. Failure is an individualized thing.

Even though this student is writing about failure, he writes from the position of the discourse of success, with talk about individual goals and achievements. Nevertheless, his professor, a colleague of mine, did not think he had written successfully. The text sounds like the ideology of individualism it means to imitate, and it even understands that one must add a new twist to the commonplace—here, a belief in failure. What has gone wrong? And why did this particular paper bother my colleague enough that he made it an example of what is wrong with student writing? *Could* the student simply have added concrete, personal detail and turned failure into success? Empiricism falters as a model for this student, who cannot imagine the self as the subject of an experience he could substitute for the covenant he has reworked. The professor does not know, from this paragraph, what he needs to know to reduce what the student means to personal terms, and that resistance to meaning may be precisely the point. The student, on the other hand, does not know what kinds of failures the professor might acknowledge as acceptable. The student hopes that he has shown enough mastery of popular rhetoric that his failure paper will succeed, but the professor, denying that institutional conventions are the issue, marks the paper a failure. Both remain ignorant of the power struggles at work.

At such moments it seems that if only we instructors were explicit enough about what we want—if only we exposed our ideology totally?—we could demand that students learn to write our way. We could then make some progress. But instead of insisting on solutions where the problem is antagonism, perhaps we should prefer to make the difficulties explicit.

Much of the current talk about schools—the various calls for reform, the literacy movement and E. D. Hirsch, Jr.'s version of "cultural literacy," political endorsements of education as important—takes place within a liberal narrative of social progress. When, for example, Michael Dukakis addressed students at Iowa State about his views on education, he told them the familiar narrative about his immigrant parents and how schooling enabled them to make it in America. In such views education functions as the primary means of social mobility, of assimilation, and the problem for the English teacher is simply to pass on the Anglophone cultural heritage to the new immigrants flooding our schools. But there's a dark side to literacy and assimilation and social mobility. In the name of progress, the cultural other is superseded; in the name of mastery, the resistant minority is repressed. The different circumstances of women, blacks, immigrants, the rural poor, Native Americans, the homeless—the failure of anyone not to make it in the American way—can be chalked up to individual responsibility. Fearing failure, students hide their differences.

Some kind of resistance to a monolithic cultural literacy is important. But student resistance too often appears as ignorance, stupidity, or willful misunderstanding. Resistance to the mechanisms of progress may have more to do with the instructor than with the student.

Critical theorists have found resistance fruitful, including the notion that theory can speak from the position of the oppressed and the disenfranchised. For instance, Judith Fetterley has described the feminist "resisting reader," who uncovers the sexism of a text by reading against the grain. In *Women Teaching for Change*, Kathleen Weiler has argued that a feminist position can allow teachers to open a classroom to critical thinking and make a place for differences. These feminist notions of resistance have certain overlappings with the Marxist tradition, whose power derives, Louis Althusser contends, from the political repositioning of the young Marx from a petit-bourgeois to a working-class discourse, and so to a discourse of resistance. Such changes of position open up a political unconscious, making class differences appear in discourse. Similarly, Paulo Freire's organization of literacy programs tries to empower students by changing classroom relationships; the teacher moves from a position of authority to a position of dialogue that asks the students to participate as masters of their own culture, resistant to the domination of the instructional situation. Literacy then becomes not just a skill, but an act of emerging consciousness. Henry Giroux and Stanley Aronowitz have worked to define resistance as more than oppositional thinking—as a way to theorize new discourses of possibility. Resistance seems to hold great promise, in other words, as a mode of critical thinking and instruction.

New modes of classroom organization seem to reflect this commonality in spite of political differences. Advocates of a critical classroom such as Ira Shor organize programs that look very much like the teacherless writing class Peter Elbow describes, or the dialogic classroom of both Freire and the postmodernists. Shor hopes to promote class consciousness, critical thinking, and resistance to capitalist ideology. Elbow hopes to empower students as free individuals—a liberal ideology permeates his theorizing of writing pedagogy. Bartholomae, working with postmodern theory to situate composition, in particular the instruction of basic writers, advocates an open-ended undecidability about the construction of knowledge. The Marxist, liberal, and post-structuralist approaches are so variously at odds that their commonality tends to be overlooked, but they all converge on a single implication for pedagogy: students (like the oppressed) have had a master-slave relationship with educational institutions, and theorists have problematized their own relationship to mastery to situate themselves as students, always engaged open-endedly (and uncertainly) in learning. Moreover, they position themselves as a resistance within the institution. Criticism as resistance allows the instructor to critique the authority of the discipline.

Nevertheless, critical theory faces pedagogical difficulties because resistance positions students and teachers differently. The question of agency remains part of the problem of the subject, particularly pressing in American culture because of our long commitment to individualism and the idea of self-development. While theory has embraced resistance, students and the public have come to a somewhat different point. As the global economy demands more and more workers, and economic marginality seems more apparent in the United States, a significant number of students are experiencing a desire for economic aptitude—very different from a desire for learning, or for self-development, or even for learning about their cultural traditions.

For the economically anxious, the desire for literacy must correspond to the desire for economic power: literacy seems then strictly an instrumental good, not a good in itself. The postmodern rejection of instrumental language from such a position looks like a refusal. While theorists resist the rationalizing machinery of the institution, students are caught up in it, implicated in its operations. The desire for economic aptitude means that instruction that does not carry out imperialistic ideologies, in form as well as content, may violate the position of student agency whenever students say they want to learn "practical," "real-world" "skills." What does it mean when students resist resistance, reject critical thinking, and especially do not want to think about the uncertainty and fragmentation of postmodern culture? Is the problem here similar to the problem of feminism, confronted with many women who seem to embrace patriarchy, and with the theoretical difficulty of a discourse shaped and situated by the contradictory terms of essentializing subjectivity and needing to imagine a subjective agency that is other?

Some poststructuralists, such as Scholes, have largely avoided the problem of the subject's agency by opposing the ideology of individualism and locating power not in the individual but in the cultural text. Writing as a discipline has perhaps gained momentum recently because it is theoretically compatible with such a view. The idea that writing is disciplined not so much by the powers of an individual author as by the power of the academic discourses has, in fact, increasingly been receiving attention from writing theorists. Kenneth Bruffee has taken the social construction of knowledge to imply that students might best learn to write through collaboration rather than in isolation. But simply opposing individualism and endorsing the social construction of knowledge does not give us a critique of power. As Bartholomae and Bizzell ("Arguing" 150) have both argued, the discourses of the university are implicated in power relationships with students, a situation especially evident with respect to basic writers. What happens to the way we can think about the teacher and the student and their material circumstances when we recognize the power of discourse to produce knowledge? How are we to conceive of resistance?

Seeing resistance as a kind of critical thinking assumes that it is conscious. What in the classroom looks like ignorance or even irrationality may be, on the other hand, a resistance to that very view of resistance. What is inscribed in the classroom discourse is unacceptable difference, the crack in the mirror. Within the available means of expression, it seems unspeakable, like an unconscious. Thus the psychotherapeutic dialogue offers a model for addressing such resistance. Shoshana Felman has described how the resistance of the patient in psychoanalysis resembles that of students in the classroom.

What the therapist practices both locates and opens up resistance, providing access to the unconscious. "Teaching," Felman argues, "like analysis, has to deal not so much with *lack* of knowledge as with *resistances* to knowledge" (30). The teacher seems to know something out there in the world, facts, information, referential knowledge. But what the teacher knows is what Jacques Lacan has called "textual knowledge," knowledge about interpretation, not things. This kind of knowing cannot be passed from one to another like coins, but can only be used or practiced, and every situation will elicit a new interpretation. So ignorance, Felman argues, "is not a simple lack of information but the incapacity—or the refusal—to acknowledge *one's own implication* in the information" (30). Learning, and not just classroom management, has everything to do with the subject-positions students and teachers occupy. It is understandable that a student might be willing to write, "I believe in failure," and yet not be willing to go on to make that statement personal and specific, even though the writing might improve. The student refuses "to acknowledge [his] own implication" in what he writes, and failure multiplies. But this is not a straightforward failure to follow directions. The student must have felt that he was giving the instructor what was called for, stating the correct belief. If asked why he didn't go on to describe in concrete detail the specifics of personal failure, he probably would not say anything that sounded like resistance. He would say, "I didn't know what the professor wanted."

Pedagogy and Difference

> The way to see the fish and to write the fish is first to see how one's discourse writes the fish. (Scholes 144)

In his account of its textual history, Scholes demonstrates how Ezra Pound's exemplary tale about Louis Agassiz's method of teaching works to produce a certain kind of writing (129-48). According to the story, Agassiz taught his students to be good observers by making them look and look again at the bones of a fish until they began to see what was there and could write a full and careful description. What Scholes points out is how the story hides its reliance on texts. Although the tale appears to prove the merit of empiricism, of close observation, it shows instead the way a certain kind of discourse produces discipline. The discourse itself constrains and directs what a student might say, or a teacher admit. The fact was that Agassiz's students had a textual source in the teacher's own writings for the perception, for example, of the fish's bilateral symmetry. But this textual origin is obscured in the account of close inspection—the students appear to discover what they had already learned.

As repeated by Pound and then by a number of books on writing, the story has played its part in constructing a writing discipline based on observation and concrete description, a discipline that denied the importance of reading, or of membership in a discursive community with shared texts, to the would-be writer. We are now struggling as we teach writing with the realization that different and unequal communities of discourse exist in a university, and that these discursive habits of mind indeed function to produce the texts that the disciplines are willing to acknowledge as objects of inquiry.

The subjects of classroom discourse—students and teachers—are also implicated in disciplinary textuality. What Althusser calls the "problematic" of the text writes us. We are the other fish. If we think of difference as merely textual, somehow innocent of other context, we are dealing with an illusion of leisurely recreation, and we are all in danger of merely being on a fishing expedition. Rather, we must interrogate our own positions in the discourse. But how can we talk about the interaction of classroom differences of gender, race, or class with the production of writing? If students are the fish, we who speak as the subjects of teaching profess a discourse that would rewrite them. Students might well see us as out to eat them alive.

Overtly political discourses such as Marxism and feminism make ideology visible, but the ideal of objective, rational inquiry is also political. Teachers produce and reproduce culture within the constraints of discursive possibilities, in particular constrained by literate discourse. We teach within the boundaries of a history of *reading* that defines us and our relationships to students. It is not a personal power that determines our authority—if it were, we would find it easier to extricate ourselves from the oppressive features of teaching. But neither is our authority based upon an ideologically neutral objectivity.

If we suspect that we too are the fish, we can at least see how our interests might propel us into elusiveness. This elusiveness is at work even in Scholes's analysis. When we recognize the "power of the text," do we then deny that we have any personal responsibility or agency? If we acknowledge, that is, that we are both subjects of and subject to the disciplines we teach, we may have a tendency to view this positioning as disregarding our personal interests and putting us outside the operations of power, much like the old stance of neutral objectivity. Reducing all discourse to the symbolic, to a textuality without reference, can make difference seem purely structural, without attachments to human agency. Teacherly disinterestedness can then deny that it is out to eat anyone alive.

However, as Bartholomae points out in "Inventing the University," the academic context of student writing is often precisely the issue, and beyond the basic writer's reach. There is no neutral ground for the study of discourse, and the desire of students within the discourse of the university produces effects such as pressing for good grades, or trying to avoid classes that are neither irrelevant nor alien to the discourses they are trying to learn. As Michel Foucault puts it:

> Neither the relation of discourse to desire, nor the processes of its appropriation, nor its role among non-discursive practices is extrinsic to its unity, its characterization, and the laws of its formation. They are not disturbing elements which, superposing themselves upon its pure, neutral, atemporal, silent form, suppress its true voice and emit in its place a travestied discourse, but, on the contrary, its formative elements. (68)

Scholes seems to enact the kind of separation between text and context that Foucault would not allow. Developing an aspect of deconstructive and semiotic criticism that disregards the political, he is not critical enough of how the school functions as an institution to produce the available discourses and knowledge. Furthermore, he does not examine the way students and teachers enter into textuality—the way discourse addresses, and, in Althusser's term, "interpellates" students as subjects (182).

Classroom discourse frequently reduces differences to the single difference circulating around the obfuscated question of authority—the difference between student and teacher. There is, of course, more than one way that difference can seem singular and stereotypical. Ostensible recognition of race, class, gender can be equally reductive. The teacher (as authority) and the students (as audience) so frequently enter into covert arrangements to ignore all realities of power that difference may come to seem irrational, itself the other, all that keeps students, teachers, and text apart. If only, we hear again and again, we could all learn to "communicate."

At the same time, the difference between students and teachers is what keeps classrooms the same, producing adolescence as a problem of identity. A postmodern pedagogy could overthrow a number of assumptions that now seem natural in teaching, including this one, to involve us in recognizing the English teacher's engagement in power relations. Textual power extends beyond not only text but classroom, affecting teacher as well as student. But interrogation can open up a space for resistance.

Resistance and Relationship

If our classrooms represent the opportunity to find a better life—and many new immigrants obviously see them that way—why are they also the locus of failure? Is it because middle-class tyranny takes the form of *demanding* mobility, enforcing the modernist social consensus that change is good? If so, or to the extent that this is so, those who remain the same through desire or necessity—refusing to make English their first language, change their gender or the color of their skin, or even move to or from the city—are the ones who seem "different."

In the past year I have worked with a Chinese woman who came to the United States to improve her ability to teach English in Chinese schools. Her class contributions ranged from a wonderful, sensitive explanation of Chinese poetry and its relationship to visual imagery to a discouraging, seemingly stubborn failure to grasp what I wanted in interpretive essays. She had such formidable difficulties writing anything that required advancing a thesis, along with persistent small mistakes of vocabulary and syntax, that I began to think that she simply needed to learn better English, whatever that meant—that she wasn't "ready" for the advanced courses in writing or literature. Then I participated in an oral examination where she explained her interpretation of F. Scott Fitzgerald's *The Great Gatsby* (1925) and Ernest Hemingway's *The Old Man and the Sea* (1952). She had prepared meticulously, reading biographies and background materials, searching out relevant quotations from the texts.

Fitzgerald is less acceptable than Hemingway for the Chinese, she said, because it is not clear that Fitzgerald means to criticize Gatsby, even though the latter acquired his wealth through questionable means and dreams of adultery. Hemingway's old man, on the other hand, learns a valuable lesson: he lives in society like the fish in the sea; it is important to be satisfied with little fish, and not to destroy himself and hurt others by trying to catch a bigger fish than he should.

She read the works as if they were allegories of a political unconscious that we do not share with her. She read with no sense of irony; none of the American modernist knowledge about how to read our texts informed her rhetorical strategies. She assumed that a novel ought to have a moral—that it ought to serve the larger interests of society in a straightforward way. The very notion of aesthetic distance appeared to her a cultural bias. The idea that a free society could produce a reading free from lessons about class struggle and writing free from social doctrine seemed to her a political ploy, a simple matter of taking sides. To interpret in the American way might be disloyal to Chinese ways of thought, she said.

This is not a simple demonstration of ignorance. Although my student may well learn to interpret American literature in the context of American culture, it will be because she acquiesces to a cultural flexibility that we demand, one not entirely mutual, one neither innocent nor neutral. Learning to read and write our way may be assimilation, a good, or colonization, a form of violence.

If the fish in Agassiz's lesson seems to establish a certain kind of objectivity as the grounds of discursive competence, the fish in Hemingway's novel also seems to represent aspects of a code needed for "interpretive competency" in the West. The conquest of knowledge is like the conquest of nature. Our heroic gestures may fail, but we do not easily give up the effort. Our writing requires the gesture of heroic effort, even if it is in vain. And so we have a hard time thinking of ourselves as the objects of writing—fish caught up in nets of our mutual invention. Recognizing that students must write in a network of texts does not take us far enough; texts seem too innocent. We need also to recognize that teaching writing may plunge us into power struggles about cultural dominance—that teaching may not only help but also colonize. As teachers we are subject to power we are not altogether free to redirect.

The profession itself is the subject of current theoretical debate. While some departments, such as those at Duke, Carnegie Mellon, and Syracuse, have already made changes that articulate certain implications of postmodern theory, others are still exploring whether the fundamental study of an English department ought to be critical studies or textual studies or rhetoric or literature or culture. The canon is still at issue. Feminists must argue heatedly for courses in women's writing against equally heated colleagues, some of whom still claim that women's writing is too marginal to count as a requirement and still worry about the erosion of our coherence, our discipline. African-American studies may be even more frequently under attack. In spite of these stances, we are still talking. But these are times when departments have difficulty defining themselves. In the middle of this institutional discursive crisis, it would seem that at least we could not be accused of verbal totalitarianism. However, we need to remember that pluralism and acceptance of differences—even the agonistic mode of discussion—are characteristic of the dominant academic culture.

But what about the idea that English departments ought to work for excellence? Does that undermine the commitment to differences, especially in the case of basic writers? The developmental classes are places where students with wildly different cultural training can begin to acquire the specialized culture and discourses of the university. But these needs seem outside the considerations of disciplines.

It is no accident that remedial or basic classes occupy the place where an English department remains most unconscious about its curriculum. The disciplines have no interest in developing peoples—as disciplines, they cannot even recognize the nature of the conflict. At this boundary, where education and social margins mix, we can see—but do we really want to look?—the conflict not of academic discursive communities, but of interpretive communities whose relative power is very different. When students come to school, the knowledge games of the academy work to colonize them, and they feel alien. Easy resolutions such as lowering requirements have paradoxical effects, such as lowering student access to excellence. Shattering the disciplines on behalf of marginal students makes what counts as knowledge more vulnerable to elite power struggles. Easy resolutions in favor of tougher requirements also have paradoxical effects, not only by discouraging marginal students, but by forcing certain closed sets of standards on the institution that destroy its ability to engage in critical discourse. Thus the difficulties of students produce lines of fracture in the institutional totality. These intersections also produce less obvious conflict but much greater power struggles than the battles of critics and curriculum.

The university is reluctant to acknowledge such struggles, even though students must submit to discourses that colonize them as subjects, and the face of the institution itself will mirror the effects of their resistance. And by the forms of their acquiescence as well as their opposition, students enact ideological resistance.

Scholes's text-driven schooling leads us to ask what happens when the master of texts, the interpretive virtuoso, encounters students. Does the teacher not possess an authority like that of the therapist—in Lacanian terms, the "subject supposed to know"? That is, as Scholes insists, what the teacher knows is how to interpret texts. But knowing how to read texts entails a kind of ignorance as well. The words are always mumbling behind our back; like unruly schoolchildren, they have an unconscious, have other agendas. So the teacher does *not* know, as Felman points out—teaching, like therapy, is grounded in ignorance.

What teachers most scandalously do not know is what students think they do know—that is, what students know and what they will learn. No matter how many explanations and instructions teachers write, or how carefully they tailor exams to objectives or evaluations to assignments, and no matter how hard students try to provide exactly what the teachers want, teachers cannot know either what students will repeat, copy, mimic, and remember or what they will forget. It is the question of resistance to knowing, a resistance that is not merely emotional or personal but cultural. What new shapes of knowing and writing arise within that dynamic?

Pedagogy resembles both society and therapy. It may be coercive, may aim to reproduce the dominant ideologies, and yet it is also open to critical practice. Student resistance is not purely personal; it is also political. To the extent that the school functions as Althusser saw it, as an ideological state apparatus, teaching can be viewed as a powerful activity generating not only psychological resistances but resistances connected to the social and political "unconscious" as well.

Felman argues that the mode of learning in the classroom resembles therapy and is likewise characterized by nonlinear temporality:

> Proceeding not through linear progression, but through breakthroughs, leaps, discontinuities, regressions, and deferred action, the analytic learning-process puts indeed in question the traditional pedagogical belief in intellectual perfectability, the progressistic view of learning as a simple one-way road from ignorance to knowledge. (27)

What kinds of success—and failure—do we believe in as teachers? If we can't situate a student paper somewhere on the road to knowledge, how can we look at it? How can we talk about the differences resistance makes?

Bhabha uses Lacanian and Derridean approaches to explore the impact of cultural resistances on the seemingly one-way exchange of colonial discourse. Like Felman, he argues that attempts to dominate in a straightforward fashion are not only immoral but ineffective. As Edward Said has pointed out, a chief characteristic of colonial discourse is to deny dialogue, to deny that the others are capable of representing themselves—in the case of Orientalism, experts claim to "know more about Islam than Islam knows about itself" (219). Women recognize the syndrome.

What Bhabha undertakes, then, is an argument that would overthrow that self-serving construction of absolute mastery, demonstrating that the response to authoritative discourse may undermine and change it, that there is no one-way exchange. Even what is repeated and mimicked comes back as "less than one and double." In the classroom, resistances that re-form the knowledge that the teacher is supposed to convey may be seen as both psychological and political, both conscious and unconscious. If straightforward opposition does not work to end domination, domination itself does not do away with resistance.

In the classroom, the teacher as "master" practices both therapy and imperialism. Students seem to choose assimilation or cultural essentialism, upward mobility or stagnation, docility or rebellion, identity or opposition, but in fact the forms of resistance, as Bhabha points out, may introduce more difference into discourse via mimicry than via simple opposition ("Signs" 151). The situation is not simple, but its heterogeneity can be revealed.

In order to deal with its colonies, nineteenth-century England had to use power in ways that contradicted its self-representation. This produced, Bhabha argues, a splitting, a certain ambivalence in discourse made up of the difference between the progressive and liberal aspect of civil England and the oppressiveness of the colonial governance. I do not mean to suggest that American students are greatly like the nineteenth-century colonial subjects of British imperialism. However, both imperialism and American education have been articulated by liberalism. What Bhabha points out about colonialist discourse may suggest ways of looking at classroom discourse and the fate of difference in classroom exchanges.

Twentieth-century America is split over colonization not only externally but internally, as we confront the large numbers of recent immigrants and the increasing influence of other cultures on schools and businesses. Campaigns for cultural literacy and English First seek less to extend a despotic governance overseas than to defend hegemonic interests at home by asserting a discursive homogeneity in the face of radical heterogeneity. In the universities the outcry against using teaching assistants, especially in the sciences, who are not native speakers of English seems local and pragmatic. But the argument that students have a right to understand teachers gains a hearing in this instance most of all because it advances the assumption of a simple, singular language and culture native to the United States.

The ambivalence in our liberal discourse keeps arguments for empowering the oppressed at cross-purposes with arguments for multicultural dialogue, with immediate implications for curriculum and instruction. Should students read *The Color Purple*? Use Black English in the classroom? Have instruction in their native language—Spanish, Vietnamese, U-pick? Read women writers? At the cost of never reading *Hamlet*? Which comes first, assimilation or cultural differences? What does it mean that most girls never do acquire cultural literacy when it comes to football? And who decides?

One of the things Bhabha can help us with is understanding how the problem is based on an imaginary contradiction—how the illusion of a dominant, coherent "American" tradition might be constituted out of the very encounter with cultural differences. His point about the English colonial presence is that Englishness itself, like the English book, "acquires its meaning *after* the traumatic scenario of colonial difference, cultural or racial, returns the eye of power to some prior, archaic image or identity" ("Signs" 150).

I want to argue that a sense of the American text, and of what cultural literacy might mean in the United States, arises now as a repetition of the English colonial presence, prompted not by the coherence of our national identity but by the excess of multiplicity and the vigorous claims of difference within. Whatever cannot be allowed because it is too marginal is exactly what produces the discriminating presence and authority of a dominant "American culture." The urban adolescent and the children of the new rural poor make a mockery of their teachers' assertions about individual responsibility at the same time that they repeat and enhance the authority of those claims. Sitting in the classroom, day after day, doing nothing, they demand the right to fail, and recognize themselves as choosers of failure, at-risk youth, a new hybrid of individualism.

Bhabha, I must stress, makes no connection between the colonial and the American situation—he is at pains, rather, to contrast "the spirit of the Western nation" to the colonial government, and his contrast depends upon a comparison of the sense of presence and absence, of Derrida's "unanimous people assembled in the self-presence of its speech" and the people separated under the sign of colonial *writing* ("Civility" 71). The situation of a colonized people renders problematic the figure of national authority, especially the authority of a democracy. But we should consider the implication of the fact that in the United States the figure of national authority does not recall the original presence of a monarch or a stable feudal class system, but rather a text—the Constitution—whose bicentennial in 1987 reminded us that we are governed by *writing* in the place of authoritative presence, and by contentious interpretation in the place of obedience. What makes the United States a special case is that we have been decentered from the start—we have always already imagined deconstruction; we have met the text and it is us. What has never been us before is the construction of a national unanimity of culture and language in the name of which we would centralize and canonize the texts of the hybrid melting pot.

Bhabha argues that colonial hybridity involves not the desirable variety of liberal pluralism or the pleasures of a multivalent text, but repeated traces of the dominated that distort and yet mimic colonial authority. By "hybridity" Bhabha means a "*ruse* of recognition" that simultaneously imitates authority and marks the resistances at work ("Signs" 157). Like the unconscious, the cultural other brings into question authority's pretensions to a monologic identity. What makes authority problematic is *not* simple opposition or antagonism or direct resistance. Rather, the very effort to assimilate difference creates this heterogeneity. Thus the demand for a unitary discourse—a common curriculum, for example—will be undermined by the very attempt to imitate when it comes from one defined as different. As Ellen Goodman once pointed out in a column about the withdrawal of Pat Schroeder from the campaign for president, "Most cannot imagine the leader of the Western world signing letters with smiley faces," but the difference in Schroeder's style also makes us uneasy about the "packaging" of the president. Similarly, difference challenges our academic dispassion at the same time that it makes it visible.

That something like a colonial situation should appear in American classrooms is, perhaps, only to be expected. Whose culture do we wish to be literate about? We have always found ourselves in a colonial relationship with the authority of England and the English language, which American pronunciation and usage relentlessly destabilize. American culture is already hybrid, and the image of an American authority or culture is as ambivalent as the relationship between nation and culture inscribed in our appropriation of "American," confusing the figure of two continents, North and South.

What becomes of the text in our classrooms, like whatever we might mean by cultural literacy, is shaped by these cultural relationships. And our schools do not simply reproduce culture; they change it, and irritate our bad conscience. Bhabha summarizes what the native peoples of India did to the English book: imitation became a lack; mimicry did not reproduce, but doubled and distorted.

Students both imitate and subvert cultural authority. This may seem a commonplace—rebelliousness and the adolescent are at one in our minds—but I do not mean the misleading subversions of teenage culture, but rather the differences frequently hidden by adolescent discourse. "Teenager" is not the "native" culture of students, with its consumerist exploitations and economic degradations. It is rather a superimposed discourse that defines opposition to adulthood in ways that repress cultural history and reduce difference to sameness. Students then take up the stance of opposing adolescence to adulthood, repressing more diverse oppositions of class, race, or gender.

Let me return, then, to the question of resistance and Felman's assertion that what pedagogy confronts is not a problem of transmitting information, but rather a problem like resistance. As I have noted, student resistance may take the form of a disturbance, but it may also simply look like ignorance. For teachers, who are the ones who are supposed to know, these disturbances mark the traces of not-knowing—the mutual ignorance that governs the production of the texts—and represent the temptation to arbitrary denials and domination. In this situation, to take the strict psychological posture of the therapist may simply be to endorse repression, for student resistances have to do with more than hormones and preoccupation; they have to do with power, with ideologies in conflict.

When the student mimics the success-centered discourse of individualism in the midst of a falling farm economy, he produces a mottled text. The rural student who "believes in failure" may be resisting the full disclosure of his despair, but his feeling is not just personal. The Chinese student who reads messages against capitalism in Fitzgerald and Hemingway exposes our ironic biases. A student who follows every direction with flattering care resists our claims to value creativity and initiative. A woman who starts every effort with a personal confession resists the pressure of schooling toward a masculine-seeming impersonality. In any case, they return a mimicry of the discourse they imagined the professor wanted, scarred by the mostly hidden hold of other texts, other ideologies. In the fissured mirror of this prose we can see reflected the subject of the student text, and the difference it has introduced into the pure reproduction of culture. If we think of knowledge as a positivity, these differences will seem to frustrate and undermine education. If we think of education as critical, these different texts will mark a starting point for reflection.

And if such texts make us uneasy about our claims to know what we are doing, so much the better.

Works Cited

Althusser, Louis. "Ideology and Ideological State Apparatuses." *Lenin and Philosophy and Other Essays*. Trans. Ben Brewster. New York: Monthly Review P, 1971. 127-86.

Atkins, Douglas, and Michael Johnson, eds. *Writing and Reading Differently: Deconstruction and the Teaching of Composition and Literature*. Lawrence: UP of Kansas, 1985.

Bartholomae, David. "Inventing the University." *Journal of Basic Writing* 5.1 (1986): 4-36.

Bhabha, Homi. "Sly Civility." *October* 28 (1984): 125-38.

______. "Signs Taken for Wonders: Questions of Ambivalence and Authority under a Tree outside Delhi, May 1817." *Critical Inquiry* 12 (August 1985): 144-65.

Bizzell, Patricia. "What Happens When Basic Writers Come to College?" *College Composition and Communication* 37 (1986): 294-301.

______. "Arguing about Literacy." *College English* 50 (1988): 141-53.

Bruffee, Kenneth. "Collaborative Learning and the 'Conversation of Mankind.' " *College English* 46 (1984): 635-52.

Elbow, Peter. *What Is English?* New York: Modern Language Association, 1990.

Felman, Shoshana. "Psychoanalysis and Education: Teaching Terminable and Interminable." *Yale French Studies* 63 (1983): 21-41.

Foucault, Michel. *The Archeology of Knowledge*. Trans. A. M. Sheridan Smith. New York: Harper, 1972.

Goodman, Ellen. "Schroeder Shunned Political 'Packaging.' " *Corvallis Gazette-Times* (2 October 1987): A4.

JanMohamed, Abdul R. "The Economy of Manichean Allegory: The Function of Racial Difference in Colonialist Literature." *Critical Inquiry* 12 (Autumn 1985): 59-87.

Said, Edward. "An Ideology of Difference." *Critical Inquiry* 12 (Autumn 1985): 38-58.

Scholes, Robert. *Textual Power: Literary Theory and the Teaching of English*. New Haven, CT: Yale UP, 1985.

Shor, Ira. *Critical Teaching and Everyday Life*. Boston: South End, 1980.

Ulmer, Gregory. *Applied Grammatology: Post(e)-Pedagogy from Jacques Derrida to Joseph Beuys*. Baltimore: Johns Hopkins UP, 1984.

Weiler, Kathleen. *Women Teaching for Change: Gender, Class and Power*. South Hadley, MA: Bergin & Garvey, 1987.

Willis, Paul. *Learning to Labor: How Working-Class Kids Get Working-Class Jobs*. New York: Columbia UP, 1981.

SUBVERSION AND OPPOSITIONALITY IN THE ACADEMY

My topic in this essay is the rhetoric of subversion—or rupture, or disruption—that is so frequently encountered in critical discourse these days; my purpose is to raise some questions about the implications this rhetoric carries for a politically oppositional practice in the academy. I shall address some important features of poststructuralism and deconstruction, as well as certain components of feminist theory, but I shall try to minimize my focus on theory as such and instead stress a related concern that has increasing influence on our everyday critical practice and pedagogy—namely, the matter of challenging (whether opening up, jettisoning, or, as my former colleague Michael Warner calls it, busting) the literary canon. When I use the term *new scholarship* in this essay, I refer primarily to this canon-busting activity, in conjunction with its roots in post-structuralist, deconstructive, and feminist theory.

Before tackling these critical and literary-historical questions, however, I shall briefly summarize the historical context within which our current discourse about theory and pedagogy is taking place, since any recommendations about political oppositionality necessarily address themselves to a specific situation. This context is profoundly anomalous and contradictory. On the one hand, we seem to be inhabiting a wasteland that makes T. S. Eliot's spiritual desert a comparative oasis. The supersession of Cold War rivalries by a race for newly opened markets that will align emergent and declining superpowers in highly competitive—and increasingly warlike—alliances; the desperation of a declining American empire that is doggedly supporting fascist regimes around the world while creating a massive new poverty class within its own proletariat; the reestablishment of gross inequalities of race and gender, even after decades of popular resistance; the reconversion of the campuses into centers for CIA recruitment and war research: these and other phenomena signal the deepening of a capitalist crisis that can only result in increasing repression and impoverishment for a vast number of the globe's inhabitants.

On the other hand, while CIA recruitment is on the increase, in the academy we seem to be experiencing exciting and progressive developments that signal a very different sort of trend: the number of canon-busting scholars and poststructuralist theorists is also on the increase. A generation of 40ish scholars, whose social and political consciousness was shaped in the crucible of the 1960s and has now reached full maturity, is writing many of the books and articles we now read, and is attaining (or seeking to attain) tenured positions in English and literature departments. Academic Marxism is experiencing a popularity and prestige unprecedented since the 1930s. Whereas fifteen years ago it was heresy to treat literary works as anything other than apolitical, ahistorical, transcendental, and privileged, now, in the wake of poststructuralism, deconstruction, and feminism, it is almost a new orthodoxy to proclaim that everything is ideological, everything is textual and political. And in the wake of the canon-busting movement, the literary tradition emerges as variegated and full of pockets of resistance, rather than monolithic and hegemonic. Ethnic-minority, female, and working-class writers now draw the attention of many of the best younger scholars, and even the stodgy oldsters of the canon are discovered to have been secretly in rebellion against the dominant ideologies of their time.

As a result, the humanist's role as the gatekeeper of tradition seems to have undergone a profound alteration. Where once we were charged with pointing up the uniqueness of works of undisputed genius and the darkness and ambiguity of the human condition, we are now empowered—indeed, encouraged—to relativize, historicize, contextualize. Subversion is the new order of the day, and we appear to inhabit a decidedly oppositional stance in relation to dominant ideology. Allan Bloom and William Bennett may be building up a dangerous case for cultural traditionalism among the populace at large, but we in the academy know that pluralism and decentering constitute a truer and better (kinder and gentler?) approach to cultural matters.

Does this anomalous disjunction between the situation in literature departments and that in the body politic at large indicate that the academy is exempt from the rightward drift I described before? Do we in fact look to semiotics and post-structuralism for political guidance in the moral limbo exemplified by Tammy Faye Bakker and Geraldo Rivera, Donald Trump and George Bush? Is the Chapel Perilous located in departments of comparative literature? Is the canon-busting scholar the Fisher King? Or does the apparent progressiveness of contemporary literary scholarship make for only thunder over distant mountains, but no rain?

No doubt my own skepticism is signaled by my irony. Before explaining the reasons for this irony, however, I should acknowledge the most significant achievements of the canon-busting movement. First, and most obviously, the movement has profoundly democratized literary study, for students are now asked not only to read but also to understand and respect significant numbers of previously marginalized writers and traditions. No major shake-up occurs, of course, when a few women writers or writers of color are given grudging admission to course syllabi, or when old analytic paradigms remain intact. (I think here of a professor who incorporated Charlotte Perkins Gilman's "The Yellow Wallpaper" into his survey of American literature but taught it as an instance of Nabokovian unreliable narration!) But when the critic pays careful attention to those very features of neglected literary texts that have provided the basis for their exclusion from the canon in the first place, then there can occur a profound rupture in literary study—not only with inherited models of literary history but also with the elitist politics undergirding traditional notions of aesthetic value. For example, Cleanth Brooks's valorization of literary texts as setting forth not ideas, but what it would feel like to hold certain ideas (731), can take shape not merely as an expression of an aesthete's disdain for political commitments in general, but as a conservative's reaction against the leftist politics that many texts of the 1930s had worn on their sleeves.[1]

Second, the canon-busting movement invites us to rehistoricize canonical writers as well, and thus rescues them from the toils of the New Critical and archetypal interpretations in which they have been enmeshed for so many years. It becomes difficult indeed to stress Herman Melville's metaphysics to the exclusion of his materialism when "Benito Cereno" is taught not with "The Turn of the Screw" but with Frederick Douglass's *Narrative of the Life of an American Slave* (1845) or Harriet Wilson's *Our Nig* (1859). *The Adventures of Huckleberry Finn* (1884), when viewed in conjunction with Charles Chesnutt's *The Marrow of Tradition* (1901) or W. E. B. Du Bois's *The Souls of Black Folk* (1903), requires the critic to address questions quite different from those invited through a comparison of Mark Twain's novel with *Walden* (1854). As Carolyn Porter has pointed out, Ralph Waldo Emerson's early essays gain a crucial social dimension when seen in the context of the author's anguished reactions to the commodification and alienation of labor in New England mill towns of the 1830s (*Seeing*). After decades of a critical hegemony exercised by the intentional and affective fallacies, by paradox and ambiguity, by epistemological skepticism, and by archetypal patterns of Adamic innocence in a fallen world, history reenters the domain of literary study—not simply as background or source, but as a constitutive component of discourse and textuality. (See also the recent excellent revisionary readings in Karcher, Sundquist, Arac, and Wilding, as well as Russell Reising's theoretical study of the politics of traditional American literary scholarship.)

Despite the significant achievements of the canon-busting movement, however, I believe that in many ways it falls short of its emancipatory rhetoric and frequently ends up reconfirming those very structures of authority to which it purports to be opposed. There are a number of axes along which this process of co-optation and reincorporation occurs. It is to a scrutiny of these that I now turn, first focusing on more exclusively critical issues and then exploring their implication for our political practice in the academy.

Oppositionality, Aesthetics, and Politics

First, the maneuver of opening up the literary tradition—and the curriculum—to previously silenced or marginalized voices is often conflated with the notion that these voices, *because* excluded, must somehow constitute a significant threat to the hegemony of dominant social groups. Now, I do not want to be misunderstood as saying that works such as Jessie Redmon Fauset's *Plum Bun* (1929) or Rebecca Harding Davis's *Life in the Iron Mills* (1861) fail to query important facets of class, race, and gender inequality in American culture and in the discourses by which that culture represents and validates itself. But I am bothered by the argument that these writers, simply by virtue of their race and/or gender positioning, necessarily articulate a counter-discourse that is intrinsically subversive of dominant power relations.

For an instance of this phenomenon—of which there appear more and more examples every day—I refer to Sandra Gilbert's introduction to the recently issued Penguin edition of *The Awakening* (1899). This essay is in some ways politically astute, but also, in my view, injuriously one-sided. Gilbert argues—with considerable force—against the antifeminist reading that would invoke standards of "realistic" plausibility and would accordingly treat the novel's conclusion as " 'a defeat and a regression, rooted in a self-annihilating instinct, in a romantic incapacity to accommodate . . . the limitations of reality.' " Accordingly, Gilbert claims that Edna's final act of suicide represents instead "a resurrection, a pagan female Good Friday that promises a Venusian Easter." The protagonist's final gesture thus "expresses not a refusal to accommodate to reality but a subversive questioning of both reality and 'realism' " (31).

I am in considerable sympathy with Gilbert's desire to point out the oppositional, even triumphant, aspects of Edna's rejection of a patriarchal society that would restrict her possibilities for growth. I also agree with Gilbert's corollary assumption that feminist criticism should address itself not simply to textual patterns of victimization but also to representations of defiance. I would moreover second the view that the presumably "realistic" invocation of probability and common sense as criteria for evaluating Edna's character carries with it a freight of conservative patriarchal judgments. But I also think that, in treating Edna Pontellier as a kind of transcendent pagan goddess, Gilbert profoundly distorts the contradictory nature of Kate Chopin's portrayal of her protagonist—a woman marked by considerable weakness of intellect as much as by greatness of spirit, by a narrow selfishness as much as by a generous identification with cosmic regenerative forces.

In arguing that Edna engages in a "subversive questioning of both reality and 'realism,' " in short, Gilbert mistakes the part for the whole, substituting a univocal—and somewhat anachronistic—celebration of female sexual identity for what is, in my view, in fact a highly tension-filled and ambivalent representation of the cost of woman's emancipation. In particular, I would point out, it is precisely at the text's moment of closure that this conflict emerges most sharply. In its attempt to synthesize the divergent claims of individual and social identity, Chopin's valorization of her protagonist's courage is substantially qualified by profoundly ambiguous patterns of symbolism and imagery that suggest infantile regression at least as much as Venusian transcendence.[2]

The problem I have pointed out in Gilbert's introduction to *The Awakening* is repeated, I believe, in a substantial number of works of the new scholarship. Recent critics are often eager to demonstrate that a noncanonical—or, in this case, recently canonized—writer occupied (and occupies) an oppositional stance in relation to dominant institutions of power. But in arguing their case, these critics too frequently select various subversive moments in the text while overlooking the ways in which these moments are frequently subordinated to larger narrative patterns, most particularly patterns of closure, that negate or at least blunt the text's sporadic querying of hegemonic conceptions of character and social relations. The critic's own brand of oppositional politics, in other words, becomes conflated with authorial intention.[3]

Second, practitioners of the new scholarship too often conclude not only that noncanonical writers possessed subversive politics but also that long-canonized writers experienced significant sympathy with oppressed social groups—or at least ironized or otherwise problematized the more reactionary ideas that their texts would appear to assert. As I mentioned before, Porter's discovery of Emerson's awareness of the alienation of labor in 1830s New England mill towns, and her postulation that this awareness is centrally involved in his formulation of a transcendentalist epistemology, puts Emerson's philosophical enterprise in a badly needed historical context. But this discovery does not in itself demonstrate that Emerson has any particularly strong sympathy for the oppressed masses, who figure in his essays as a somewhat rowdy and undesirable presence—"the unintelligent brute force that lies at the bottom of society [and] is made to growl and mow" (Emerson 960). In Emerson's complex political epistemology, the great unwashed contribute to the anguish suffered by the all-seeing "eye" at least as much as they themselves suffer from a comparable alienation. Nor does demonstrating Emerson's awareness of alienation in itself prove that, in his own philosophical practice, Emerson managed to contest or overcome the commodification that he perceived and decried.

Moreover, Porter extends her analysis of Emerson as a radical—which, given his association with Margaret Fuller and other progressive transcendentalists, is at least plausible—to Henry James, Henry Adams, and William Faulkner as well:

> Each of them [the four cited above] responds critically to his society, and the related terms in which these several radical critiques take shape reveal at once the deepening structure of reification in American society as it moves from the nineteenth century into the twentieth, and the exemplary efforts of four of America's most formidable critical minds to overcome and resist that reification. ("Reification" 188-217)

Emerson, James, Adams, and Faulkner do indeed offer compelling analyses of the costs of living in modern industrial society, but their criticisms are largely articulated from a conservative viewpoint. It does little to clarify these writers' political stands to treat them as sympathetic participants in an essentially Marxist critique of capitalist commodification. (For an interesting discussion of the distinctly nonradical aspects of Emerson's thought, see Grusin.)

I invoke the example of Porter's *Seeing and Being* not to negate the value of her discoveries about the centrality of the problem of alienation in the works of Emerson and other American writers, but simply to point out a certain lack of dialectical thinking that is prevalent in a number of even the most valuable works of the new scholarship.

In the attempt to pull canonical writers down from the clouds of idealist critical discourse and to reground them in history, writers who have for decades been seen as bearing the standard of traditional moral values are suddenly seen as querying these values. By a curious turn of the wheel, then, the effort to historicize produces a new kind of dehistoricization, albeit on a different plane. To be sure, writers are no longer seen as espousing human truths divorced from time and space. But in their insertion into time and space they frequently take on an aura of anachronistic political correctness. Their firm commitment to elitist, sexist, or racist social values is waved aside so long as their works contain the germ of a concern with decentered subjectivity or the problematics of reference.[4]

Indeed, such a privileging of postmodernist concerns can result in a very troubling bypassing—verging on whitewashing—of reactionary politics in canonical texts. Andrew Parker, for example, argues that Ezra Pound's virulent hatred of Jews stemmed from his perception that "Judaism, writing, money and rhetoric . . . all belong to the same tropological series, each term functioning analogously as a figure of 'excess,' as an inscription that deflects any immediate connection between the sign and its intended referent" (81). Although Parker claims that his argument "will enable us to reject the widely-held critical position that considers Pound's anti-Semitism as a merely 'contingent' phenomenon, ancillary to his poetic achievement" (71), I remain skeptical of a rehistoricizing that virtually collapses politics into poetics. Parker is certainly not arguing that there is anything progressive about Pound's anti-Semitism. But his contention that Pound worked out his poetic anxieties through his social attitudes has the effect of dignifying those attitudes. Pound's obsessive concern with the relation of signifier to signified makes him "one of us"; even his repellent politics takes shape as a protest, however distorted, against the epistemological dilemma of modern humanity.

I can anticipate various objections to these arguments. It might be stated, for example, that in invoking critical categories such as "larger narrative patterns," "closure," and "intention," it is I who am reproducing dominant ideology, especially when I apply these notions to noncanonical texts. Concepts of totality, coherence, and authorial subjectivity can be seen as Aristotelian or Jamesian mediations of phallogocentric hegemony. Counterinvoking Jacques Derrida or Paul de Man, the canon-busting critic might argue that oppositional ideology necessarily asserts itself in gaps, fissures, and discontinuities in the text—that opposition itself is by definition a marginalized phenomenon. It is enough for the text to have flaunted the logocentric conventions that support patriarchy and racial domination; subversion consists not in the negation of this hegemony, but simply in its interrogation.[5]

I am bothered by this argument, even though we hear it often enough these days, uttered in a tone of radical panache. What it amounts to is an admission that subversion and oppositionality are essentially formalistic operations—maneuvers of which the target and goal remain unspecified. The *act* of rupture is valorized. But what this act is subversive of, and oppositional to, is too often left unclear—as is the extent of the text's commitment to its disruptive stance. The enemy would seem to be an epistemological nexus defined by stability, fixity, realism—but beyond this we know little else. The result of this insistently structural definition of the antagonist is that we are left with only a hazy notion of the actual political praxis involved in textual subversion. Power, in this critical paradigm, lurks everywhere; but it is not always clear where power comes from or whose interests it serves. There is no cause for despair, however, because polysemous subversion waits everywhere in ambush, forcing dominant ideology continually to cover its flanks against guerrilla harassment from what Derrida calls the "marginalized other" of the West (134-35). There are romantic echoes here of the discourse and practice of Regis Debray, so popular among certain elements of the New Left in the 1960s. We may wonder, however, whether such a formulation of subversion and oppositionality is as sure a safeguard against reincorporation as it would claim to be.[6]

It is not necessary, I believe, to throw out the subversive baby with the traditional bath: to recognize that texts do not always succeed in negating dominant ideology is not to deny that they may try to do so. Such notions as intention, totality, and closure do not rule out the importance of considering *contradiction* in literary texts. Indeed, they enable us to view the text as an ideological battleground where contradictions in representation fight out the broader struggles of the society at large. But within the dialectic of the text's unity, there are nonetheless primary and secondary aspects of contradiction. If the "pockets of resistance" in a text constitute a secondary aspect—as is, in my view, most often the case with works written in the bourgeois tradition, even with noncanonical texts—so be it. Let us appreciate these pockets for all they are worth, and point out their significance to our students. But this does not mean that other aspects of authorial consciousness may not—however unfortunately—end up winning the battle. Indeed, to posit that an insurgent, secondary aspect of a contradiction is, simply by virtue of its existence, a primary, essence-determining phenomenon is to trivialize the very urgency of the political issues that the canon-busting movement invites us to consider. Such a contention makes it appear that battles that have been bitterly waged in the historical world—and often continue to be waged—have achieved a comparatively easy victory in the realm of literary discourse.

It might also be objected, as a kind of fallback position, that even if I am right about the limited subversiveness of the majority of texts produced in the bourgeois tradition—or even at its margins—I am misconstruing literature's relation to ideology when I hold writers accountable for the formulable social views that their texts project. Some, invoking a more traditional distinction between the languages of science and poetry, might maintain that literary discourse is pseudostatement. Others, calling upon the post-Althusserian description of literary discourse as positioned midway between ideology and ordinary propositional discourse, might declare that literary texts are distanced from the politics they appear to articulate. To hold Emerson as a "subject" accountable for the views he expresses is to miss the point, because what the new scholarship is doing is precisely to demonstrate how subjectivity is constructed by discourse. Rather than affix praise or blame to the formulable politics explicit or implicit in a text, the critic's task is to reveal how the multiplicity of language continually disrupts ideology as such; indeed, the real subversiveness of literature (and of the criticism that treats it) resides in precisely this antipathy to the confinements of univocal meaning and reference.[7]

In response to this argument, I would note that it is quite illogical to assert on the one hand that "literary" texts must be understood within the fuller context of contemporaneous discourse, and on the other that there is something distinctive about "literary" language that overturns the text's apparent commitment to the ideological content it appears to set forth. Indeed, what this argument does is again not to foreground but to bracket—or at least to marginalize once again—the issues of politics and history. If poets and novelists necessarily become rebellious when they start tangling with literary language, then there must be something intrinsically subversive about literary discourse as such. Politics thus becomes an abiding feature of discourse rather than a historically specific matter of social analysis and intervention. Writers might in their personal lives (which are after all historical lives) adhere to politically retrograde beliefs—for example, Faulkner on the subject of black equality. Nonetheless, when such writers take pen in hand, they become deft interrogators of dominant ideology. Ideological contradiction is thus displaced from within authorial ideology—where I for one think it belongs—and inserted into the epistemological space between literature and ideology (see Eagleton, Macherey, Bennett). Despite its insistence that everything is political, everything textual, then, much of the new scholarship—even in some of its neo-Marxist variants—ends up hypostasizing the realm of the aesthetic as a terrain somehow exempt from the political constraints that ordinarily shape the operations of consciousness. Perhaps Brooks has not, after all, been completely left behind.

Politics, Citizenship, and Academe

We may now address the implications that this critique of the politics of the new scholarship has for our practice as citizens of the world—and, in particular, as teachers in the universities and colleges of the empire whose troubled situation I touched upon in the opening part of this essay.

There is, I believe, a distinct oppositional potential in the critical movements I have been describing here. In challenging both the makeup of the canon and the values that sustain the canon, we are in a position to subvert key tenets of dominant ideology. We therefore do potentially occupy an adversarial position in relation to the centers of power in American society—centers that are represented, among other places, on the boards of trustees of the colleges and universities that pay our salaries. And while it is our colleagues in the sciences and social sciences who are called upon to do weapons and counterinsurgency research for military escapades in Central America, we should not minimize our importance to ruling-class hegemony. After all, it is our job to furnish—and make compelling, beautiful, and inevitable—views of the human condition that, if they do not glorify, generally justify and permit social inequality and the separation of personal morality from public policy. The humanities, Herbert Marcuse once observed, serve to inure people to their own and others' want of bread by demonstrating that man does not live by bread alone (109). If we successfully undermine such assumptions, pointing up their specious universalism and ahistoricity, and bringing to our students' attention entire submerged subcultures that have queried such values, then we pose a threat to ruling-class hegemony.

But if this is the case, why do our boards of trustees generally tolerate—indeed, actively cultivate—our presence? Why, indeed, has the move for integrating race, gender, and class into the curriculum been promoted—over the objection of harshly hostile elements—at major universities such as Duke and Stanford, where the sons and daughters of the wealthy receive their training? This happens, I believe, not because financiers and industrialists shed their crude commercialism when they enter the groves of academe, but because we oppositional scholars by and large make ourselves safe—and because, to some extent at least, the captains of industry actually need us to do much of what we do. I shall now translate my earlier criticisms of the canon-busting movement and the new scholarship into a critique of the political practices, both liberal and neo-Marxist, that they imply.

To begin with, the movement to open up the canon to new voices and traditions is readily enough assimilable to the myth of American democratic pluralism: the melting pot has simply finally made it to the academy. What a celebration it is of "representative" American institutions if female and minority writers now receive "representation" in anthologies and course syllabi! Even if the largest poverty class in the United States consists of families headed by single women, and even if millions of unemployed and working-class people of color confront continually worsening prospects for housing and jobs—what a testament the new cultural pluralism is to the "sensitivity" of the leading institutions in our society! My sardonic tone here should not be taken to signify, of course, that I think it negative that such an opening up has occurred. (On the contrary: we should always recall that the decisions about inclusion and exclusion that take place nowadays in the quiet halls of W. W. Norton are the fruits of the very unquiet decisions—and demonstrations—about inclusion and exclusion that took place in other halls some twenty years ago.)

My point is simply that, if we really want to "politicize" the study of literature, we should juxtapose Richard Wright's *Uncle Tom's Children* (1938) with William Faulkner's *Absalom, Absalom!* (1936) in a way that fully recognizes the fundamental antipathy between the two. Unless we incorporate a re-creation of social struggle into our presentation of these writers to our students, we are simply perpetuating—and doing nothing at all to subvert—quintessentially logocentric conceptions of the American body politic. Wright and Faulkner are not simply two sides to the democratic coin. The social views articulated in their texts are as irreconcilable now as they were in the 1930s. Any pedagogical strategy that simply juxtaposes them in a pluralistic exploration of literary representations of race and racism violates the motives that prompted both writers to take pen in hand.

By no means, however, are all scholars involved in opening up the canon so conventionally liberal as I have just suggested. Rather than validating the myth of the melting pot, some of the new scholars would claim, they are blasting it open and demonstrating that social life—and discourse—are constituted not by unity and consensus, but by difference, alterity, heterogeneity. Indeed, they would argue, the politics implied by their critical practice is emancipatory, even revolutionary. They are seeking out pockets of resistance and envisioning social change coming from autonomous groupings of dispersed elements—women, blacks, Hispanics, Native Americans, gays—who fashion what Stanley Aronowitz calls a "micropolitics of oppositional movements" (123-26) or what Félix Guattari calls the "proliferation of marginal groups" that will bring about "molecular revolution" (268-72).[8]

Traditional Marxism, according to this analysis, is logocentric and authoritarian, because it posits the primacy of production in determining social relations, situates change in the class struggle rather than in the activities of "interest groups" such as those cited above, and makes the fatal mistake of supposing that a "third term"—revolution—will synthesize and resolve the destructive binary oppositions upon which bourgeois society founds itself, and by means of which it justifies itself. True resistance, in short, can come only from "pockets" that take the "refusal of mastery" as a guiding political principle. If these pockets should turn into phalanxes, much less armies, then the margins would become the center, and logocentric structures of authority would reassert themselves, albeit in a different guise. According to this argument, which is endorsed by a number of feminists and neo-Marxists involved in the new scholarship, to overturn the canon is neither to reaffirm liberal democracy nor to contribute to a class-based movement for social revolution, but rather to carry on rearguard guerrilla actions that will interrogate hegemonic discourses without superseding or replacing them.[9]

Such a politics, in my view, amounts to little more than a rewarming of the liberal pluralism I mentioned before, although I know its adherents would strenuously disagree with me. To be sure, many feminists and neo-Marxists are quite correct to point out the fatal failure of the "old left" to understand the centrality of questions of race and gender within the overall class contradiction. And a class-based Marxism need not—indeed should not—seek the eradication of plurality, which is not the same thing at all as pluralism. But to concede that race and gender cannot simply be collapsed into class does not mean that the class struggle is no longer the main contradiction shaping historical processes. Nor does it mean that provisional coalitions of dispersed and molecular interest groups can successfully confront the powers that be, which have proven themselves remarkably efficient in accommodating—at least rhetorically—demands for cultural self-determination. Indeed, our political experience of the past decade or so reveals that this presumably radical politics of heterogeneity and difference is readily enough absorbed into the conservative pluralism of *E pluribus unum*, which celebrates the openness and flexibility of American capitalist democracy while guaranteeing the continuing segregation and subjugation of the great number of its citizens. Interrogation from the margins is kept safely at the margins.

Indeed, in its extreme form this politics of decentering and marginality becomes a politics that actually enshrines impotence as a positive good, for the "refusal of mastery," apparently an act of heroic disengagement from the epistemology that fosters oppression, can lead to a kind of defiant passivity. This passivity may console the conscience of the individual, but it forecloses in advance the possibility of engagement in a praxis that will encounter hegemony on its own turf. The adherents of this refusal of mastery become avatars of Eliot's Fisher King—incapable of determinate action, but by their very presence continually emanating the promise of a redemptive rain that will magically fall from the sky. One might note, indeed, that some practitioners of the new canon-busting scholarship seem actually to relish the continuing existence of ruling-class hegemony, insofar as they take their own marginality as a condition of their scholarly being and conceive of themselves as a kind of loyal opposition. Fearing that, should the margins become the center, they would be transformed into sites of a new power that would be, *qua* power, as oppressive as the old, these scholars prefer to engage in skirmishes that never take as their goal the actual reconstruction of textual value and literary tradition—let alone the seizure of power in the society at large—according to a new plan.[10] Better, they counsel, to drop in our lines from the dock behind the gashouse, turn our backs on the devastation of the global wasteland, and restrict ourselves to setting our own lands—demarcated by the new pluralistic geography—in order. What starts out as a radical refusal to engage in the co-opting discourse of power can easily enough end up as a resort to the solaces of the word processor and the conventional prestige rewards of the profession.[11]

I'd like to point out, however, that such questions of *how* most effectively to oppose the machinations of power are frequently rendered moot—for liberals and neo-Marxists alike—by what I have argued to be the greatest drawback of much of the new scholarship: namely, the tendency to find subversion under every textual bush. If it is true not only that marginalized texts subvert the established canon, but also that canonical texts subvert the traditional and conservative ideologies that they seem to endorse, then bourgeois ideology—at least when embodied in literary texts—really poses no sort of threat at all. It self-destructs when touched—or, at least, when touched by the poststructuralist critic or pedagogue.

However inadvertently, the scholar who holds such a view of literature actually ends up bolstering bourgeois hegemony. For if literature *qua* literature offers, when deconstructed, such a trenchant critique of dominant values, and if it takes the oppositional scholar to point out the full extent of this critique, then what are universities and colleges if not privileged zones where the mysteries of textual subversion can be plumbed? The logic of the new scholarship *ought* to extend to a critique of those institutions that help to maintain hegemony. But it can actually end up legitimating the hegemonic view that campuses are apolitical centers where disinterested research and pedagogy take place, and, moreover, where the future leaders of society can receive the humanistic enlightenment that will equip them to respond effectively to the discursive plurality—if not the material needs—of the citizenry.

Poststructuralist scholarship thrives on the perception of ironic incongruities. I can think of no more ironic incongruity, however, than the situation of poststructuralist scholars who affirm the latently self-critical capacities of bourgeois culture while their campus administrations are recruiting students for the CIA or training officers to lead working-class G.I.s into battle in Central America—or, on the more mundane level, preparing the new generation of business leaders to meet the challenge posed by an increasingly multicultural work force. The view that both literature and criticism subvert and disrupt dominant ideology implies that the discourse carried on in departments that teach these subjects is somehow not complicit with the discourses and operations in which the university as a whole is engaged. Despite its up-to-date post-Saussurean dress, then, and its insistence that literature purveys not sweetness and light but counterhegemonic subversion, much of the new scholarship ends up valorizing literary study on grounds that are hardly unfamiliar. As I noted before, the numbers of both canon-busting scholars and CIA recruiters are increasing on our campuses these days; let us not be content with a conception of either literature or literary study that facilitates a peaceful coexistence between the two.

Notes

1. For a discussion of the problems minority and female writers have encountered with the ideological premises encoded in inherited genres, see, respectively, Reilly and Abel. The definitive treatment of the relation of questions of aesthetic value to the activity of canon revision remains the final chapter of Jane Tompkins's *Sensational Designs*.
2. Similar dynamics and difficulties underlie Deborah McDowell's recent introduction to the reissued edition of *Plum Bun*: "*Plum Bun* has the hull but not the core of literary conservatism and convention. . . . It passes for conservative, employing 'outworn' and 'safe' literary materials while, simultaneously, remaining suspicious of them. . . . *Plum Bun* dares to explore questions about unconventional female roles and possibilities for development using the very structures that have traditionally offered fundamentally conservative answers to those questions. Fauset's answers were risky, in the literary marketplace, but powerful, liberating alternatives nevertheless, both for herself as a writer and for the image of blacks and women in literature" (xxii). (For this example I am indebted to conversations with Carla Kaplan during our joint explorations of Harlem Renaissance literature in a graduate independent-study course at Northwestern University.)

   There are abundant examples of these sorts of radical claims in recent feminist scholarship. See also, for example, Lee Edwards, who encounters a dilemma frequently found in works of scholarship that aspire to demonstrate the oppositionality of a submerged tradition in women's writing. On the one hand, Edwards asserts that her study, unlike Sandra Gilbert and Susan Gubar's *The Madwoman in the Attic* (1979), finds not "covert reappraisals" of patriarchal domination but "overt and radical attacks" (15). On the other hand, she is forced to conclude that in work after work of nineteenth-century fiction, the female hero ends up a "heroine," safely reincorporated into the dominant system of patriarchal marriage. I agree that many nineteenth-century novels featuring woman heroes *do* exhibit this contradiction—and therefore wonder at Edwards's claim to be discussing works that unequivocally contain "overt and radical attacks." For a considerably more dialectical assessment of the strengths and limitations of the "cult of domesticity" in nineteenth-century women's fiction, see Baym (esp. 22-50).

3. See the final chapter of Foley's *Telling the Truth* (233-64). For a discussion of ideological reincorporation in African-American literature, see Hogue. For a description of the ways in which an excluded cultural tradition develops its own oppositional poetics and countertraditions, see Gates. In stressing the issue of ideological reincorporation, I am not denying that it has been a salutary development in feminist criticism to move from analyses of women's distorted lives, anxious authorship, and conservative social roles (for instance, Heilbrun) to explorations of their strategies of cultural survival and resistance. I am simply arguing that it is crucial that we not heroize the achievements of victims of oppression in such a way as to end up minimizing the nature and extent of that oppression. What seems to me a very sensible analysis of the relationship between oppositionality and reincorporation is presented in Radway.
4. For arguments along similar lines regarding the presumably self-reflexive (and hence antilogocentric and antiauthoritarian) quality of the American literary tradition in its entirety, see Dauber and Riddel. Porter avoids the solipsism of Dauber and Riddel but mistakes the *foregrounding* of the problem of reification in classic American literature with a *radical opposition* to that reification.
5. For altering views on the extent to which the novel form itself is irrevocably patriarchal, see, on the one hand, Jehlen and Fetterley, and, on the other hand, Tompkins.
6. For a valuable critique of the psuedo-oppositionality of the leftist panache accompanying much poststructuralist criticism, see Graff, Meyerson, and Larson. It is important to note, however, that poststructuralism can produce the diametrically opposed claim that literature—or at least narrative—is intrinsically so co-optative as to preclude opposition of any kind, deriving from either authors' explicit politics or their implicit subject positions. See Davis.
7. For an intelligent discussion of literary conventions as carriers of ideology—a discussion that both acknowledges the force of dominant ideology and at the same time allows space for oppositional activity—see Rabinowitz.
8. Interestingly, Guattari notes that "it is impossible to make a clear cut distinction between the fringe ideas that can be recuperated and those that lead down the slippery slope to authentic 'molecular revolutions.' The borderline remains fluid, and fluctuates both in time and place" (269). This argument is similar to Michel Foucault's contention that power and opposition are often indistinguishable from one another (141).
9. See Foley, "Politics," and, for the poststructuralist/Marxist critique of dialectics, Ryan. Among poststructuralists/Marxists who attempt to retain dialectics as an analytic category, a common operation is to assert the importance of identity rather than struggle within contradiction, and thus to evade the necessity of determining which aspect of the tendencies locked in combat is essence determining. See, for example, Jameson, who argues that in both literary texts and social experience, utopian gratification and ideological manipulation often become virtually indistinguishable from one another (281-99). It seems to me crucial for the Marxist critic—for any critic—to make distinctions in this arena.
10. For an instance of a critical stance that takes the refusal of mastery as both premise and goal, see Craig Owens's description of Martha Rosler's photographs of the Bowery, in which she purposefully undermines her own authority as photographer in order to impress upon her audience "the indignity of speaking for others" (her words; Owens 69). There is an urgent need for further inquiry into the extent to which such statements articulate not simply an antipathy to hegemonic discourses but also an unacknowledged anticommunism, one that conceives of Marxism as a reductionist discourse threatening to engulf all difference not immediately subsumable to class. Until such inquiry is undertaken, there is the continual possibility that current

research into the intersections—textual and historical—of race, gender, and class will be inhibited by the assumption that these intersections are merely conjunctural, with the consequence that the last of these categories will, by a curious turn of the wheel, almost automatically be subsumed to either of the former two.

11. The extent to which careers are now built around this politics of marginality is exemplified in a 1987 *PMLA* advertisement that heralded the new collectively written *Columbia History of the United States*, which presumably embodies much of the new concern with canon busting. We are told that the new survey is "thoroughly up-to-date in understanding and attitude . . . refreshingly contentious and crammed with bright and bold [scholarship]. . . . intellectually challenging and socially and politically provocative." Interestingly, the ad was headed by the following in boldface: "**Meet the New Authority**."

Works Cited

Abel, Elizabeth, et al. *The Voyage In: Fictions of Female Development*. Hanover: UP of New England, 1983.

Arac, Jonathan. "The Politics of *The Scarlet Letter*." Bercovitch and Jehlen. 247-66.

Aronowitz, Stanley. *The Crisis of Historical Materialism: Class, Politics and Culture in Marxist Theory*. New York: Praeger, 1981.

Baym, Nina. *Woman's Fiction: A Guide to Novels by and about Women in America, 1820-1870*. Ithaca, NY: Cornell UP, 1978.

Bennett, Tony. *Formalism and Marxism*. London: Methuen, 1979.

Bercovitch, Sacvan, and Myra Jehlen, eds. *Ideology and Classic American Literature*. Cambridge: Cambridge UP, 1986.

Brooks, Cleanth. "Irony as a Principle of Structure." Morton D. Zabel, ed. *Literary Opinion in America*. New York: Harper, 1951. 729-41.

Dauber, Kenneth. "Criticism of American Literature." *diacritics* 7 (March 1977): 55-66.

Davis, Lennard J. *Resisting Novels: Ideology and Fiction*. London: Methuen, 1987.

Derrida, Jacques. *The Margins of Philosophy*. Trans. Alan Bass. Chicago: U of Chicago P, 1982.

Eagleton, Terry. *Criticism and Ideology*. London: Verso, 1976.

Edwards, Lee R. *Psyche as Hero: Female Heroism and Fictional Form*. Middletown, CT: Wesleyan UP, 1984.

Emerson, Ralph Waldo. "Self-Reliance." *The Norton Anthology of American Literature* I, 3rd ed. 956-72.

Fetterley, Judith. *Provisions: A Reader from 19th-Century American Women*. Bloomington: Indiana UP, 1986.

Foley, Barbara. "The Politics of Deconstruction." *Genre* (Spring-Summer 1984): 113-34.

———. *Telling the Truth: The Theory and Practice of Documentary Fiction*. Ithaca, NY: Cornell UP, 1986.

Foucault, Michel. *Power/Knowledge: Selected Interviews and Other Writings 1972-77*. Ed. Colin Gordon. Trans. Gordon et al. New York: Pantheon, 1980.

Gates, Henry Louis. " 'The Blackness of Blackness': A Critique of the Sign and the Signifying Monkey." Gates, ed. *Black Literature and Literary Theory*. New York: Methuen, 1984. 285-321.

Gilbert, Sandra. Introduction. Kate Chopin, *The Awakening*. Harmondsworth: Penguin, 1986. 7-33.

Graff, Gerald. "American Criticism Left and Right." Bercovitch and Jehlen. 91-121.

Grusin, Richard A. " 'Put God in Your Debt': Emerson's Economy of Literature." *PMLA* 103 (January 1988): 35-44.

Guattari, Félix. *Molecular Revolution: Psychiatry and Politics*. Trans. Rosemary Sheed. Harmondsworth: Penguin, 1984.

Heilbrun, Carolyn. *Reinventing Womanhood*. New York: Norton, 1979.

Hogue, W. Lawrence. "Literary Production: A Silence in Afro-American Critical Practice." Weixlmann and Fontenot. 31-45.

Jameson, Fredric. *The Political Unconscious: Narrative as a Socially Symbolic Act*. Ithaca, NY: Cornell UP, 1981.

Jehlen, Myra. "Archimedes and the Paradox of Feminist Criticism." Elizabeth Abel and Emily K. Abel, eds. *The Signs Reader: Women, Gender, and Scholarship*. Chicago: U of Chicago P, 1983. 69-95.

Karcher, Carolyn. *Shadow over the Promised Land: Slavery and Violence in Melville's America*. Baton Rouge: Louisiana State UP, 1980.

Larson, Neil. *Modernism and Hegemony: A Materialist Critique of Aesthetic Agencies*. Theory and History of Literature Series, Vol. 71. Minneapolis: U of Minnesota P, 1990.

Macherey, Pierre. *A Theory of Literary Production*. Trans. Geoffrey Wall. London: Routledge & Kegan Paul, 1978.

Marcuse, Herbert. *Negations: Essays in Critical Theory*. Trans. Jeremy J. Shapiro. Boston: Beacon, 1968.

McDowell, Deborah. Introduction. Jessie Redmon Fauset, *Plum Bun*. New York: Pandora, 1985. ix-xxiv.

Meyerson, Gregory. Review of *Universal Abandon: The Politics of Postmodernism*. Ed. Andrew J. Ross. *Ariel* 20 (October 1989): 192-96.

Owens, Craig. "The Discourse of Others: Feminists and Postmodernism." Hal Foster, ed. *The Anti-Aesthetic: Essays on Postmodern Culture*. Port Townsend, WA: Bay, 1983. 57-82.

Parker, Andrew. "Ezra Pound and the 'Economy' of Anti-Semitism." Jonathan Arac, ed. *Postmodernism and Politics*. Minneapolis: U of Minnesota P, 1986. 70-90.

Porter, Carolyn. *Seeing and Being: The Plight of the Participant Observer in Emerson, James, Adams, Faulkner*. Middletown, CT: Wesleyan UP, 1981.

______. "Reification and American Literature." Bercovitch and Jehlen. 188-217.

Rabinowitz, Peter J. *Before Reading: Narrative Conventions and the Politics of Interpretation*. Ithaca, NY: Cornell UP, 1989.

Radway, Janice. *Reading the Romance: Women, Patriarchy, and Popular Literature*. Chapel Hill: U of North Carolina P, 1984.

Reilly, John. "History-Making Literature." Weixlmann and Fontenot. 85-120.

Reising, Russell. *The Unusable Past: Theory and the Study of American Literature*. London: Methuen, 1987.

Riddel, Joseph. "Decentering the Image: The 'Project' of 'American Poetics.' " Josué Harari, ed. *Textual Strategies*. Ithaca, NY: Cornell UP, 1979. 322-58.

Ryan, Michael. *Marxism and Deconstruction: A Critical Articulation*. Baltimore: Johns Hopkins UP, 1982.

Sundquist, Eric J. "Benito Cereno and New World Slavery." Sacvan Bercovitch, ed. *Reconstructing American Literary History*. Cambridge: Harvard UP, 1986. 93-122.

Tompkins, Jane. *Sensational Designs: The Work of American Fiction 1790-1860*. New York: Oxford UP, 1985.

Warner, Michael. "Recanonization." Paper delivered at the meeting of the Midwest Modern Language Association, Chicago, November 1986.

Weixlmann, Joel, and Chester Fontenot, eds. *Studies in Black American Literature, II: Belief vs. Theory in Black American Literature*. Greenwood, FL: Penkevill, 1986.

Wilding, Michael. *Political Fictions*. London: Routledge & Kegan Paul, 1980.

ENTITLEMENT AND EMPOWERMENT: CLAIMS ON CANONICITY

THE POETICS OF CANONICITY

The best academic work on poetry during the 1960s and 1970s dealt with questions of technical poetics, especially the discovery of systemic dimensions of linguistic and rhetorical structuration. In the early 1980s, work shifted toward larger, more abstract questions of generic and historical definition; the central question—how to define the characteristic poetic gesture of modernity—remained within the general arena of poetics. But the most interesting academic work on poetry these days is not in poetics—the study of the structure and structuring of verbal art—but in a radical challenge to the canon, which is defined variously with reference to terms such as "selection" (Lauter) or "consensus" (Quasha), or to a generalized alignment of ideology, prejudice, and taste (Collins). My own sense is that any discussion of the canon has to take into account both its manifest passivity, as a museum of all literature that has proven value in the culture it represents, and its latent activity, as a set of criteria and economic influences applied whenever a poem is conceived, written, revised, offered for consumption, edited, anthologized, or taught. It has been common to hear of the "opening" or "broadening" or "diversifying" of the canon in the past several decades, but only recently has there been talk of chucking it altogether, whatever that might mean.

The need for doing something constructive with the canon has become obvious to anyone and everyone, and any anthology of poetry or discussion of poets provides the clearest evidence of such need.[1] To take a few obvious cases from our not-too-remote history: of the 130 entries in Louis Untermeyer's *Lives of the Poets*, covering a period that extends from Chaucer to Dylan Thomas, eleven represent women. There are no African-Americans, no Hispanic-Americans, no Native Americans, Chinese-, Japanese-, or Portuguese-Americans. But that is an old book (1959), and we've learned not to expect too much of the old.

Still, when we consult instead a more recent work by someone who ought to know better—Richard Howard's *Alone with America,* written in 1969 and "enlarged" in 1980—we can't feel a great relief at discovering that of his "comprehensive studies of 41 contemporary American poets" six are women and one is black. Characteristically, Howard speaks interestingly about the poets he chooses; but his selection—his silent process of choosing these forty-one poets from among the thousands of people in this country who write what may be called poems—clearly is discriminating in matters of race and gender as it discriminates among poems.

A final example is William Heyen's 1984 anthology, *The Generation of 2000*, which adds to its prejudices of taste the arrogance of prognosis: these poets, all gathered around a reasonably well-defined set of dispositions toward image, line, music, and statement, will be the poets of the millennium. One perceives at first a sort of affirmative action at work: of the thirty-one poets represented, ten are women, three are African-American, and one, I believe, is Native American. But the dominant voice remains white and male. Black, white, red, male, female—the overall effect is remarkable not for any splendid variety but for a kind of creeping sameness; we seem to be reading here the multiracial death of poetry, its whimpering, prosaic, academic last gasp. Similarly, Diane Wakoski notes that the "new" poets added to the latest edition of the *Norton Anthology of Modern Poetry*—among them significant numbers of women and ethnic minorities—reflect the conservative poetic values associated with the white male poets of the previous generation favored by that anthology. As she writes of Afro-American poet Rita Dove, her "material does not stretch or extend one little bit the canon of good poetry" (30).

Like the anthologies treated by Wakoski, *The Generation of 2000* fails to reflect anything close to the full range of significant poetries available in the United States today. What it does reflect is a certain set of biases of theory and technique that have in a great number of ways cemented themselves in most English departments and many poetry journals in the country. It should not surprise us that such a source of criteria fails to choose a higher proportion of minority products for its anthologies than it chooses for its literature faculties. In Cary Nelson's words, "We deal with the canon through a culturally articulated network of pedagogical and professional discourses" (40).[2] The same forces, authorities, and prejudices remain at work, and the canon—as a broadening, opening, diversifying set of criteria for what counts as poetry—is a direct construction of the same social forces that subvert the lives and minds and hopes of minority professionals and minority students: the canon vibrates to the same frequencies as criteria like "collegiality" (as in "Her publications are fine, but she doesn't know how to take a joke") and courses like "English 101."

This is to say that the canon has power—even that it *is* power, that it has the effect in the present of allowing expression to some voices (through publication, grants, and hiring practices) while suppressing others.[3] In this view, outsiders enter the canon by matching their voices to those already selected—the canon seems to open, broaden, and diversify, but in fact grows by suppressing difference, constraining radical impulses, and coercing the vulnerable. In the best book written on the canon of poetry to date, *Repression and Recovery: Modern American Poetry and the Politics of Cultural Memory, 1910-1945* (1989), Nelson argues that the essential conservatism of any canon must ultimately result in a cultural amnesia in which minority texts, their conditions of production, their value, their meaning, and even their audiences are condemned to oblivion. He is right; he is also right in his perception that in any culture built upon a hierarchical structuring of institutions, canonicity will be unavoidable.

There is no use pretending we can "chuck the whole thing"; something else that suits the ideological needs of the culture's bases of power will rush in to fill the void (54-56). For this reason, any responsible effort to overturn the criteria of the canon must propose and support another set of criteria.

The principal argument against the established canon of poetry in America derives from its having built into itself certain racist, sexist, and classist biases connected with the underlying ideology of the historical crisis called modernism. Wakoski's summary is succinct to the point of brutality:

> The Modernist canon enshrines four American poets: Eliot, Pound, Stevens and Williams. Four white males. None first-generation American. All from the East. Two who became ex-patriot [*sic*?] Americans, none from the lower classes, all with extensive formal education and only one—William Carlos Williams—with an explicitly democratic interest in the people of the American culture or its language. (25)

But it is also important to note the best defense of modernism and the trajectory of modern poetry, that is, belated white male poetics. The reason that modernist poetics retains a significance for minorities, the underdeveloped, and the systemically repressed is that, in Jerome Rothenberg's words, it "sees itself as challenging limits and changing ways of speaking/thinking/doing that have too long robbed us of the freedom to be human to the full extent of our power and yearnings" (Rothenberg and Rothenberg xiv). At least in part, every time the modernist poet submits him- or herself to the criteria of judgment implicit in the established academic canon of poetry, this ideal—formulated by Ezra Pound in his scriptural exhortation to "make it new"—must be approached.

But the ideal is frankly inadequate, and has been co-opted and trivialized: "Make it new" currently applies more to the commodification of increasingly scarce natural resources than to the spirit of human beings. Perhaps W. H. Auden was seeing more clearly than Pound in his comment on Shelley's idea that poets are "the unacknowledged legislators of the world": the real unacknowledged legislators are the secret police, and as poets we had better face up to that fact (27). Nevertheless, the ideal is good to keep in mind, in view of the alternatives, for it assumes some possibility of redemption for our species and for the planet, while the alternatives tend either to be local and regressive—essentially retreating into some variant of tribal poetic—or culturally imperialistic, blindly impelling all marginal voices toward a supposedly utopian monoculture.

Nelson supports his argument in *Repression and Recovery* with specific examples of kinds of poetry produced in the United States in this century that the explicit and implicit criteria of the established canon have led us to forget. Probably through his explicit intention, most of us will feel a measure of tedium and even resentment that centers on Nelson's choice of poems to rescue from cultural oblivion.[4] Especially his preference for the ideological poetry of working-class poets of the 1920s and 1930s weighs heavily on the senses. By conventional standards these tend, with some few exceptions, to be lead-footed, tin-eared, soulless exercises in banal singsong. Nelson's claim, substantially undemonstrated, is that these poems deserve our attention because they did great cultural "work," and that their repression prevents other such poems from doing comparable cultural work in the present.[5] I would claim that what cultural work they were capable of was slight, was achieved largely *because* of their noncanonical status, and is irrelevant to the problem of getting cultural work done in the present. In fact, there are numerous avenues open for the achievement of cultural work in the present, many of which depend for their success upon being noncanonical (witness the fate of "graffiti art," for instance). The idea of the jangly rhyming of proletarian clichés having a significant effect on the potential counterculture today seems to me a determined (and painfully nostalgic) misreading of the contemporary audience for noncanonical poetry. But what is really at issue here is a difference of perspectives on the canon: on the one hand a scholarly concern for recovery of lost poems and poets, and on the other a concern about recovering for poetry the power to recognize what its real job of cultural work is.

This difference of critical perspective is decisive, focusing as it does on a temperamental and methodological split between the criteria espoused by contemporary Marxists like Nelson and those of the group of poetic theorists and practitioners associated with the wide-ranging multicultural perspectivism that Jerome and Diane Rothenberg have named "ethnopoetics." Both modes of study (and they are in many ways related) have developed in opposition to the increasingly stubborn closure of modernist poetics. In general, this poetics has delivered us to a point where considerations of "poeticalness" are determined formally, not substantively.[6] While modernist poetics has its various branches, emphases, and concentrations, there is a general tendency toward framing the question of poetic value in terms not of what is said in or done with a poem, but of the richness, strangeness, and complexity of the verbal form. Wakoski notes this explicitly: "Formalists? Experimenters? Are they not in the same camp? Both care more about the way a poem is written than the subject matter or content" (21-22). Yet her own critique is contaminated by a preoccupation with criteria that are precisely formal:

> The claim [informing the new Norton anthology] seems to be that a wider range of poetics is going to be represented. More women, more ethnic minorities, more experimental poets, more kinds of poetry. That's the claim. However, it seems to me that as we move, supposedly, Left and look at all these new additions, we *stop looking at verse practices, or aesthetics,* and start looking at race, gender, politics, population distribution and everything but poetics. (28; italics mine)

On the other hand, Wakoski wishes to promote those poets whose crucial concern is with content rather than form, poets who "are primarily concerned with telling the tale, the story, the myth of the culture, which is far more important than the form of the language with which they tell it. Needless to say, there's form and content in everything. The crucial point is where the emphasis is placed and therefore what the first criteria are that a poet uses to judge his and others' work" (24). There is a contradiction here, stemming at least in part from Wakoski's dedication to the monocultural grandiosity of the poetics associated with "the Whitman Tradition and its attendant earth mythology":

> The self that Whitman sings of is the new pure man/woman who democratically is everyone, white or black, slave or free, woman or man. Each man/woman is free to make him/herself into a god/goddess/hero of the American culture. Each one must break new ground to do it. Each one must take risks, as all heroes risk themselves for their enterprise. (23-24)

The contradiction of these perspectives is irreducible, and demonstrates the difficulty of attacking the canon from within.[7] In order to move beyond her point of view, truly to open the canon, it would be necessary to admit that the myth of a single American culture ("*the* American culture") must give way to a clear-sighted exploration of the systemic forces that prevent such homogeneity. Such an exploration might well require that we need to "start looking at race, gender, politics, [and] population distribution" as factors that point first of all to significant differences of poetics.

Nelson tries to remain rigorously outside the canon while acknowledging the difficulty of sustaining such a position while being, in an important sense, "in literature."[8] Specially concerned with the canon's capacity to obliterate certain kinds of thought, his rejection of the criterion of form is more consistent than Wakoski's. The canon has been shaped by formal criteria to such an extent that even a very good idea may be judged too malformed to earn a place in it, so it is no surprise that an effort to recover texts excluded from this canon would attempt to shift the emphasis of canonical criteria from form to meaning: in this perspective, form is effete, and "cultural work" involves the expression of meanings that censorious forces in the culture would tend to repress.

But if an emphasis on politically repressed meanings satisfies critics like Nelson, it does not satisfy the poets, linguists, anthropologists, and philosophers loosely assembled under the rubric of Rothenberg and Rothenberg's "ethnopoetics." Generally concerned less with global theorizing and more with local analysis of the ways poetry works in a variety of cultures, this project—which Sherman Paul, quoting Eliot Weinberger, calls "the most fruitful and interesting configuration in American poetry in the last 20 years" (72)—finds in its scrutiny of alternative, tribal, primitive, and suppressed poetries of the world a range of functions unimagined and unimaginable in any theoretical model based simply on the distinction, which remains a formal one, between form and meaning.[9] Paula Gunn Allen articulates a crucial principle of ethnopoetics in her analysis of differences between Western and Native American poetics:

> Western cultures lean more and more heavily on technological and scientific methods of maintenance, while traditional cultures such as those of American Indian tribes tend toward mystical and philosophic methods. Because of this tendency, literature plays a central role in the traditional cultures which it is unable to play in technological ones. Thus, the purpose of a given "work" is of central importance to understanding its deeper significance.[10]

As John Crawford notes, Allen is arguing "for a 'functional' definition of genre into 'ceremonial and popular, as opposed to the Western prose and poetry distinction' " (158). Allen is interested in defining only a Native American poetics—she is essentially unconcerned with the dispositions of the macroculture.[11] But the macroculture cannot be expected to relinquish its present shape and power of its own accord, and its canon, as Nelson makes clear, will continue to exert its aesthetic and economic pressures on Native American, Chicano, African-American, Asian-American, women, gay, disabled, and proletarian writers; and inasmuch as this holds true, it behooves us to determine that the canon must be developed progressively. The overarching message of ethnopoetics is that this need for progressivism means applying to all poetry the kind of "functional" analysis of genre that Allen prescribes for Native American poetry.

The two discourses that might be expected to articulate this variety of functions are history and anthropology. The first of these, which is Nelson's method, delivers us to a diversity of poetries operating (and sometimes competing) at any one time in the historical arena under study. But this localization may lead to presumptions of uniformity of function. Thus Paul Lauter, one of its sharpest proponents, avers that "all working-class art (perhaps all art) must be explored precisely in terms of its use" (65).[12] But unless *use* is given an extremely broad application—use is beauty, beauty use—*function* seems a more adaptable term. *Use* seems to bend toward a view of poems as ready-made tools, for instance, and it seems clear that not only the poem as finished object, but the very act of creating, has a function for individuals and cultures.

As to the second method, a basic underlying principle of anthropology is a presumption of potential difference—assuming commonality, or even intercultural correspondence, is held to be methodologically naive. But so are nostalgia, sentimentality, and precipitous analogizing, which sometimes befog Rothenberg and Rothenberg's version of ethnopoetics. If ethnopoetics intends to organize itself into a richly useful model of analysis and critique, it must shake itself free of the "folkloristic conception of anthropology, with its assumptions of stability and traditionalism of culture content in non-Western or marginal societies" noted by Vera Zolberg, and heed her suggestion: "Rather than accept a view of traditionalism as a fixed attribute, it is important to recognize that traditions too are created and re-created" (68).[13] A related warning comes from anthropologist Victor Turner: "There are not a few *ethnoi*, both past and present, and not all of them are poets or prophets. There are many tribal Archie Bunkers, antiritualists, village atheists, and not a few philistines and despots" ("Review" 340). Nevertheless, if ethnopoetics as a whole does not perfectly sustain an adequate anthropological skepticism in its analyses, it insists in principle upon a determined multicultural, reflexive analysis that articulates varieties of poetic function better than any other available methodology.

Besides Rothenberg and Rothenberg's *Symposium of the Whole* and *Alcheringa*, the journal edited throughout the 1970s by Jerome Rothenberg and Dennis Tedlock, data in support of a functional poetics have been gathered in *A Gift of Tongues*, edited by Marie Harris and Kathleen Aguero, and Denys Thompson's *The Uses of Poetry*. Thompson several times quotes Johan Huizinga's *Homo Ludens* (1938): "Certainly in the oldest culture of which we have knowledge poetry was at the same time 'ritual, entertainment, artistry, riddle-making, doctrine, persuasion, sorcery, soothsaying, prophecy and competition' " (26). He also describes the philosophical poems of Empedocles and Lucretius, cites poetries that were vital to successful navigation and weather forecasting, and notes, "In the Irish bardic schools . . . which flourished with scarcely a break from A. D. 590 to the seventeenth century, magical incantations were part of the course for poets" (47). What is important in all this is not that poetry has *represented* such diverse functions—modern poetry can, within the shadowy limits of representation in general, represent anything—but that the functions of poetry far exceed representation: poetry elsewhere has performed and performs a wide range of cultural functions. Thus he cites T. B. Macaulay's claim about working people in the England of 1685—that "a great part of their history is to be learned only from their ballads" (110-11).

These texts present dozens of paths one might follow, including a variety of roads toward ethnic poetics by Paula Gunn Allen and Chicano critic Juan Bruce-Novoa. Richard Dauenhauer, for instance, presents elegant translations and analyses of Koyukon (Eskimo) riddle-poems, Kofi Awoonor discusses Ewe (African) dirges and insult poetry, and Ruth Finnegan discusses African drum literature and Ifa divination poetry. We find poems that are used for healing, both psychological and physiological. (Thompson notes that "this form of healing [poetry therapy] has been practised at the Philadelphia Hospital for nearly two centuries, and is used at 3,500 mental health centres" in the United States [214].) Poetries are essential to religious ceremony, the transference of political power, the establishment of laws, and the definition of cultural standards of behavior. Poetries are intricately interwoven with the articulation of alternative cultural or political systems of belief. Poetry has provided proverbial intelligence its decisive forms; likewise love charms, spells, and curses. And of course it has importantly established rhythms and images of work, play, hunt, war, and domestic wisdom in virtually every culture, including, in a watered-down way, our own.

What is a poetics based on a simple dichotomy between form and content to make of any of these functions? And what would the functions poetries serve in their cultures tell us about the feeble efforts of contemporary American academic poetry to say something "useful"? What can we learn from these poetries, in the specifics of their service to and commentary upon their cultures, that can be made to address significantly our own experience? Is it conceivable that the canon as it now stands could withstand such an assault? Given the complex history of poetic forms and functions, it at least seems self-evidently narrow-sighted to arrive at the focus applied by Nelson. To determine that the canon imperatively needs to open itself—or to be radically converted—to a specific set of utterances that have been politically suppressed *because of their meanings* is to disregard the much larger range of voices that have been forgotten, and seems like ideological special pleading. Clearly enough, as Wakoski notes, women and members of minority groups who have been willing and able to work within the parameters of the canon have already been admitted; it is only radical sentiments that have been barred. Such sentiments remain a relatively local phenomenon, defined differently in different historical epochs. Urging now the legitimation and admission of such a historically determined set of radical meanings according to a further extension of the form/content distinctions of modernist poetics is a gesture that can be justified without challenging the structure of that poetics at all, simply by referencing the liberal assumption that all varieties of sincere expression ought to be tolerated in an open society.

Nelson is deeply aware of poetic diversity, yet his summary employs the same monocultural assumption as Wakoski's: "In the competition to define and dominate our sense of what poetry is and can be, quite different notions of what poetry can do *within the culture* are validated and rejected" (245; italics mine).[14] This assumption, he considers, sharply limits the range of poetry's use, purpose, or function—in Nelson's term, work. Dismissing "a narrowly aesthetic history of the conflicts between different kinds of poetry," he summarizes his own sense of "what is at stake":

> We need to recognize that poetry throughout the twentieth century is the site of a much broader cultural struggle. It is a struggle over whether poetry can be an effective and distinctive site for cultural critique, over whether poetry will offer readers subject positions that are reflective and self-critical, over whether poetry can be a force for social change, over what discourses poetry can plausibly integrate or juxtapose, over what groups of readers will be considered valid audiences for poetry, over what role poetry and the interpretation of poetry can play in stabilizing or destabilizing the dominant values and existing power relations in the culture as a whole. (245)

But I can discover no argument in Nelson's book that urges an opening of the canon to the full range of possibilities inherent in the history of poetic functions, where meaning plays only a partial role. Moving poetics in this direction changes the question from one of moral and political urgency to one of a skeptical empirical historicism: setting aside the local positivist biases that have infiltrated the poetic canon by way of the academy, what are the cultural functions that poetry has shown itself able to serve?

The anthropological approach that ethnopoetics takes to this question requires close attention to psychology, linguistics, political dynamics, history, and, in a necessarily broad application of the term, philosophy. Such an applied anthropology also articulates different paths toward several disciplines. The first stage in the application of an ethnopoetics would involve learning the specific poetics of a given culture and regarding its poetic output only in terms of that culture. The work done by Bruce-Novoa on Chicano poetry, by Houston Baker on African-American poetics, by Olatunde Olatunji on Yoruba poetics, and by Allen and Joseph Bruchac on Native American poetics points up a development shared by this poetics and the larger study of anthropology itself—a significant shift toward self-study by members of cultures once only studied by outsiders, which involves the recognition that intimacy with political and historical substrata of the culture is necessary for such an "immersed" and localized theory to be significantly realized. Still, the work of some few committed persons—Gary Snyder is clearly the most decisive example—has made it clear that an outsider can become an insider. But the example also makes it emphatically clear that this is more easily said than done, and that far from being a chronological "first stage," this kind of knowledge of a culture is an always elusive goal.

A second stage involves a more abstract cross-cultural analysis, with a view toward comprehension. Though such a strategy appears modernist and crudely assimilationist in disposition, comparative ethnology—for this is what is in question—is necessary to prepare the way for the third stage: adaptation, in the sense that one studies not only to master, but to restructure one's life. Modern anthropologists from Claude Lévi-Strauss to Turner have held this out as an ideal. So much depends on this—that Rilke's implication is correct, that our encounter with the truly alien (an archaic torso, a red wheelbarrow) insists that we change our lives, insists that such a change is both possible and necessary: precisely inasmuch as adaptation in this sense *is* possible, it exists as the most vital promise that the study of culture offers, and its most persuasive justification.

Finally, one further path: instead of passing from a cultural poetics to comprehensive comparison to cultural adaptation, one might pursue the path of reducing audience—from the macroculture to the regional culture to the subculture to the subdivisions of the subculture (Chicano poems in English, in Spanish, and in both languages, for instance; or "academic" versus folk-oral poems of the same subculture). But here, having focused one's attention on the local phenomenon, instead of moving through the various processes that might lead to comprehension and adaptation, one might instead come to see that a specialized understanding of a given poem may be derived by reducing it further toward the terms of its most specific audience: the author's gender group, or her race, or her locale, or her village, or even her family (there is a kind of criticism corresponding to each of these). Following this reduction, one comes to the ultimately reduced audience for any poem, the poet herself, and to the psychoanthropology of biography. While the limitations of this reduction are clear and decisive, we have to keep in mind that the reduction *has its function*, that poems persistently express a psychology as well as a sociology, and that those two levels are vitally interactive. The poem as self-expression—although not complete and not an end in itself—is neither dead nor functionless.[15]

Certainly it is not possible to address all the poetries I've mentioned or all the questions I've raised here, but a brief comparison of three kinds of insult poems may illustrate the sense of urgency I feel. The first, Eskimo "contest-songs," Thompson notes, "gave vent to poisonous grudges and supplied an outlet for pent-up aggression. . . . The process actually took the place of judicial decisions" (212-13). The second example is the African song of abuse, exemplified by the *halo* tradition of Ghana, a poetry of seasonal carnival, when villages or "rival sections of the same town" (Anyidoho 18) visit one another for a variety of celebratory entertainments.[16] Awoonor explains:

> Each side commissioned its poets to dig into the history of the other group for all the scandalous details about their leaders, true or false. The ingredients constitute the material for verbal assault on the ugliness of the opponents' leadership, juicy bits about whose grandmother was a whore or whose great-grandfather built a wealth on stolen goods. (*Breast* 86-87; quoted in Anyidoho 18)

Kofi Anyidoho notes that while these poems are produced and consumed in a celebratory spirit, they remain "a poetry of dramatic confrontation," partly by maintaining a "tone of combat" (19). They are "a game governed by aesthetic norms which mingle reality and fantasy" (19), but also do the social work of providing a kind of public shaming, warning, and discharge of animosities. In addition, the songs stand as a kind of challenge for a response from members of the opposing group (who are present while the performance takes place). As Anyidoho explains, "Everyone looks forward to the next performance when today's harassed spectator will in turn take the stage and launch a counter-offensive" (20).[17]

The "tone of combat" underlying (or overlaid upon) a carnival performance depending upon "the combined arts of singing, drumming, and dancing" (Anyidoho 19) makes for provocative resonances between the African song of abuse and my third example, the insult poetry embedded in African-American rap music.[18] This has been a terrific burden for liberal commentators to have to bear, because it violates all sorts of rules of respect, propriety, decorum, thoughtfulness, nobility, manhood (much rap insult is visited by male rappers on women), and so on. In general (the feeling runs), the whole thing has gone beyond good taste and common decency; there is, in short, no appeal to art here. From a Marxist point of view, too, something is wrong with the fact that these black men and women expend so much energy insulting not their oppressors but each other.[19] From this perspective, rap insult poetry does no productive social work, but on the contrary must be seen as yet another instance of the proletariat turned against itself.

From the perspective of an anthropology, however, it must be clear that all three of these modalities of insult function with reference to questions of cultural space or territory, though differently. The issue in Eskimo culture is that of shared, enclosed territory and the necessity for resolving differences—hence the explicit contest, staged in view of a community that stands to lose when its members fail to resolve their differences. In the case of *halo*, the opposing parties in question are not necessarily bound together either in interdependence or in physical proximity to the same extent as the Eskimo. And where the Eskimo ritual attains a kind of judicial seriousness, the African version plays more freely along the axis of truth and fiction, work and game, and formally appears less dependent upon prior formulas and more upon imagination and a will to shared entertainment.

I would suggest that an analysis of the function of the rap insult must take into account (1) the seriousness of conflict in the hip-hop subculture and the nature of social bonding there, (2) the relation between the status attained through one's art in this culture and social mobility (few poetic forms, it seems to me, can match rap in its confrontatory mix of self-dramatization and self-reflexiveness), and (3) the value attached to abstracting the material realities of this culture—including the omnipresent mythology (and sometimes present reality) of physical violence—into verbal forms. Beyond the explicit poetry of abuse rappers visit upon one another, this abstraction of violence underlies highly publicized intercultural flash points like Ice T's "Cop Killer." Outside the community of rap listeners, the artist's claim—that the sociopath of that song's title should not be felt as a real threat (i.e., a set of instructions for killing actual police officers) but as a kind of symbolic warning that such mentalities are being produced by contemporary distributions of social power—was generally not felt to be sufficiently reassuring. And thus, while still a carnivalized aesthetic form for the resolution of conflicts between or within communities, rap (at least in this highly politicized form) situates itself differently from Eskimo and African insult poetry along the axis of fantasy and social truth. Thus the insult function subdivides culturally and aesthetically, and raises questions for poetics that are also questions pertinent to the ways in which cultural groups symbolize their differences. Most simply, they raise questions of the verbal symbolization of violence. The next question is, How do these symbolisms function systemically with reference to the needs of this culture, and to the demands or challenges of the other? Then, from the formal point of view, one might want to examine the structural relations between and among Eskimo, African, and rap poems of abuse and others—Italian "flyting" and Irish curses, for instance. Is the rap insult more formulaic or more dependent upon spontaneous imagination? And do these forms demonstrate any systemic variation—a process of cultural adaptation—as rap publication (recording and distribution) reaches an audience beyond the immediate community? Finally, the adaptive level—the great sign of vigorous health in the poetics attaching to American popular musical forms is that they have provided a space in which a great variety of intercultural adaptations have been enabled.

Teaching Differences

It seems to me that an ethnopoetics must finally confront a crucial social paradox or crisis, namely, that two powerful and antithetical forces are at work in all social inscription. We may call them mythic and rational, or conservative and evolutionary, or localizing and globalizing. There are more names than we really need. Clearly a culture that conserves nothing of itself to call a past, or myth, or dream time, or tradition, or history is no culture at all; just as clearly a culture that has no mechanism for adapting to environmental change is already dead, awaiting burial. Every functional culture exhibits both capabilities—conservation and adaptation.[20] But this paradox, conflict, or dialectic is far from politically neutral, for environmental change in the form of a lake's drying up, for instance, is qualitatively different from that of an omnivorous macroculture's demanding of a smaller culture that it adapt by surrendering the very heart of its being. This is what is in question in the work of someone like Native American theorist Allen, whose work finally comes down on the side of the local, the conservative, the tribal. She registers no objection in principle to the poetics of the macroculture, but instead plants herself separate: to each tribe its own poetry. And as the worn-out myth of the melting pot has given way to a reality of divergent, multiply alienated cultures, the possibility of a fragmentary poetics, a patchwork of uncorrelated poetries and theories, is not beyond imagining.

This is why at the outset I ambivalently offered a defense of at least one principle of modernist poetics—its desire to articulate, through something like a freshness of language, a set of possibilities through which men and women might strip themselves of the dull, thoughtless, and oppressive baggage of the world. That this original impulse has degenerated into niggling mandarinism and intellectual one-upmanship is a scandal, and that its determination to "make it new" seems to disregard the positive values attaching to tradition and custom in nonindustrial cultures presents serious philosophical problems; but these important reservations don't justify abandoning the impulse itself. Opposite Allen's isolationist sensibility is the assimilationism that Bruce-Novoa and Carmen Tafolla discern as constitutive of Chicano poetics.[21] Bruce-Novoa notes that "the essential situation of creating from at least two major cultural sources is a defining characteristic of Chicano literature" (240), and describes contemporary Chicano poets as committed to "craftsmanship, quality, and dedication to personal vision" (244); Tafolla situates these poets in immediate proximity to the macroculture:

> Chicano literature has gone beyond beginnings in many respects—it has gone beyond a definition of our cultural origins, it has gone beyond the beginning stages of myth creation and symbol kinship, it has gone beyond its own awareness of the literary action itself, and, perhaps most significantly to those who struggled for years to be read and to read, it has gone beyond the beginnings of its acceptance and recognition by the literary world as a whole. (223-24)

Virtually every culture today experiences some sort of tension between tradition and assimilation—again, between conservation and adaptation. To resolve this tension in a humane way is a crucial task that falls by default upon our educational system. In every culture, education means not only preserving the past, but also making it new. In one sense, every culture educates its children strictly into itself, its own ways of being and knowing. But the other, adaptive side of the picture is just as important; every culture teaches its adaptive possibilities, its ways of confronting the new and alien, to its young. For this reason education in a culture like ours presents the paradox in a specially vivid way. Fred Rodriguez, in *Education in a Multicultural Society*, expresses it clearly as he defines "multicultural education," which not only "values" but "endorses cultural pluralism." It "recognizes cultural diversity as a fact of life in American society, and affirms it as a valuable resource." Yet it also "recognizes that each group exists as part of an interrelated whole" (3). The implied praxis, it would seem, is a kind of liberal appeal to mutual respect; economic inequities, meanwhile, will presumably take care of themselves in the fullness of time.

This precarious balance is nothing to mock in the name of any political ideology. It is impossible for me to imagine a near future in which alternative cultures flourish independently, given the present localization of political and military power and imminent battles over diminishing natural resources. The future holds engagement and conflict. Meanwhile, we must all learn to adapt without losing ourselves in the process. We cannot imagine that anyone's canon—anyone's reserves of power—will simply disappear. We have to use our language, establish rules by which we can understand each other, recognize what cultural functions and capacities are shared, try to educate each other. We have to create boundary conditions in which our adaptive abilities are put to the test—in which we experiment with new possibilities of community. It seems to me that the academy, with all its faults, has the potential of becoming a kind of laboratory for conducting those experiments in community.

This brings me to the question of the participation of the academy in the conservation and adaptation of cultures. If it is necessary to throw out the entire history of poetics to establish a new canon entirely predicated on the straightforward expression of subcultural attitudes, the academy will just be in the way. Why should the academy—the institutional source of power of that history—be the scene of its overthrow? The interests of the academy and of those who would repudiate the history of poetics conflict essentially, for the academy as an institution depends on the marketing of knowledge, which in turn depends upon the conservation, the stockpiling, of knowledge.

And this knowledge-commodity will not go away, though it may transmogrify. No matter what poets do, the academy will deliver its analyses: as Nelson notes from his quite different perspective, poetics and the canon, in some form, will persist. The problem at present is not that poetics is inaccurate in its analysis, but that it has become shortsighted. Looking no further than the narrow range of poetic values it has institutionalized in the classist, racist, sexist history of its academic affiliation, poetics has hardened into the very shape of the systemic patterns of prejudice that constitute today's academy. As Nelson notes, literary theory has conspired with a narrow canon to reinforce the prejudices of that canon and make it impenetrable by texts whose emphases differ from its own. The bracing diversity of poetry and poetics gathered under the canopy of Rothenberg and Rothenberg's ethnopoetics makes it clear that to the extent that such a canon ignores or omits verbal productions that various communities recognize as poetry, it is radically incomplete, and its supplementation requires a reconstruction of its poetics to articulate the new cultural criteria. It is only through a forced extension beyond the narrow bounds of academic ideology that poetics can redeem itself. The academy today hardly deserves poetry, but it does have the potential to earn it.

The canon didn't happen by accident, nor did it evolve by conscious design. When Michael Castro notes that American mythic images of Native Americans—Caliban or Uncas—"serve underlying psychic needs of Western culture" (quoted in Bruchac, "Survival" 196), he has his finger on a much more general pulse. Thompson notes the "cheap books and the popular press that [were] devised to meet the social and psychological needs of an industrialized country" (180). Both point to the important truth that modern poetry and poetics have behind them the force of such needs; if the poetry of the macroculture is introspective, for instance, introspection has served a crucial function for poets writing in an alienating culture. These things will not disappear, nor can they be ignored into oblivion.

It is also important to see not only that this functional tactic has benefited only a minority, but also that it has privileged that minority's imaginative life by denying the validity—the canonicity—of alternative responses to cultural alienation.[22] In a word, the canon tells us to learn to get along with loneliness and powerlessness rather than mount a communal effort that might lessen them: the cliché goes, "It's lonely at the top," but on the underside of the canon is written, "To wield power one must reject the claims of the Other."

Thompson sounds an optimistic note, however: "In the last quarter of the century we are much humbler, and this is a most hopeful trend; we are more open to take hints from any source, to learn for instance from non-industrialized peoples" (202). One of the important learnings he calls "the collaboration of the old style": the relearning of a poetry in which poet and audience experience one another more directly, without the gap of modernist alienation and privilege dividing them. Against the solipsism of modernist poetics there exist several powerful counterexamples, one of which is the poetry program or workshop. More than any other group of students I've encountered, student poets come to us not looking for a set of skills, but yearning to know *what they are*. And this interrogative drive—which can, of course, be knocked out of them by exclusive emphasis on "the poet's craft" or "the poetry marketplace"—can best be nurtured by recognizing and using the special quality of the workshop, its open-ended potential for developing an interdisciplinary and, ideally, multicultural sense of community.[23] Nowhere before or after such a workshop does the academy provide a comparable sense of where one's art comes from, how it affects others, and what it means. In this community of intense and intimate interaction, writers learn what their work means, *how* it means, and, most important, how it functions culturally, through the responses of the members of a concerned group whose differences are as important as its shared premises.

The poetry workshop is a special instance of the more general case of the dramas of economics and power (political, professional, aesthetic) that mark the relationship between the academy and the canon. This drama articulates along the axes of two imperatives, two claims, that may be termed *entitlement* and *empowerment*.[24] Entitlement marks the domain of the claim on the future, a narrative of "rights," in which a principle of tolerance is imagined for meanings that cultural forces acting in the present might otherwise declare intolerable. Northrop Frye provides a lucid instance: "No discussion of beauty can confine itself to the formal relations of an isolated work of art; it must consider, too, the participation of the work of art in the vision of the goal of social effort, the idea of a complete and classless civilization" (*Anatomy of Criticism* 346-47; quoted in Denham 33). This "vision" and "idea" anticipate Fredric Jameson's dependency upon "utopian meta-narratives" that guide neo-Marxist critique, and inform the impulse of modernist poetics to aim itself toward a purified homogeneity framed by formal criteria (see McHugh 6). Perhaps Frye and Jameson are right, and such a monocultural idea is an ultimate principle. The claim of entitlement—in its starkest form, that every cultural narrative is entitled to unprejudiced attention—involves attempts to disassemble the systemic apparatus of bias against cultural conventions outside the mainstream. This is to say that ultimately (according to something like a utopian meta-narrative), a future must be imagined and built in which all repressive structures disappear: if the canon suppresses, then *ideally* it should be scrapped.

In practice, however, the liberal claim of entitlement has been co-opted to participate in the suppression of minority poetics, as the monocultural ideal precipitates monocultural expectations. To "disassemble the systemic apparatus" means to disempower some in service to the general claim—projected always into an ideal future—of entitlement. This cultural ideal needs reinforcement and balancing as a working principle by a principle of practical skepticism that allows for continuous attention to the actual literatures diversely produced. This second claim, that of empowerment, involves attempts to assure the most talented individuals that their process of adapting to the system that is given will be completed, to assure that avenues they have chosen to success or power—of expression, first of all—will not be interrupted. Partly such a claim signifies a distrust of the utopian narrative that relies on the power of collaborative adaptation. To speak only of poetics here, if Frye's "idea of a complete and classless civilization," although clearly a goal worth maintaining, has the effect in the present of embedding ethnocentric criteria in the poetic canon of the macroculture, then only a determined insistence upon concrete, immediate mechanisms of empowerment based on extracanonical criteria—"race, gender, politics, population distribution and everything but poetics," in Wakoski's words—can protect the truly eccentric.

The academy, as a source and base of institutional power over the dissemination of cultural attitudes toward the canon, needs to balance these two claims. The ultimate goal of entitlement needs to be reconciled with an immediate goal of empowerment. Given the hierarchical disposition of power and authority in the definition and enactment of canonical criteria, such reconciliation cannot be accomplished without ongoing conflict. But minority poetics should not be expected to aim themselves toward a future when they will attain legitimacy by dissolving themselves in a macrocultural monopoetics; nor is there any sense in dismissing or discouraging the adaptive potentialities of multicultural interpenetration. Somewhere on a distant horizon may perhaps be imagined a world in which differences have been fairly eliminated to everyone's satisfaction; then we can live out our utopian future. Until then, the realities of social life at every level present us with an array of human difference—that in this learning environment is literally *all we have to work with*—that we must learn to attend to and contend with.

Notes

1. See Diane Wakoski's discussion of the "new conservatism" of several recent anthologies.
2. "From book reviews to scholarly journals, from normalizing critical histories to anthologies and reference works, from student handbooks and class reading lists to graduation requirements that emphasize 'major' authors, from faculty hiring priorities to tenure decisions that privilege certain authors and disparage others, from convention programs to publishers' lists" (Nelson 40).
3. See Nelson (56ff. and passim) for a discussion of the relationship between the canon and power.
4. Nelson is aware of a greater variety than he treats here: "The full range of modern poetries is so great that it cannot be persuasively narrativized in any unitary way. . . . No single story can be told about modern poetry and its varied audiences that is even marginally adequate" (7).
5. Nelson's general argument for including such texts is complex, and is strengthened by this example; I would claim that they deserve attention (from a particular audience) because they *attempted* to perform an unusual cultural *function*.
6. Wakoski affiliates "left" ("the avant-garde") and "right" ("conservative poets") under the sign of "form" ("because both . . . are deeply concerned with the surface form of the language used"), creating "a new Left side of the balance," which "has to be called 'content' " (23).

7. Wakoski notes that her ambivalence about the anthology partly derives from Norton's having doubled the number of her poems in this edition.
8. "If we want a field that is open to intellectual challenges, canon formation and literary historiography should cultivate a productive antagonism. . . . Another reason I recognize that hierarchical, canonizing cultural impulses cannot so easily be swept away is that I realize I have a number of internally canonized and devalued texts" (Nelson 54-55).
9. Wakoski calls ethnopoetics "a real change that diminishes the importance of the white male Christian, European tradition" (26). Nelson disregards it and the Rothenbergs entirely.
10. See also her comments on a "poetics of use" in Bruchac (*Songs* 2), and Rayna Green's discussion of her and other Native American women poets (1-12).
11. Houston Baker adopts a similar disposition toward a "sui generis poetics" (172) in *Afro-American Poetics* (1988).
12. Similarly, Wakoski: "If the Right wing is conserving the values of the culture, and those values are seen most clearly in the 'forms' that a culture creates, then, as we move Left on the scale, we become less and less concerned with form and more and more concerned with what use the form is put to" (23-24).
13. More radically challenging—though perhaps more abrasive than persuasive—is Edward Said's claim that anthropology is immedicably contaminated as intellectual theory and practice by its intimate affiliation with the systemic imperialism of America's military-political apparatus.
14. This "monocultural assumption" is related to the "utopian meta-narrative" discussed by Patrick McHugh.
15. In *Symposium of the Whole* Albert Lord's dismissal of originality in oral song is immediately followed by Kofi Awoonor: "What is very striking about the Ewe oral tradition is the individuality of the poets. Even though their work has full meaning only within the all-embracing scope of the folk tradition, the individual genius and talent of the poets come into full play, contradicting the popular notion that performers are generally following rigidly laid down patterns in their art" (163).
16. See Turner, *Celebration*, for a wide-ranging discussion of the cultural dynamics of festival, carnival, and ritual. For a suggestive discussion linking traditional festival and African drama, see Etherton.
17. This carnival phenomenon seems to invoke an African tradition of festival "misrule" (see Etherton 30; also Turner, *Celebration* 27) as it inverts the traditional African praise poetry (the genre *Oriki* among the Yoruba—see Olatunji 67-107); but it is also clearly related to the *Halo* (insult poetry) tradition of the Ewe described by Awoonor.
18. A highly publicized example is the sequence of "Roxanne" songs, especially "Roxanne Roxanne" (UTFO) and "Roxanne's Revenge" (Roxanne Shanté).
19. A broader discussion, of course, would consider also the empowering, celebratory dimension of rap.
20. A relevant discussion (again, with different terminology) appears in Robert Denham's treatment of Northrop Frye's dialectic of the "myth of freedom" and the "myth of concern" (35ff.).
21. This claim is challenged by work in progress by Justo Alarcon.
22. "Poetry for a minority can never be a satisfactory aim or recipe." Thompson (180) is taking the long view, perhaps, and his "minority" is an educated, sensitive one opposed to dull masses of semiliterates. Clearly limiting access to poetry to such a group is undesirable, if poetry is a good thing. He does not, however, perceive the alternative picture in which society appears as numerous subcultures, each a potential reservoir of poetic expression in its own terms.
23. Nevertheless, poetry programs are marketed; see any issue of *Poets and Writers* for evidence of graduate programs' marketing focus on craft and competitive success.
24. I am grateful to Robert Miklitsch for advice on clarifying this terminology.

Works Cited

Alarcon, Justo. Private correspondence.

Allen, Paula Gunn. "The Sacred Hoop: A Contemporary Indian Perspective on American Indian Literature." Rothenberg and Rothenberg. 173-87.

Anyidoho, Kofi. "Kofi Awoonor and the Ewe Tradition of Songs of Abuse (*Halo*)." Lemuel A. Johnson et al., eds. *Toward Defining the African Aesthetic*. Washington: Three Continents, 1982.

______. Prefatory note to poems in Bruchac, ed.

Auden, W. H. *The Dyer's Hand and Other Essays*. New York: Random House, 1962.

Awoonor, Kofi. *The Breast of the Earth*. Garden City, NY: Doubleday, 1975.

______. "Some Ewe Poets." Rothenberg and Rothenberg. 162-68.

Baker, Houston. *Afro-American Poetics*. Madison: U of Wisconsin P, 1988.

Bruce-Novoa, Juan. "Chicano Poetry: An Overview." Harris and Aguero. 226-48.

Bruchac, Joseph, ed. *Songs from This Earth on Turtle's Back*. Greenfield Center, NY: Greenfield Review P, 1983.

______. "Survival Comes This Way: Contemporary Native American Poetry." Harris and Aguero. 196-205.

Clark, John Pepper. Private correspondence.

Collins, Billy. "Literary Reputation and the Thrown Voice." Harris and Aguero. 295-306.

Crawford, John. "Notes Toward a New Multicultural Criticism: Three Works by Women of Color." Harris and Aguero. 155-95.

Dauenhauer, Richard. "Koyukon Riddle-Poems." Rothenberg and Rothenberg. 121-24.

Denham, Robert D. "Northrop Frye and Wayne Booth: (New) Ideologies and (Old) Traditions." *Perspectives* 20.1 (Spring 1990): 32-42.

Etherton, Michael. *The Development of African Drama*. New York: Africana, 1982.

Finnegan, Ruth. "Drum Language and Literature." Rothenberg and Rothenberg. 129-39.

Green, Rayna, ed. *That's What She Said: Contemporary Poetry and Fiction by Native American Women*. Bloomington: Indiana UP, 1984.

Harris, Marie, and Kathleen Aguero, eds. *A Gift of Tongues: Critical Challenges in Contemporary American Poetry*. Athens: U of Georgia P, 1987.

Heyen, William. *The Generation of 2000: Contemporary American Poets*. Princeton, NJ: Ontario Review P, 1984.

Howard, Richard. *Alone with America*. New York: Atheneum, 1980.

Lauter, Paul. "Class, Caste, and Canon." Harris and Aguero. 57-82.

McHugh, Patrick. "Capitalist Logic and Cultural Critique: The Dialectical Limits of Postmodernism." Unpublished paper delivered at University of Utah Humanities Center, 30 March 1990.

Nelson, Cary. *Repression and Recovery: Modern American Poetry and the Politics of Cultural Memory, 1910-1945*. Madison: U of Wisconsin P, 1989.

Olatunji, Olatunde O. *Features of Yoruba Oral Poetry*. Ibadan, Nigeria: University P, 1984.

Paul, Sherman. *Hewing to Experience: Essays and Reviews on Recent American Poetry and Poetics, Nature and Culture*. Iowa City: U of Iowa P, 1989.

Quasha, George. "From 'DiaLogos: Between the Written and the Oral in Contemporary Poetry.' " Rothenberg and Rothenberg. 461-74.

Rodriguez, Fred. *Education in a Multicultural Society*. Washington, DC: UP of America, 1983.

Rothenberg, Jerome, and Diane Rothenberg, eds. *Symposium of the Whole: A Range of Discourse toward an Ethnopoetics*. Berkeley: U of California P, 1983.

Rothenberg, Jerome, and Dennis Tedlock, eds. *Alcheringa*. 10 vols. New York and Boston, 1970-80.

Said, Edward. "Representing the Colonized: Anthropology's Interlocutors." *Critical Inquiry* 15.2 (Winter 1989): 205-25.

Tafolla, Carmen. "Chicano Literature: Beyond Beginnings." Harris and Aguero. 206-25.

Thompson, Denys. *The Uses of Poetry*. London: Cambridge UP, 1978.

Turner, Victor, ed. *Celebration: Studies in Festivity and Ritual*. Washington, DC: Smithsonian Institution P, 1982.

______. "A Review of 'Ethnopoetics.' " Rothenberg and Rothenberg. 337-42.

Untermeyer, Louis. *Lives of the Poets: The Story of One Thousand Years of English and American Poetry*. New York: Simon & Schuster, 1959.

Wakoski, Diane. "The New Conservatism in American Poetry in Spite of the 'Expanding Canon.' " *New Letters* 56.1 (Fall 1989): 17-38.

Zolberg, Vera. *Constructing a Sociology of the Arts*. New York: Cambridge UP, 1990.

Canon: New Testament to Derrida

The *New York Times Book Review* recently carried a clever piece by Henry Louis Gates, Jr., on canon formation titled "Canon Confidential: A Sam Slade Caper." After splashing some bourbon into his coffee mug and putting his feet on the desk, Sam meditates:

> Seemed there was some kind of a setup that determined which authors get on this A list of great literature. Payout was all perks, so far as I could make out. If you're on this list, they teach your work in school and write critical essays on you. Waldenbooks moved you from the Fiction section to the Literature section.

Estelle, who sets Sam off on this case and who later turns out to be Thomas Pynchon in drag, is a bit ambivalent concerning the canon: "I got no beef with the canon as such. It serves a legit purpose. What I'm telling you is, it's fixed. It's not on the level" (1).

In the foreword to the Schomburg Library of Nineteenth-Century Black Women Writers, Gates has argued, less playfully,

> Literary works configure into a tradition not because of some mystical collective unconscious determined by the biology of race or gender, but because writers read other writers and ground their representations of experience in models of language provided largely by other writers to whom they feel akin. It is through this mode of literary revision, amply evident in the texts themselves—in formal echoes, recast metaphors, even in parody—that a "tradition" emerges and defines itself. (xviii)

Who decides what we read and on what basis? What makes some texts canonical and others noncanonical? Although these questions have until recently received mainly the specialist attention of textual scholars, they are now being widely discussed, if not easily answered.

I propose to look at three episodes in canon formation, two selected from what might be called the high canons of sacred and secular literature—the New Testament and Milton—in the interest of recovering something of the dynamics of traditional canon formation. My third episode may seem an idiosyncratic choice, but I hope to show that Jacques Derrida's famous but little-read *Of Grammatology* (1976) has much to contribute, both as example and as theory, to an understanding of processes of canon formation. The specific questions that have led me to investigate these examples are as follows: What precipitated the forming of the New Testament canon, and does that process serve as a model for understanding the formation of the canons of secular literature? Why has Milton been so often invoked by feminist and black readers, while being so often condemned in recent critiques of canonicity? Do deconstructive textual processes, such as those Derrida examines, extend to the positioning of entire texts within a canon or tradition? Finally, I hope by these examples to inquire into the adequacy of "canon" as a metaphor for understanding textual tradition.

Canon is a curious word, an uncanny word. The six columns of small type devoted to it in the *OED* serve to distinguish four fundamental meanings: (1) canon, from Latin and Greek by way of Old English, signifies "a rule, law, or decree of the Church; esp. a rule laid down by an ecclesiastical Council," thus "canon law," that body of ecclesiastical law derived from papal decrees and council statutes; (2) canon may also denote "the collection or list of books of the Bible accepted by the Christian Church as genuine and inspired" and thus, by analogy, "any set of sacred books," a usage dated by the *OED* in the first instance from John Wyclif in 1382 and in the analogous instance from Max Muller in 1870; (3) in music, a canon is "a species of musical composition in which the different parts take up the same subject one after another, either at the same or at a different pitch, in strict imitation"; (4) finally, canon may indicate "a clergyman . . . living with others in a clergy-house . . . or in one of the houses within the precinct or close of a cathedral . . . and ordering his life according to the canons or rules of the church." These definitions are linked by a sense of law and rule. Canon law governs the life of the resident of the clergy-house; canonical texts are judged acceptable to the Christian Church; the musical composition repeats the same subject in strict imitation.

It is rather unsettling, however, to move from these accounts of the word *canon* to either ancient or modern accounts of how the New Testament came to be. Although one might well expect to find that some formal decree of the early Church established the list of books that we now call the New Testament, the process of sacred canon formation was quite different from what one might suppose from a too-literal application of the later sense of "canon law" to a process that occurred before the Church established the formal practices of papal and council decrees.

For modern readers to imagine the earliest bibles, it is necessary to abandon many of the assumptions we take for granted about books. Although it is often said that Christianity was born with a bible already in its cradle—that is, the Hebrew scriptures in the Greek translation—such a cradle would have been a crowded place, full of either separate scrolls or individual codices. The closest approximation to the modern sense of the Bible as a single bound book is the fourth-century A.D. Codex Sinaiticus, which was discovered at St. Catherine's Monastery, Sinai, in 1844 and is now one of the treasures of the British Museum. For the first 200 years after the death of Jesus, the written texts of his sayings and the other texts related to his teaching were distinctly heterogeneous. There were individual letters by the several apostles, sectarian texts such as those discovered in 1945 at Nag Hammadi, records of the sayings of Jesus such as those to which Matthew may have had access for the Sermon on the Mount, and the various gospels.

Furthermore, as early Christians struggled to sustain their beliefs in what remained until the fourth century a hostile Roman climate, the relationship between Christianity and Judaism was a major problem. Were Christians Jewish sectaries, like the Pharisees, Sadducees, and Essenes, or was theirs a distinctive faith? The bible in the cradle—that is, Jewish scripture—complicated this issue in the minds of many early Christians. Two of the most important figures in second-century Christianity to wrestle with the problem of whether the teachings of Jesus constituted a definitive break with Judaism or a supplement to it were Marcion and Irenaeus. Although the quarrel between them directly precipitated the New Testament as we now know it, the works of both have passed into obscurity, only a fragment of Marcion's *Antitheses* having survived, and Irenaeus's writings being available neither in most libraries nor in the Penguin Classics.

Although the supposed model of the biblical canon is a continual source of metaphor for students of the politics of literary tradition, the recoverable second-century processes that shaped the New Testament are more curiously interesting than usually assumed. In his magisterial study *The Formation of the Christian Bible*, Hans von Campenhausen writes that "the idea and the reality of a Christian Bible were the work of Marcion" (148).[1] The path to this conclusion is not an easy one. Because of Marcion's excommunication as a heretic in A.D. 144, most of what is known of his thought has to be recovered from the denunciations of his work, particularly Irenaeus's massive polemic, *Contra Haereses*. To recover Marcion's thought requires the same processes of reconstruction that were necessary for Valentinian Gnosticism before the discovery of the Nag Hammadi Library.

Marcion's fundamental conviction appears to have been that there was an intolerable contradiction between the Law and the Gospel. On the one hand there was the God of the world, of creation, of the old covenant, of Jewish scripture; on the other hand there is the Father of Jesus, who is mysteriously unknown to the world except through faith in the Gospel of Christ. Thus, for Marcion, Christianity is a polemical religion. Its true texts are those that resist the teachings of the old Law and promote the faith that is the only means of knowing God the Father of Jesus. Here is a portion of Irenaeus's polemic against Marcion's polemical theology:

> Marcion . . . impudently blasphem[es] him who is declared to be God by the Law and the Prophets; calling him a worker of evils, delighting in wars, inconstant in judgement and self-contradictory. . . . He alleges that Jesus came from the Father who is above the God that made the world; that he came to Judaea in the time of Pontius Pilate . . . and was manifest in the form of a man to all that were in Judaea, destroying the prophets and the

> Law and all the works of that God who made the world, whom he calls also the Ruler of the Universe. (Bettenson 53)

Marcion cannot find a gospel untainted by the Old Testament's Law and Prophets; all have been already perverted and distorted, blighted in the bud. What he considers necessary, therefore, is a careful sifting of the texts in order to remove the extraneous and contaminated matter. The only writings that come through his tight mesh are a single, definitive gospel—that is, a de-Judaicized version of Luke—and ten exclusively Pauline letters. Here is Irenaeus's account of what would have been Marcion's New Testament:

> Moreover he mutilated the Gospel according to Luke, removing all the narratives of the Lord's birth, and also removing much of the teaching of the discourses of the Lord wherein he is most manifestly described as acknowledging the maker of this universe to be his father. Thus he persuaded his disciples that he himself was more trustworthy than the apostles, who handed down the Gospel; though he gave to them not a Gospel but a fragment of a Gospel. He mutilated the Epistles of the Apostle Paul in the same manner. (Bettenson 53)

This, then, was to be the eleven-book canon: no Old Testament, no distinction among the points of view of the four gospels, no non-Pauline epistles. Marcion, its first reformer, was determined to rescue true Christianity from Judaism's God of the World at its textual source. He wrote a dogmatic exegetical treatise to justify his canon, but it is no longer possible to recover the structure or system of his argument.

Two curious consequences followed from Marcion's attempt at rigorous canon formation. The first was that his followers adopted his method but not his list, canonizing other epistles by mistakenly attributing them to Paul, and reintroducing passages from the other gospels back into Marcion's Luke. This prompts Tertullian to write against the Marcionites, "Day after day they remodel their gospel, as day after day we refute them once more" (quoted in Campenhausen 163). An entire genre with the title "Against Marcion" is a legacy of this contravention of Marcion by Marcionites.

The second consequence is far more important. Marcion's reformer's zeal prompted the Church to adopt a canonical strategy of inclusion. The principle that informs this strategy runs through the anti-Marcionite literature and is inscribed in the New Testament itself, when in 2 Timothy 3:16 it is written, "All scripture is inspired by God and profitable for teaching, for reproof, for correction, and for training in righteousness." This claim of universal scriptural inspiration, particularly if considered in the context of the Marcionite move to establish a more limited canon, serves not only to embrace Pauline and non-Pauline texts, but also to make a virtue of their heterogeneity. "The main contents of both the Old and New Testaments," Campenhausen writes,

> were never officially instituted or determined. The Old Testament had come

> with the Church at her birth; the New was consolidated in the process of the use which individual churches—with the critical and controlling participation of their intellectual leaders—made of the corpus of primitive Christian writing. The regular use of a book for liturgical reading was a pre-condition of its later *reception*. . . . Official decisions by the Church are not involved. Synodal judgements and episcopal pastoral letters concerning the contents of the Bible become usual only in the later fourth century. (331)

Important traces of this canonical fluidity remain in the New Testament.

Mark, the earliest of the gospels, displays a remarkable sense of the indeterminacy of signs. Although his text argues the urgency of being watchful and of attempting to interpret Jesus' words and the signs of his second coming, Mark is equally urgent in his warnings against false prophets and signs. Especially in his version of the parable of the Sower and the Seed, Mark emphasizes the problematics of interpretation: how the word is received, whether it takes root in the self of the listener, how the multiple fruits of interpretive reception grow—these are central concerns in his gospel. Whereas Luke, in his version of this parable, cheerfully promises that "nothing is secret, that shall not be made manifest; neither any thing hid, that shall not be known and come abroad" (8:17), Mark's Jesus retains his messianic mystery. Also in contrast to Mark, while still depending on him, Matthew is meticulously intertextual, carefully citing exactly the relevant portion of Old Testament prophecy that establishes not only the interpretive link but also the cause of individual events in the life of Jesus. John's gospel, in contrast to the three synoptics, not only offers yet another version of the processes of the word—especially in his chapter 15—but also radically purges his text of parables. There are sixteen parables in Mark, fifty in Matthew, forty-three in Luke, and six in John. Because John's Jesus interprets and allegorizes his parables, even these six are not parables in precisely the sense indicated by the parable on parables (the Sower and the Seed) in the synoptic gospels. In contrast to the reticent Jesus in the synoptics, Jesus in the Gospel of John declaims his message in authoritative, commanding discourse. He orders his followers to love one another. The New Testament epistles are similarly heterogeneous, both in relation to the narrative books and in their often open debate with each other. Paul's emphasis on salvation by faith and grace prompts James's counter, "Faith, if it hath not works, is dead" (2:17), which in turn invites Paul's attack on James by name in Galatians 2. But Acts 13 provides a rare glimpse of Paul among the Jews, speaking in the synagogue and placing Jesus in a line of descent from the patriarchs.

Marcion was indeed correct in the perception of multiplicity in these texts and in his understanding that this multiplicity is a legacy of the Old Testament. The canon he unwittingly precipitated, however, celebrates that multiplicity and the Jewish legacy to Christianity. What is most instructive about the example of the New Testament for an understanding of processes of canon formation is that a canon necessarily consists of more than one text and is therefore, from the moment it comes to be, dialogic. Here the musical canon, "in which the different parts take up the same subject one after another," becomes a relevant if not an exact metaphor for intertextual tradition. By rejecting Marcion's attempt to establish a single-voiced New Testament, Irenaeus and Tertullian affirm the principle of revision, looking again, as a fundamental process of tradition and canon formation.

Milton and African-American Literature

For Milton the reading and study of ancient texts, including the Bible, are occasions that manifest the interpretive freedom of the human mind and its powers of canonical revision. In his "First Prolusion," which he wrote as an undergraduate at Cambridge, Milton insists that he reads the ancients in order to apply the test of truth to their work. No institution, not the Church, not the state, not the university, can or should make that judgment for him. In his much later *A Treatise of Civil Power in Ecclesiastical Causes* (1659), he states the case boldly by imagining a situation in which an individual's reasoned convictions are in opposition to the entire authority of the Church and to the entire tradition of interpretation as handed down by the church fathers. To capitulate to authority in that situation is, in his view, unforgivable. Such interpretive liberty as he envisions requires totally open access to books, because censorship assumes a transcendent and infallible judgment superior not only to that of all potential authors but also to that of all potential readers.[2] The act of reading, as he envisions it in his manifesto for textual freedom, *Areopagitica* (1644), reverses the processes of textual production. Orpheus is his image of the author. The canonical works of an individual author—and of all authors whose works survive—are as the parts of Orpheus's dismembered body. As these embodied texts come toward the reader, however, they are transformed in the mythology of *Areopagitica* into the fragments of the body of Osiris, which have been spatially and temporally scattered. The task of the friends of truth is to regather Osiris's body and to re-member his limbs.

Although she does not specifically echo Milton's Orpheus-Osiris myth of texts, truth, and tradition, Phillis Wheatley, the mother of the African-American literary heritage, wrote poems that manifest the Orphic and Osirian desire nonetheless.[3] "To Maecenas," the poem that opens her volume and that is probably addressed to Alexander Pope, with whose epistolary poems hers have a strong affinity, identifies in her mentor a process of reading, identification, and creativity that her poems long to express as well. Indeed, Maecenas has done what all poets must do:

> Maecenas, you, beneath the myrtle shade,
> Read o'er what poets sung, and shepherds play'd.
> What felt those poets but you feel the same?
> Does not your soul possess the sacred flame?

> Their nobler strains your equal genius shares
> In softer language, and diviner airs. (lines 1-6)

His achievement and that of Terence—an African by birth, Wheatley notes—inspire her poetic quest:

> O could I rival thine and Virgil's page
> Or claim the Muses with the Mantuan Sage;
> Soon the same beauties should my mind adorn,
> And the same ardors in my soul should burn:
> Then should my song in bolder notes arise,
> And all my numbers pleasingly surprize;
> But here I sit, and mourn a grov'ling mind,
> That fain would mount and ride upon the wind. (23-30)

Even without considering Wheatley's biography, the poetic accomplishment here is remarkable. The accommodation of Pope's form to Milton's poetic aspiration in creating an anatomy of the African-American imagination exhilarates her mind. Although she claims that she is unable to "raise the song" and that "the fault'ring music dies upon [her] tongue" (35-36), like Milton she does magnificently well precisely what she is in the process of declaring herself unable to do. Wheatley turns to classical literature, to Milton, and to Pope for what she can use. When she berates her muse—"But say, ye Muses, why this partial grace, / To one alone of Afric's sable race . . . ?" (39-40)—she seems to long for the tradition to which she is in the process of giving birth. But her final couplet carefully sustains the ambiguity of her relationship to Homer, Terence, Milton, and Pope. They are both her fathers and her lovers, the sexually textual source of the "paternal rays" necessary for the generation of her poems. Tradition—that is, the literary canon from Homer to Pope—is alive in the body of her poems, just as it constitutes a standard of inspired achievement that she desires to equal.

Wheatley's remarkable life complicates the task of reading the politics of canonicity. She was called Phillis after the slave ship that brought her from Africa to America at the age of 7 or 8. Wheatley was the name of her owner, John Wheatley, who somehow provided her with an education in English and Latin, encouraged the development of her remarkable talent, and assisted in the difficult task of getting her poems published. In 1772, at the age of 18, Wheatley was given an oral examination by eighteen worthies of Boston, including Thomas Hutchinson and John Hancock, to determine the authenticity of her poems. Although no American publisher would print the poems, the examiners provided an authenticating letter to accompany John Wheatley's. Still a slave, Wheatley sailed for England with Nathaniel, her master's son, where her poems were published under the patronage of the Countess of Huntingdon. There Wheatley was visited by Benjamin Franklin and presented with a handsome edition of Milton's poems by the Lord Mayor of London, but most important, because of a recent legal decision in the English courts, as soon as she set foot on English soil, she ceased to be a slave. Just as European and especially English literary tradition had liberated her imagination, so now English soil liberated her body. All of this she associated with Milton, whose book she kept, even through poverty, until her death.

"The experience of defeat," as Christopher Hill has recently shown in a book with that title, haunted Milton's life and the lives of his contemporaneous revolutionaries after the Restoration of 1660. Wheatley experienced that same sense of defeat after her return to America. Having been freed from slavery simply by setting foot in Britain, she was ready to become a slave to Isaac Newton and to Milton, whom she addresses as the "British Homer," once she was back in America:

> The generous plaudit 'tis not mine to claim,
> A muse untutor'd, and unknown to fame.
>
> The heavenly sisters pour thy notes along
> And crown their bard with every grace of song.
> My pen, least favour'd by the tuneful nine,
> Can never rival, never equal thine;
> Then fix the humble Afric muse's seat
> At British Homer's and Sir Isaac's feet. ("Reply" 9-16)

Here is a tragic instance of the muse of inspiration being transformed into the anxiety of influence. Milton, once her father or lover, is now Wheatley's slave master. Her poems were not published in America until 1786, thirteen years after the London edition and two years after her death.

In 1788, two years after the first American edition of Wheatley's poems, Mary Wollstonecraft appropriates Milton for the English feminist tradition by assigning him an important place in *The Female Reader*, which she edited for the radical London publisher Joseph Johnson (for whom she also collaborated with William Blake in issuing books with her text and his illustrations). Wollstonecraft's daughter, Mary Shelley, manages to deal productively with Milton's poetic legacy at age 18, like Wheatley, in her brilliant book *Frankenstein, or, The Modern Prometheus* (1818), which creatively revises and transforms *Paradise Lost*. Wheatley, Wollstonecraft, and Mary Shelley find imaginative liberation in their appropriation of Milton's poetic legacy. Except for Blake, who writes an entire epic poem on the subject of how productively to manage Milton's influence, the response to Milton by male writers has typically been one of resistance and defensiveness. In this T. S. Eliot is perhaps the most notorious:

> While it must be admitted that Milton is a very great poet indeed [he writes in 1936], it is something of a puzzle to decide in what his greatness consists. On analysis, the marks against him appear both more numerous and more significant than the marks to his credit. As a man, he is antipathetic. Either

from the moralist's point of view, or from the theologian's point of view, or from the psychologist's point of view, or from that of the political philosopher, or judging by the ordinary standards of likeableness in human beings, Milton is unsatisfactory. (258)

In his second Milton essay, Eliot finally gets to the heart of his quarrel with the earlier poet: "We cannot, in literature, any more than in the rest of life, live in a perpetual state of revolution" (273).

In African-American literature, Milton has similarly fared better with women than with men. Ishmael Reed, even more than John Boyd and Charles Waddell Chesnutt, defines his own creative position in opposition to Milton's. Reed's *Mumbo Jumbo* (1978) rightly sees Osiris as central to Milton's mythology, but for Reed this means that Milton and Christianity are adversaries of a black culture that is polytheistic and life-affirming. This black movement he calls "Jes Grew," and Milton epitomizes the Osirian religion of "Atonism" that opposes it. This passage from *Mumbo Jumbo* locates the center of the dispute in some verses on the routing of the pagan gods in Milton's "On the Morning of Christ's Nativity":

John Milton, Atonist apologist extraordinary himself, saw the coming of the minor geek [magician] and sorcerer Jesus Christ as a way of ending the cult of Osiris and Isis forever.

The brutish gods of Nile as fast,
Isis and Horus, and the dog Anubis haste.

Nor is Osiris seen
In Memphian grove, or Green
  Trampling th'unshower'd Grass with lowings loud:
Nor can he be at rest
Within his sacred chest,
  Naught but profoundest Hell can be his shroud;
In vain with Timbrel'd Anthems dark
The sable-stoled Sorcerers bear his worshipt ark.

This from his Hymn "On the Morning of Christ's Nativity," which is nothing but a simple necktie party out to get Osiris' goat. And those "Timbrel'd Anthems dark" is the music that old Jethro played, the music of the worshipers of those festivals where they had a ball. Boogieing. Expressing they selves. John Milton couldn't stand that. Another Atonist; that's why English professors like him, he's like their amulet, keeping niggers out of their departments and stamping out Jes Grew before it invades their careers. It is interesting that he worked for Cromwell, a man who banned theater from England and was also a hero of Sigmund Freud.[4] (95)

Here Reed's narrator joins a distinguished tradition of anti-Miltonists including Samuel Johnson, Eliot, and William Empson, each of whom counters Milton's ideology with an ideology of his own. Reed carefully avoids suggesting any link between Osiris's appearance in Milton's "Hymn" and his appearance in *Areopagitica*. He prefers the stereotype of the repressed Puritan who despises music and theater. But to create this picture of Milton, he needs the music that Milton himself provides: the "Timbrel'd Anthems dark."

There seem to be basically two distinguishable theories of Milton's place in English poetry. For Harold Bloom the reception of Milton epitomizes the anxiety of influence, the powerful imaginative impact of a strong poet on his readers that first creates the panic of imaginative claustrophobia in the face of the extent and power of the poet's achievement (32). This fear is followed by willful misprision, misinterpretation—by such later strong poets as Eliot and Reed—in the interest of cutting the poet down to size and making room for new creative effort. The other position is one that Bloom knows but rejects—or revises or misinterprets—and is the one that Blake builds into the poem he calls *Milton* (1804-10).[5]

The central drama in this poem is the reception of a song, or poem, written by Milton, here a character in Blake's poem, and received by a female reader, Ololon. Blake was only 16 when Wheatley briefly visited London, and despite his great interest in black Americans, there is no reason to think that he knew of her existence. But the similarities between Wheatley's use of Milton and Ololon's response to Blake's Milton are striking, just as both are on a continuum with Wollstonecraft's and Mary Shelley's creative appropriations of Milton. After struggling with Milton and his text for some verses, Ololon first asks, "Are we contraries, O Milton, Thou & I?" Then, apparently realizing the creative benefits of otherness, she asks: "O Immortal, how were we led to War the Wars of Death? / Is this the Void Outside of Existence, which if enter'd into / Becomes a Womb?" (pls. 41-42). Ololon's two insights would seem to be necessarily related. Before her realization of their productively contrary states, she sees between herself and Milton only the "Wars of Death." Sameness or oblivion. What she comes to see, however, is that he offers her a void outside the contours of her own existence, a text she can enter. Here the imagery requires the complete overthrow of sexual stereotype and biological literalness. The otherness of his text becomes a creative place for her to engender when she recognizes it precisely as other but not alien to her.

Anna Julia Cooper's *A Voice from the South* (1892), without drawing on Blake, knows independently these two ways of reading.[6] Cooper successfully manipulated the administration of Oberlin in the early 1880s to give her free tuition and to allow her to take what was then called the "Gentleman's Course." (She wryly observes that neither event caused the college to collapse.) She moved on in 1887 to teach in the Washington Colored High School, which later became the famous Dunbar High School. There her feminism ran up against the male hostility of Washington's black middle class, which led to her expulsion. She was a magnificent woman of great tenacity, living to the age of

105. She adopted five orphaned children when she was 57, resumed her teaching of Latin at the school from which she had been fired, and overcame the humiliation of that dismissal by taking up the doctoral course at Columbia. Despite her family and teaching responsibilities, she did summer study at the Sorbonne, defended her dissertation in 1925 at the University of Paris, and thus became the fourth American black woman with a Ph.D. One of the others was her former student, and all three were from the high school where she taught.

A Voice from the South, which has recently been reissued in Gates's superb series, includes a fully formed theory of canon set forth in the context of a clearly recognizable feminism and antiracism. "Can any one conceive a Shakespeare, a Michael Angelo, or a Beethoven putting away any fact of simple merit because the thought, or the suggestion, or the creation emanated from a soul with an unpleasing exterior?" Cooper asks, leaving the reader no doubt as to the acceptable answer. She proceeds to distinguish two motives for writing. In the first category she places

> those in which the artistic or poetic instinct is uppermost—those who write to please—or rather who write because *they* please; who simply paint what they see, as naturally, as instinctively, and as irresistibly as the bird sings—with no thought of an audience—singing because it loves to sing,—singing because God, nature, truth sings through it.

She goes on to say that for these writers, "to be true to themselves and true to Nature is the only canon." Such writers "cannot warp a character or distort a fact in order to prove a point" (114, 181-84). Shakespeare heads her list of these writers, with George Eliot second.

The second group she calls, not disparagingly, "the preachers." They "have an idea to propagate, no matter in what form their talent enables them to clothe it, whether poem, novel, or sermon,—all those writers with a purpose or a lesson, who catch you by the buttonhole and pommel you over the shoulder till you are forced to give assent in order to escape their vociferations." At the head of this list she puts Milton "in much of his writings," with Thomas Carlyle in "all of his." She proceeds to warn that although the first class "will be the ones to withstand the ravages of time," the others risk having their day and passing away. She cannot, however, leave Milton there. Thus she distinguishes Book Three of *Paradise Lost*, "in which Milton makes the Almighty Father propound the theology of a seventeenth century Presbyterian," from the first stirrings of consciousness in Eve (a passage she quotes in full), where "Eve with guileless innocence describes her first sensations on awaking into the world." Such passages as these, she says, "will never cease to throb and thrill" (185). Apparently unaware of Wollstonecraft's *The Female Reader*, she is nevertheless drawn to the same passages. Cooper is also steeped in the Bible, which she often quotes in her book, although—as one would expect even from what little I have said about her—she resists any narrow doctrine, whether of Christianity or of anything else. Her generous spirit reaches out especially to Wheatley, a classicist like herself, and her imaginative picture of the young Phillis is better than anything that we can substantiate:

> Visiting the slave market in Boston one day in 1761, Mrs. John Wheatley was attracted by the modest demeanor and intelligent countenance of a delicate looking black girl just from the slave ship. She was quite nude save for a piece of coarse carpet she had tied about her loins, and the only picture she could give of her native home was that she remembered her mother in the early morning every day pouring out water before the rising sun. (274)

Here two Miltonists meet over a gap of more than a century.

In their different responses to Milton, all the writers I have mentioned have a vision of a large, multivoiced, polyvalenced canon within which the possibilities range from Wheatley's appropriation of Milton to Reed's Osirian critique, with Cooper selecting from Milton what she can use by applying to him the test of truth. Milton, of course, does all of these things himself. In all his poems he puts together pieces of the past—re-membering Osiris—in preparation for his own Orphic dismemberment; like Reed, he is an accomplished polemicist; and like Cooper, he insists, in the language of the "First Prolusion," that he is "only attempting to bring them [the ancient poets] to the test of reason, and thereby examine whether they can bear the scrutiny of strict truth" (224).

Derrida, Milton, and the Bible

Although he has read apparently as much as Milton, I doubt that Derrida has read his predecessor for the Ph.D. at Paris, Cooper. In their writings about textual history, feminism, racism, and aesthetic ideology, they nevertheless have much in common. Derrida's *Of Grammatology* argues with great care several of the points I have advanced in my separate episodes: that texts write more than one message; that what is on the margins or in the metaphors may be as important as what is at the supposed center; that careful reading involves not only entering into—or giving oneself over to—the textual structures of argument and metaphor, but also finding within the text its own potentialities for movement beyond itself.

Derrida's first chapter counters by anticipation many misreadings of his work that have nevertheless appeared in several handbooks on literary theory and postmodernism. For reasons that soon become clear, Derrida does not ask the question, "What is deconstruction?" but rather, "What does deconstruction do and what doesn't it do?" Here are some of the answers offered in chapter 1. Deconstruction does not "illustrate a new method" (lxxxiv); it does not discount history while freeing itself from "classical historical categories," but rather considers history "as a text" (lxxxix); it contributes to the movement to dislocate logocentrism, a movement "always already" begun, but it works toward such liberation in an underground, marginal, oppositional way (4); it takes shape within, yet works against, "the historico-metaphysical epoch" of which the closure rather than the end is visible (4); it presupposes a privileged concept of the sign, which it works to undermine (4); it is allied with the future to break with "constituted normality" and is thus proclaimed to be—and is resisted as—a "monstrosity" (5); it focuses upon the "as if," the metaphorical, the metonymic in discourse (8); it questions, therefore, the dream of history and metaphysics to make the subject present in language (10); it "inaugurates . . . the de-sedimentation" of truth that is dependent on the logos (10); it "designate[s] the crevice through which the yet unnameable glimmer beyond the closure can be glimpsed" (14); it works to free "the text . . . as a fabric of signs" from its confinement in secondariness (14); it challenges at every turn the question "What is . . . ?" (18-19) as part of a move against essentialism, which is a logocentric fiction of presence; it explores the ways of *différance*, "the production of differing/deferring" (20); and—most important, as demonstrated in Derrida's exemplary readings of Martin Heidegger and G. W. F. Hegel—deconstruction does not destroy structures from the outside but takes account of structures by inhabiting them, by borrowing all the subversive resources of the old structure, and by falling prey, in turn, to its own work (24).

Derrida's stake in the processes of canon formation can be seen not only in his repeated demonstrations of how these deconstructive processes work, but also in his identification of a number of exemplary texts that enable him to write a history of the Age of Rousseau, an era we still inhabit. In its turn, as he plans that it will, Derrida's own text becomes exemplary of the problematics of canon. It tempts us repeatedly to ask the very questions it overtly suspects: What sort of book is this that Derrida is writing? Philosophy, history of ideas, sociology of knowledge, literary theory? At what point in the text are we reading Derrida's reformulation of the arguments of texts he is interpreting, or his inhabiting of the metaphorical and other rhetorical structures of those texts, or his first attempts to move through the openings the texts themselves provide to a poststructural space beyond them? Then again, at what point are we reading *his* arguments and his metaphorical and rhetorical structures? Yet again, is the uncertainty part of his strategy to get his reader to question textual property and intellectual territorialism?

The principal texts Derrida reads in this book are Ferdinand de Saussure's *Course in General Linguistics* (1916), Claude Lévi-Strauss's *Tristes Tropiques* (1955), and Jean-Jacques Rousseau's *Essay on the Origins of Languages* (1781). He shows how these texts are simultaneously suspicious of and fascinated by writing, how they see writing as a monstrous imposition on speech (Saussure), as an instrument of enslavement (Lévi-Strauss), as a dangerous supplement to speech when speech can no longer protect and sustain natural presence (Rousseau). Two remarkable features of his readings are Derrida's recognition in each text of a dangerous potential in his own thought, which the text before him manifests also, and his generous praise—in the midst of critique—for the desire of these texts to reach beyond the argument and ideology they seek to promote.

Derrida wants to resist what he calls the "European hallucination." This hallucination is engendered by a generous liberal impulse to value otherness: Saussure's longing for preliteracy, Lévi-Strauss's nostalgic recollection of tribal societies in Brazil that are now extinct, Rousseau's desire to find in non-European languages the natural innocence of humanity. Derrida's warning is that such desires manifest ethnocentrism at the very moment when it may be least suspected. The longing for psychic wholeness, for a harmonious relationship with nature, for nonexploitative social arrangements (all in certain obvious ways innocent motives), can easily lead to the hallucination that these conditions already exist in the not-I. What I desire—and therefore lack—is in the other culture, the other race, the other gender. Such attribution of unproblematic wholeness to the Other hallucinates a solution to *my* problem; it does not invoke the presence of an authentic otherness. Marcion desires a unified, non-Jewish Christianity and proceeds to hallucinate a canon that gives presence to what he wants. On the other hand, from Wheatley to Cooper, many readers passionately interested in developing an African-American tradition have seen in Milton a potentially creative otherness epitomized by Ololon's "void outside existence."

Derrida explicitly suspects the kind of textually inhabited theology that Marcion's work displays. Marcion's idea of the canon is a longing for the presence of the mysterious Father of Christ. The ultimate realization of his textual desire is a private audience with a monolithic and unambiguously present other, the logos without history. Derrida reminds us that such desires are ubiquitous. We want our language and our knowledge to make present what we seek. Such is the urgency of desire. But to want what we seek only on our own terms is to frustrate that desire by insisting that we already have—or are—that hallucinated other that perfectly fits our desire. Such is to dwell in a universe alone with a text that speaks in only one voice, our own.

Texts and canon, however perversely, manifest their rigorous multiplicity. In biblical studies at present, two of the most prominent voices in the debate over canon are those of Brevard Childs and James Barr.[7] At the risk of oversimplifying their complex convictions, one might distinguish their views in this way: Childs sees canonicity as already written into the individual texts that make up the New Testament, as though Matthew, for example, were writing Jesus' genealogy for the first chapter of a first gospel at a transitional point between the Old Testament and the New, or John were writing a mediating gospel between the synoptics and the acts and epistles of the apostles. Barr, on the other hand, sees only individual books. He points out that New Testament texts quote freely from books not included in the Bible at all, and he argues that there is no basis in scripture for the position taken, for example, in the sixth of the 39 Articles, that only sixty-six books—and no more—are inspired. Although some may wish to call Wheatley, Cooper, and Reed noncanonical authors, it is difficult to read them as though they do not think of themselves aspiring to, or holding, or exceeding the canonical position of Milton. In that sense, to borrow Childs's argument, they are writing as though they are already canonical, and we do them an injustice not to read them that way. Barr, however, would warn us against glossing over Reed's antagonism toward Milton. (Incidentally, Barr is a very antagonistic writer himself, especially when he writes about Childs.) His view of the canon nevertheless celebrates the openness of many texts and many voices, which may combine in chorus or shout at each other in opposition.

Although Derrida has not been much invoked in the current debate over canon, he offers the best of what Childs and Barr, in their more limited arguments, are able to contribute to what has become a larger cultural debate. One might imagine Derrida, on this issue, observing that the texts that we know constitute a structure that aspires toward closure but does not constitute an end. To come to terms with the structure of those works—call that structure a canon, if you will—is also to identify those points at which the structure refuses to be self-contained, or the points at which it turns in on itself, or the points where the accumulated structures of its metaphors break the structure open.

The translators of the 1611 Authorized Version of the Bible, already knowing some of these disputes, observe in their seldom reprinted "Preface to the Reader":

> The Scripture is a tree, or rather a whole paradise of trees of life, which bring forth fruits every month, and the fruit thereof is for meat, and the leaves for medicine. It is not a pot of manna or a cruse of oil, which were for memory only, or for a meal's meat or two, but as it were a shower of heavenly bread sufficient for a whole host, be it never so great, and as it were a whole cellarful of oil vessels; whereby all our necessities may be provided for, and our debts discharged. In a word it is a pantry of wholesome food against mouldy traditions.

Seeds grow into many fruits, texts invoke contexts, structures have crevices that let in light from outside themselves, some texts sing while others preach. And somewhere a young woman with the name of a slave ship, against all probability, learns Latin, admires Milton and Pope, overwhelms the worthies of Boston and an English countess, and writes poems that move us after two centuries.

Notes

1. Athanasius is usually credited with first applying the term *canon* to a list of New Testament books. See his Festal Letter of A.D. 367, which gives the texts of the New Testament in the usual order, except for the Catholic Epistles.
2. Milton himself, however, becomes a censor under Cromwell. See Blum (74-78).

3. In his general foreword to the Schomburg Library, Gates writes, "The birth of the Afro-American literary tradition occurred in 1773, when Phillis Wheatley published a book of poetry" (vii).
4. I am indebted to Carolivia Herron for directing me to Reed. She quotes this passage also in her fine paper "Milton and Afro-American Literature." Her reading of Wheatley is more negative than mine, however. Gates has written a detailed commentary on *Mumbo Jumbo*'s critical response to the history of the black novel and of all forms of intertextuality (*Signifying* 217-38). Reed's text simultaneously takes on sacred and secular canons in its unsparing critique of tradition.
5. See David Riede's Miltonic reception history.
6. I incorporate here material from Gates's general foreword and Mary Helen Washington's introduction to Cooper's *A Voice from the South.*
7. See Frank Kermode's account of their views, which was written before Childs's book on the New Testament (189-207).

Works Cited

Barr, James. *Holy Scripture: Canon, Authority, Criticism.* Oxford: Oxford UP, 1983.

Bettenson, Henry, ed. *Documents of the Christian Church.* Oxford: Oxford UP, 1943.

Blake, William. *Milton. William Blake's Complete Writings* I. Ed. G. E. Bentley, Jr. Oxford: Clarendon, 1978.

Bloom, Harold. *The Anxiety of Influence: A Theory of Poetry.* New York: Oxford UP, 1973.

Blum, Abbe. "The Author's Authority: *Areopagitica* and the Labour of Licensing." Nyquist and Ferguson. 74-78.

Campenhausen, Hans von. *The Formation of the Christian Bible.* Philadelphia: Fortress, 1972.

Childs, Brevard. *Introduction to the Old Testament as Scripture.* London: SCM, 1983.

______. *The New Testament as Canon: An Introduction.* London: SCM, 1984.

Cooper, Anna Julia. *A Voice from the South.* Ed. Mary Helen Washington. New York: Oxford UP, 1988.

Derrida, Jacques. *Of Grammatology.* Trans. Gayatri Chakravorty Spivak. Baltimore: Johns Hopkins UP, 1976.

Eliot, T. S. *Selected Prose of T. S. Eliot.* Ed. Frank Kermode. London: Faber, 1975.

Gates, Henry Louis, Jr. Foreword. Cooper. vii-xxii.

______. *The Signifying Monkey: A Theory of African-American Literary Criticism.* New York: Oxford UP, 1988.

______. "Canon Confidential: A Sam Slade Caper." *New York Times Book Review* (25 March 1990): 1-2.

Herron, Carolivia. "Milton and Afro-American Literature." Nyquist and Ferguson. 278-300.

Holy Bible (Authorized Version 1611). London: Robert Barker, 1613.

Kermode, Frank. *An Appetite for Poetry.* Cambridge: Harvard UP, 1989.

Milton, John. *The Complete Prose Works of John Milton* I. Ed. Don M. Wolfe. New Haven, CT: Yale UP, 1958.

Nyquist, Mary, and Margaret W. Ferguson, eds. *Re-membering Milton: Essays on the Texts and Traditions.* London: Methuen, 1988.

Reed, Ishmael. *Mumbo Jumbo.* New York: Macmillan, 1978.

Riede, David. "Blake's *Milton*: On Membership in the Church Paul." Nyquist and Ferguson. 257-77.

Wheatley, Phillis. *The Collected Works of Phillis Wheatley.* Ed. John Shields. New York: Oxford UP, 1988.

FREUD, LACAN, AND THE SUBJECT OF CULTURAL STUDIES

> The greatest closure now threatening literary criticism is the tendency toward monolithic theory, abstract rational inventiveness . . . that overlooks the evaluative function of critical judgment.
> (Merod 93)

In a recent article titled "Being Interdisciplinary Is So Very Hard to Do," Stanley Fish argues against what he takes to be overblown claims about the new cultural studies, especially its idea of engendering in education a new "liberation, freedom, [and] openness" (21). He is not against the enthusiasm generated by this new movement, but he nonetheless challenges the viability of cultural studies because the "impossibility of authentic critique," he concludes, "is the impossibility of the interdisciplinary project" that constitutes cultural studies (21). Cultural studies cannot be done, and he argues that because we can never escape the confines of a discipline, the erasure of disciplinary boundaries always has the effect of drawing new boundaries, even if they are more encompassing. Therefore, thought will always be confined within some form of a discipline, which ensures that the prisonhouse of closed disciplines will always exist. Fish may be correct in claiming that the breakdown of a discipline eventually establishes a new discipline, but he misses the extensive critique of how and what we know—the critique of the "subject"—at the core of cultural studies as conceived by Stuart Hall, Richard Johnson, Gayatri Spivak, Janice Radway, and others.[1] This critique depends not on traditional approaches to interdisciplinary research and teaching but on a reinvention of knowledge as constituted in "interdisciplinary" terms, as it is being reformulated in current attempts to understand the Western subject of knowledge—what it is to know and also how we go about knowing anything. The cultural studies project is actually based on a critique of the investigating subject of inquiry and knowledge, on a newly emergent sense of knowledge within an institutional context.[2]

In fact, a new "subject" of inquiry—what it means to know something—is precisely the preoccupation of "oppositional criticism," the cultural critique produced by many left-leaning intellectuals who work within European and American universities. Since the early 1980s this group has included what Henry Louis Gates, Jr., calls "the [new] cultural left . . . that uneasy, shifting set of alliances formed by feminist critics, critics of so-called minority culture and Marxist and post-structuralist critics generally—in short, the rainbow coalition of contemporary critical theory" (1). Challenging the adequacy of formal and isolated "academic" critiques of culture and social practices, these critics are shifting cultural and political priorities in such areas of the academy as pedagogy, literary criticism, women's studies, and legal studies.

Common to all of these changes is an emphasis on theory and a reformulation of traditional conceptions of inquiry and the social use of knowledge in light of what Raymond Williams calls the "politics" of intellectual work. The point is not only that cultural studies and its reformulation of the subject may be the future of English as a discipline, but that English as traditionally conceived, in its rhetorical dimension as applied to texts, is also the future of cultural studies—in some ways the most challenging dimension of a new "performative," rhetorical conception of knowledge. Henceforth culture cannot be the accumulated "best" of what is known in an Arnoldian sense of tradition but must be recognized as a staging for struggle, what Williams calls the "struggle" of "whole ways of life" in the complex interaction of the social texts in which we live (63).

What is striking about this redefinition of cultural critique is precisely what Fish criticizes as the groundless optimism (what he calls "openness"), in both Europe and the United States, about "cultural" theory and the prospect of working to shape the culture from within the academy. There is something of this "openness" among early contributors to cultural studies such as Matthew Arnold and F. R. Leavis, as is evident in Leavis's belief in how the "placement" of a literary work's cultural value opens an ethical channel for advancing actual "judgments about life" (Hayman 115). Leavis's aim to safeguard what in *Nor Shall My Sword* he terms "cultural continuity" (quoted in Hayman 115) may be an attempt to resist many of the early effects of modernism, but it also foreshadows Williams's bolder move toward "interested" and profoundly ethical intellectual work as a response to the fragmentation of modern culture.

This line of cultural theory, starting with Arnold and Leavis, also finds negative expression in the reluctance of Michel Foucault and Paul de Man to focus on the political dimension of cultural theory. Focusing on the general problem of academic isolationism in modern intellectual work, Ira Shor notes in *Culture Wars* (1986) that subsequent to the political strife of the 1960s, a tremendous loss of institutional prestige plagued the American academy through the early 1980s. Official pronouncements about a "literacy crisis" and the subsequent need for schools to solve the problem appear to Shor to be intended to restore purpose and authority if not prestige to the academy. Even so, Henry Giroux, David Shumway, Paul Smith, and James Sosnoski describe the post-1960 period in America as failing to produce effective cultural critiques in part because interdisciplinary programs have had little or no impact on the academy (see "The Need for Cultural Studies"). They argue that the proliferation in American universities since the 1960s of interdisciplinary programs (women's studies, African-American studies, American studies, and so on) happened because proponents thought they had found a way of countering the hegemonic exercise of power in American life. But many of these new programs gradually "succeeded," became permanent departments, and thereafter began to harmonize with institutional expectations. They were thus denatured as they were institutionally assimilated past the point of having any oppositional critique to advance.

Many key figures in the current resurgence of cultural studies—Edward Said, Cornel West, Gates, and Spivak—tend to be critics with strong ideological ties outside the academy, whose collective personal histories tend to map the terrain of an "other" America and whose intellectual commitment has been to acknowledge and theorize the social and political context of education and, in the process, to expose the ideology implicit in Western ways of knowing. Indeed, the impetus of this movement, as Spivak argues in *In Other Worlds* (1987), springs from the repeated mapping of cultural margins for those whose socioeconomic circumstances have separated them from privileged access to cultural and intellectual power. Spivak, West, and Said speak with a particular legitimacy that cannot be separated from their role as cultural agents for particular ideological frames, voices at or near the site of social marginalization.[3]

These theorists are optimistic about the cultural studies critique as an oppositional criticism. But can a white male, for instance, represent an "oppositional" position in the American academy? Does the legitimacy of the oppositional discourse include speech *for* the oppressed of other classes, such as speech on behalf of oppressed African-Americans? This is a difficult issue in that by helping to assimilate the discourse of oppression into a dominant discourse, an academic critic inevitably serves the institutional interests that produced oppression, and thus may be helping to assimilate the "other" into the "same" of institutional affiliations. An alternative scenario—one I am reluctant to accept—is that only participants in a particular culture (conceived in the narrowest sense) may speak for their own condition.

At issue here is the question, as Fish raises it, of whether critique is possible, the broad question of an oppositional critique of the dominant culture and the constitution of a critical subject who can perform that critique. In the United States, academics traditionally go about their work estranged from other sites of struggle and, in the process, often fill a merely legitimating role in society. When this happens, however, doesn't an intellectual become "in some undismissible sense," as Jim Merod says, simply "an agent of that power" that supposedly was being critiqued (157)? Is it possible for an intellectual to speak about struggle and to struggle at the same time—in other words, to have a significant impact on culture in addition to a legitimating function? Alternatively, can oppressed people be in a position to "speak for themselves" and, in so doing, apparently bypass altogether the need to be "represented"—even though "they" inevitably speak, or at least will be heard, in a discourse actually constituted by the dominant culture? These issues, concerning who speaks for the culture and to what end, actually point to an underlying question of cultural studies—what, after all of the curriculum reform, cultural studies is all about.

I am suggesting that the current rise of so many cultural studies programs in the United States, within English departments and in their own right, results from the perception of a historical opening—a moment of "freedom," to use Fish's term—that many critics and educators see as offering the prospect of getting answers to the questions I am raising. Emerging on the current scene, in other words, are a new model of the subject and an agenda for cultural studies. In what follows I will explore this model of the subject, which informs most cultural studies programs, including semiotic projects and even recent moves toward a transnational cultural studies for the 1990s. As a case in point I will examine a principal modern text about the reading of texts, Sigmund Freud's account in *The Interpretation of Dreams* (1900) of his dream about a patient called "Irma," the dream experience and interpretation that Freud thought actually founded psychoanalysis as an institution. This influential text defines a strategy of interpretation—an important formulation of the subject—that is crucial to cultural studies, both for what the text claims to do and for what it fails to accomplish. In view of that tie to cultural studies, I want to examine Freud's Irma text as a prelude to discussing what cultural studies tries to know about the world—how, in fact, cultural studies is trying to reconstitute the act of "knowing." My conclusion, I will say now, is that cultural studies in one of its key dimensions is the formulation of a strategy for critique—that is, a major reformulation of how to know and study culture—and this reformulation is what I mean by the "subject" of cultural studies in my title.

Freud's Subject

In *The Interpretation of Dreams* Freud writes about one of his own dreams, producing the primary insights about the unconscious that founded the discipline of psychoanalysis. This text, designated by Jacques Lacan the great Freudian "dream of dreams" (*Seminaire* 178), advances possibilities for semiotic interpretation that Freud only partially achieves. Freud's narrative at crucial points subverts his semiotic reading practice when he forecloses his interpretation in reductively personal terms. Freud's narration of the dream of Irma's injection is as follows:

> *Dream of July 23rd-24th, 1895*
>
> A large hall—numerous guests, whom we were receiving.—Among them was Irma. I at once took her on one side, as though to answer her letter and to reproach her for not having accepted my "solution" yet. I said to her: "If you still get pains, it's really only your fault." She replied: "If you only knew what pains I've got now in my throat and stomach and abdomen—it's choking me"—I was alarmed and looked at her. She looked pale and puffy. I thought to myself that after all I must be missing some organic trouble. I took her to the window and looked down her throat, and she showed signs of recalcitrance, like women with artificial dentures. I thought to myself that there was really no need for her to do that.—She then opened her mouth properly and on the right I found a big white patch; at another place I saw

> extensive whitish grey scabs upon some remarkable curly structures which were evidently modelled on the turbinal bones of the nose.—I at once called in Dr. M., and he repeated the examination and confirmed it. . . . Dr. M. looked quite different from usual; he was very pale, he walked with a limp and his chin was clean-shaven. . . . My friend Otto was now standing beside her as well, and my friend Leopold was percussing her through her bodice and saying: "She has a dull area low down on the left." He also indicated that a portion of the skin on the left shoulder was infiltrated. (I noticed this, just as he did, in spite of her dress.) . . . M. said: "There's no doubt it's an infection, but no matter; dysentery will supervene and the toxin will be eliminated." . . . We were directly aware, too, of the origin of her infection. Not long before, when she was feeling unwell, my friend Otto had given her an injection of a preparation of propyl, propyls . . . propionic acid . . . trimethylamin (and I saw before me the formula for this printed in heavy type). . . . Injections of that sort ought not to be made so thoughtlessly. . . . And probably the syringe had not been clean. (139-40)

This text divides the dream encounter with Irma into four narrative moments. First, meeting at a party, they accuse each other of misbehavior in the therapy relationship. He thinks she has irrationally rejected his therapeutic "solution" (left unstated) to her problem. She charges that he will not recognize the pain in her throat and abdomen and that she is continually "choking." Next, "alarmed" at her "pale and puffy" appearance, he reexamines her and finds a "white patch" on the side of her throat and "whitish grey scabs" on "curly structures" attached to the sides of her throat. In a third moment, Freud calls in "Dr. M." for additional diagnosis, and then "my friend Otto" and "my friend Leopold" appear and give advice, too. Leopold examines Irma "chastely"—that is, without removing her clothes—and discovers an infection in her lower left abdomen and another one on her "left shoulder." Dr. M. then gives the mistaken diagnosis that "dysentery will supervene" to cure the infection and that the "toxin [of the infection] will be eliminated" automatically through her bowels. In the final section of the narrative, Freud indicts Otto for actually causing the infection. It turns out that Otto has previously injected Irma with "trimethylamin"—a fluid sexual in its implications and "not to be [injected] so thoughtlessly"—while using a "syringe" that "probably . . . had not been clean."

In *The Interpretation of Dreams* Freud advances three broad tenets of interpretation—suppositions, as he says, for approaching what he calls the "characters and syntactic laws" of such a dream text (312). He first proposes a bracketing of the manifest text, the apparent "pictographic" text with its intrinsic and evident meanings. He writes that "if we attempted to read these characters according to their pictorial value instead of according to their symbolic relation, we should clearly be led into error" (312). Needing to be taken into account are the dream elements as signifiers requiring *interpretation* in relation to other elements of the dream.

Second, he announces the need to assemble the narrative structure of the text, commenting that "we try to replace each separate element by a syllable or word that can be represented by that element in some way or other" (312). In other words, the signifying segments of the dream will be interpreted by ordering them in a sequence that limits their interaction and stabilizes them as referents within the dream. Like Vladimir Propp in his different but related analysis of narrative, Freud here makes narrative sequence—the order of occurrence—a distinctive feature of narrative and its interpretation.

Third, Freud proposes that other syntactic and symbolic restraints on the dream text will combine to produce what he calls a dream "wish," a center, or structural intention, that implies a dream "subject" who is the embodiment of this intention. Viewing the entire text as working to signify this intention, Freud says that "*when the work of* [dream] *intention has been completed, we perceive that a dream is the fulfillment of a* [single] *wish*" (154), suggesting that as an organized textual system the dream narrative evokes a functional pattern that brings into view its own enunciation and import.

Freud projects texts, in other words, as being constituted by signs within a narrative structure. Further, a "subject" for the text—how the text is ordered and interpreted—is constructed in the moment that one reads or listens to the dream text. Based on these precepts, he depicts psychoanalysis as an account of and a strategy for interpretive procedures—a strategy that he applies to an extremely wide spectrum of social texts in addition to dreams. In each case, whether "reading" the deployment of jokes, literary texts, female sexuality, or religious devotion, he approaches cultural texts as semiotic constructs conveying a dream wish, or subject of understanding, made evident through analysis.

In the Irma dream Freud focuses on elements having to do with "contamination," specifically the suggestion that Irma has been violated as part of her therapy through the inappropriate "injection" of fluid into her body. Leopold and Otto signal behavior toward Irma that in fact mirrors that of the "Freud" figure in the dream and that of his double, the incompetent "Dr. M." Whereas Leopold, a "good" doctor, approaches Irma chastely and advances her treatment with insight and efficiency, Otto, the inept doctor, violates medical precepts with a sexual violation of Irma and, as a result, makes her more ill. This "contamination" of therapy explains Irma's symptoms and the infection of her shoulder and abdomen.

In this way, piece by piece, Freud constructs a set of semiotic references for interpreting this dream. He eventually concludes the analysis with the illumination of a dream wish connected to his anxiety two years earlier over the "serious [nasal] illness" of his daughter (143), a period in which he had also encouraged cocaine usage by patients who later suffered under the drug—indeed, in one case, "the misuse of that drug had hastened the death of a dear friend of mine" (144). The dream text, he concludes, now can be seen as expressing a wish to reconcile himself to his guilt over bad advice he had given. He remarks that "certain other themes played a part in the dream, but when I came to consider all of these, they could all be collected into a single group of ideas and labelled, as it were, 'concern about my own and other people's health—professional conscientiousness' " (153).

In locating this dream wish analytically, Freud does attempt to fulfill his itinerary for semiotic reading. If there is a lapse in his method, however, it is the certainty with which he supplies an empirical account of the dream content and dream wish. Remember that the professed aim of *The Interpretation of Dreams* is to treat all elements of interpretation as facets of a psychoanalytic semiosis, based on the interpretation of narrative relations rather than psychological essences. He does not apply this standard, however, to the so-called actual struggle about his daughter and cocaine use. These purportedly real-life events are not analyzed in the semiotic, textual manner that *The Interpretation of Dreams* promotes, and in this lapse Freud actually shifts from the problematics of a dream text to a supposedly nonproblematic text located in "actual" experience. In effect, the dream interpretation as Freud performs it in this case is positioned as predating the dream, just as, in classical models of interpretation, an object of cognition predates any knowledge or perception of it.

This is a significant lapse in that in momentarily abandoning the semiotic implications of psychoanalysis, the semiotic nature of experience he defines so carefully, he is "reducing dreams," as Jeffrey Mehlman argues, "to the stability of a fixed meaning assimilable to the ego" (180). Freud's underlying claim here, contrary to the stated aims of *The Interpretation of Dreams*, is that he has uncovered the nonrepresentational, preexisting or "essential" origin for the dream in a nonanalytic handling of his experience. To the extent that Freud reads the dream as an unambiguous representation of an already constituted experience, like a picture with a familiar but hitherto hidden figure in it, he deploys the apparatus of semiotic dream interpretation in this instance, as Mehlman adds, in "the subtlest ruse of narcissism" (181). In effect, Freud substitutes a "real" story for a semiotic puzzle in a moment of subtle resistance to the analytic, semiotic force of psychoanalysis.

In the seminar called *The Self in Freudian Theory* (*Le moi dans la theorie de Freud et dans la technique de la psychanalyse*), Lacan reads the same dream segments Freud did—the examination of Irma's throat, Otto's misbehavior, Irma's symptoms, and so on—but focuses on Freud's resistance to the dream as integral to the text. He looks particularly at the first half of the dream, in which Freud peers into Irma's throat at a mysterious image—"a big white patch . . . whitish grey scabs upon some remarkable curly structures." In this image of Freud as examiner, Lacan finds a "horrible discovery" and an insight into Freud's resistance to the dream. The "talking cure" of psychoanalysis is plagued from its beginning, as signified repeatedly in this text, by the body's materiality. That is, psychoanalysis sets out to understand symptoms expressed through the body but attempts its cures exclusively through words; in the process, it must effectively repress the body, ensuring that psychoanalysis will forever be haunted by the body's ghostly corpse. Freud's response to the corporeal elements in the Irma text is to make the "body" abject, to set it off bounds and make it the target of Otto's unethical transgression. He also erases the specific subject of the dream *as a text* by invoking the authority of his empirical experience. His aim in this repressive reading of the dream, given this dream's function in his work, is to make the special instance of this dream the general case of a scientific interpretive model.

By contrast, Lacan rereads the Irma text to understand it in relation to Freud's own subjective, interpretive activity, the instance of Freud's evasion of the dream's textual dimension, that aspect of the dream not adequately reformulable in direct connection with Freud's life. This is precisely the point of Freud's strongest resistance to the dream, the part of the dream he rushes to make narrowly biographical, the point where he forecloses semiotic interpretation in his own exemplary encounter with the resistance to psychoanalysis.

Lacan's reading, by contrast, and without any attempt at empirical science, self-consciously fictionalizes the dream by ventriloquizing Irma's throat with the supposed voice of psychoanalysis itself. In Lacan's version the voice of Irma's throat says to Freud, "You are thus—that which is least you, that which is most unformed" ("Tu es ceci, qui est le plus loin de toi, ceci qui est le plus informé" [*Seminaire* 186]). This voice says, in effect, "You must find your own place in language amid all that is foreign and 'other' to you." In "true" speech, in other words, you will find your own alienated position—that is, the dream conveys the condition of meaning only when the limits of meaning are approached, "meaning" being that which is constituted by the marking *and* transgressing of certain limits. In this way, Lacan reads Freud's dream as a theatricalization of psychoanalysis's encounter with language and its suppression of the body—as both an acknowledgment and an evasion of limits.

Central to Lacan's conceptual framework in such a reading is the model of the "subject" not as the classical, autonomous agent of perception and "experience"—based on the Western model of the great individual—but as a linguistic and rhetorical effect, a construct analogous to the effect of the viewer's perspective in representational painting. In this view, the subject is posited not as a natural or inevitable viewpoint but as a particular "effect"—a set of relationships that creates phenomenal appearances as the further development of instituting certain effects. Interpretation and narrative understanding are, in this way, strategies that allow the subjective effect to take place. As Claude Lévi-Strauss and Lacan both suggest, we are born into a network of such linguistic effects that condition "experience" even when experience seems immediate and knowledge self-evident—so that our basic senses of subjectivity, subjective experience, and true knowledge are historically determined as "effects" rather than as essential and transcendental aspects of ourselves and our world.

In Freud's reading of his own dream, for example, there is an interpretive misrecognition and blindness, like something stuck in the throat, important for understanding the function of interpretive schemes—namely, Freud's repression of the body and of the material ("bodily") nature of the text. Following Lacan, I am rereading Freud's dream precisely to reinstate it materially, *as a text*, and to lay bare its *constituted* subject of power in the synthetic nature of critique. By "synthetic" here I mean the articulation of one narrative with a different narrative text, the "synthetic" critique contrasting with Freud's "analytic" reading of the Irma dream, wherein he merely substitutes "real" events for dream signifiers. The whole point of critiquing Freud's analysis, as I am attempting to do, is to break the circle of Freud's formalism, to show, as Robert Young writes, that "the ego is not a totality that can assimilate unconscious processes" (177). The subject of observation and inquiry, rather, is an economy of relations, a construct, and this construction promotes and conveys the cultural values that constitute it in acts of interpretation.

This perspective is especially evident in Lacan's analysis when he discusses four dimensions of the dream suggested by what he calls the Schema L. The Schema L is an interpretive device that articulates four structural relationships in texts. The first position is the role taken up by the speaker, the voice, or the principal viewpoint in the dream, such as the role of "Freud" himself. Second is the role of an "other," or unknown, object in the dream text, that which creates the occasion for the speaking subject to define itself, in this case the enigmatic throat that Freud tries to decipher. Third is the more general and absolute sense of otherness in the dream, the system of differences that structures the dream as a sequential narrative. And fourth is the emergent sense of what the dream means or can mean once the other positions become an articulated "reading" or interpretation.

The Schema L in relation to the Irma dream can be depicted as follows:

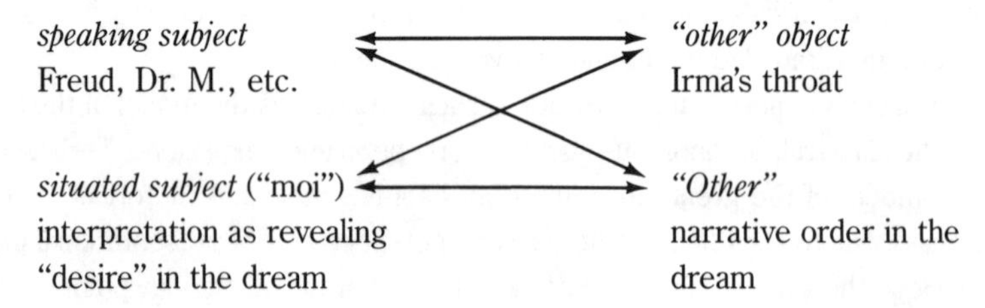

This use of the Schema L to interpret the Irma text points up an intellectual debt traceable from the pre-Socratics and Aristotle through Hegel, Marx, Antonio Gramsci, A. J. Greimas, and Fredric Jameson. This tradition of "oppositional" thinking formulates specific strategies for thinking about what it means for ideas to oppose one another dialectically and at what point opposition becomes neutralized and then reappropriates its opposition. Drawing on this tradition in his reformulation of psychoanalysis, Lacan has argued that "psycho-analysis[,] neither a world view nor a philosophy that claims to provide the key to the universe . . . is governed by a particular aim, which is historically defined by the elaboration of the notion of the subject" (*Concepts* 77).

In this elaboration of an economy of relationships, each position further defines a hierarchy of values and maps relational pathways along particular lines. Such an economy is visible as a representation of ideology when heavily encoded representations of power serve as cultural references. Lacan claims, for instance, that experience is uninterpretable without such textual markers and the ideological relations they bind us to, because these markers render cultural discourse within a grid of cultural reference—hence interpretability. Such markers or signifiers—as with the "father," for example—convey hierarchies and relations of value that will seem to be inherent and self-evident within particular narratives. Lacan attributes to the paternal metaphor, the *nom-du-père*, precisely this weight of cultural marking and authority. And yet at our historical remove from Lacan's work, as many post-Lacanians have argued, it is clear that he never fully grasped the implications for gender politics of trying to guarantee the authority of the paternal metaphor, the "name-of-the-father," as always orienting culture and instituting the speaking subject's position in every text.

The fourth term of the Schema L concludes the ideological critique with what Lacan calls the "moi," the historically situated subject. This term suggests an entirely new interpretation of all that has come before. The "moi," the new "subject," is a perspective on the ideological values the square represents, and it marks the *instituted and constructed* nature of the seemingly "self-evident," or natural, understanding. This fourth position in effect goes beyond the other oppositional relations by formalizing the reconception of their relationship as interpretation. In so doing, it demonstrates that what seems to be natural and inevitable is in fact always the activity of understanding. The "moi" creates the possibility of reconceiving the nature of all the relationships the Schema L describes so that the seemingly natural subject conceived as a subject-of-knowledge is seen to be the special case of the wider category of subject-of-knowledge *and* power.

In his discourse on the Irma dream, Lacan claims that the power to narrate—strictly speaking—belongs to language itself through the impersonal and symbolic authority of the father. But if we follow Lacan's thinking about language, the positioning of the father—like the positions and relations of the Irma dream—is necessarily a mere effect in an economy of relations, the effect of a particular narrative. The "father" as authority cannot be accepted as in any way "natural." The "natural" empowerment of the father, or any such figure, amounts to a distinctly political use of language—a mere assignment of authority to a signifier that is not "naturally" authoritative, a grotesque suturing of "phallic" authority to an otherwise empty paternal form—phallic authority here being the act of interpretation positioned so as to seem "natural."

As Lacan positions the figure of Freud in relation to the Irma text, I am here trying to position Lacan in relation to his own narrative. That is, whereas Freud missed his own reintroduction of an empirical perspective into semiotic interpretation, Lacan also misses something—the reintroduction of an idealized paternal subject into the analysis of subject relations. While Lacan assists in calling into question the empowerment of the father in psychoanalysis, the male will to cultural dominance, he himself remains patriarchal in orientation. By this I mean that the understanding of subjectivity that the Schema L represents is intended to analyze precisely such notions as paternal authority, which Lacan fails to engage with or question seriously. And yet by seizing the semiotic import of Lacan's analysis, we find an opportunity to use him against himself and against the patriarchal dimension of psychoanalysis.

Cultural Studies and the Subject

My comments about the Irma text, I hasten to add, are not intended to argue for psychoanalysis at all. But as a major modern critique of the subject, in both its failures and its successes, blindnesses and insights, psychoanalysis is a principal twentieth-century elaboration of the subject. The semiotic version of the subject that Freud calls for but misrecognizes in his own dream text is precisely the subject-of-understanding, the subject as a construct, defined currently by theorists of cultural studies such as Hall and Spivak. This subject of knowledge, not reducible to the objective recollection of supposed empirical events, can be formulated in three interpretive propositions that in fact have been incorporated into the cultural studies project. This connection to cultural studies exists in part because psychoanalysis, from Freud's work through that of Teresa de Lauretis and Kaja Silverman, has had a decisive influence on cultural studies, as is currently evident in film and women's studies. At present, both disciplines contribute to the critique of the subject—psychoanalysis and cultural studies being major strategies for situating the Western subject who is supposed to know something.

The first of these propositions, and here Freud's and Lacan's interpretations of the Irma dream serve as examples, is that cultural studies will be subjective. "Subjective" here does not mean non-"objective" or nonrigorous. Rather, it reflects an emphasis on one of two fundamentally different conceptions of culture in cultural studies. The first—I will call it "culture I"—is advanced by Raymond Williams, who holds that the concept of culture depends on the idea of a fundamental "structure of feeling," a basis for culture in actual experience. Williams projects a common human experience as the absolute ground of all cultural elaborations and formations—an essentialist construction of experience as the irreducible "terrain of the lived" (quoted in Hall, "Studies" 66). In this perspective "culture" is the outgrowth of "experience" in the sense that the common experience, as Hall says, is where "all the different practices [of culture] intersect" (63).

What can be called "culture II"—Hall's designation of "structuralist" culture (64)—posits rather that "experience" constitutes no ground of culture at all, but in its substantiated form is the effect of specific cultural texts and practices. That is, a particular culture at a particular moment produces experience in a specific configuration—culture, in effect, having a kind of priority over experience. In this second model, wherein constructedness and not experience is the foundation of culture, it is important to define and situate the constructed viewpoint, or subject, that constitutes any instance of experience being investigated. Analysis of the subject as a cultural construction within the frame of culture II begins with the critic's own subjective historical placement, the investigator's own insertion into a historically and ideologically specific moment, which Freud tried to achieve in interpreting his dream. Never simply personal, the subjective moment—the situating and constructing of a subject at a historical juncture—is a crucial reference for cultural studies according to culture II, the rigor of critique that this version of culture uses instead of "disinterestedness" or "objectivity."

The second proposition says that, given the implications of subjective understanding, cultural studies will be undertaken by interested participants. In "The Principle of Reason: The University in the Eyes of Its Pupils," Jacques Derrida has argued that institutional knowledge as produced in the Western university is a product of the eighteenth-century Kantian separation of pure knowledge from the practicality of ethics. Aesthetics and art, not categorizable purely as knowledge or power, are the crucial mediators between knowledge and ethics. Rigorously playing out Kant's logic, Derrida therefore projects social and cultural experience as having textual and aesthetic dimensions and then locates the object of cultural studies in precisely that mediating position—between and also constituted by knowledge and power. This organization of "disciplines" creates a definite sense of what it means for an inquiry to be interested. The cultural studies critic, for instance, will not inquire in a strictly disinterested sense but is committed to the "interested" task of mediating power in relation to knowledge. The critic, in other words, is never an innocent bystander passively recording an "other" world but always stands in a relation to knowledge and power. Knowing anything, in this cultural studies sense, necessarily entails ethical responsibility for the discourse of inquiry itself. It follows that intellectual scrutiny, as Freud's interpretation of the Irma dream shows, is always ethical engagement. In that there is rigor but not disinterested objectivity from this viewpoint, it is paramount to acknowledge the roles the participant/observer can and cannot occupy—that is, can *actually* occupy and be responsible for in ethical and ideological terms. Nonblacks can legitimately address African-American oppression, but only when they have discovered their own interests in African-American concerns, and I do *not* mean those who are benevolent or altruistic in relation to a fantasized and reified black "other."

The third proposition, it follows, is that cultural studies—professedly "subjective" and "interested"—will be ideologically oriented and work to acknowledge that orientation. Again, Freud's reading of his dream illustrates this point. That is, whereas rational and traditional scientific inquiry stipulates empirical and detached observation as instrumental to the testing of a hypothesis, in cultural studies there is instead a profession of commitment to the participants' interests within a historical frame. By "participants" I mean those subject to the particular constraints of a sphere of possibility in terms of what is thinkable and doable—what Foucault means by "power," *pouvoir* not as the ideal of Power with a capital *P*, but simply as that which is possible in the world as we know it. (The limits of "possibility" as they consistently constrain action, by the way, suggest a fair working definition of ideology.)

On this important point, think, for example, of Gulliver's situationally imposed limits in *Gulliver's Travels* (1726). In Lilliput, or really in any of the "other" worlds Gulliver is inserted into, there is an outlandish asymmetry between his subjective intentions and the material conditions that constrain him. The tale's frequent and satiric reversals as Gulliver encounters enormous and tiny people suggest nothing so much as the fundamental lack of any natural isomorphism between Gulliver-as-subject and the social and material discourses into which he is inserted. That is, Gulliver's own capability in every instance depends on the possibilities of knowledge and power. That textual relation, Gulliver's mediate distance between knowledge and power, is the ideological relation that Gulliver never quite understands. This misrecognition of ideology, what can be called the "Gulliver Effect," is the constitutional instability, the inevitable misrecognition, of ideology as a merely cognitive awareness of a text. A kind of anti-Gulliver is Paulo Freire's version in *Pedagogy of the Oppressed* of that impossible ideal person who recognizes perfectly the implications of ideological and class struggle and who has the unerring ethical and critical ability, as Freire says, "to perceive social, political, and economic contradictions" in society and culture (19).

In summary, the development of these propositions about the subject, consistent with Freud's particular misrecognitions, begins with the acknowledgment of the constructed subject within a cultural and historical context—cultural studies as always "subjective." Next, that acknowledgment of subjectivity facilitates an awareness of the social and economic ties that define an interested participant—cultural studies as always an "interested" inquiry. Finally, the cultural critique is made possible through a continual resituating of the inquiring subject as exerting power within discourse—cultural studies inquiry, in other words, as an interested and purposeful activity. Indeed, the power (*pouvoir*) to speak about oppression comes from the recognition, or misrecognition, of economic and ideological interests within history—of one's commitment, finally, to a valued social situation and the responsibility defined by that commitment.

This cultural studies itinerary suggests something quite different from the "disinterested" observation or benevolence exercised by members of powerful classes to "assist" the oppressed. Rather, here there is also the cultural and political stance wagered on an always-to-be-enacted *interpretation* of a social text. The possibility of success for such a practice depends on the continual refinding of texts—texts that are virtual rather than actual—within historical flux. (Hence the need of ongoing "struggle" to achieve cultural knowledge and change.) In this way, the subjective and ideologically motivated interest of cultural studies derives from a continual resituating within Western history.

CRITIQUE OF THE SUBJECT

In these observations I am proposing that the critique of the subject is a key to cultural studies and that in this critique cultural critics are reading the discourses and texts of contemporary culture to expose crucial oppositions and contradictions that govern the exercise of power. Through such critiques Hall, West, and Spivak try, in effect, to maneuver themselves into strategic conflicts with oppressive cultural practices in the oppositional style of one working from within an institution—as theorists and teachers in the academy—to enfranchise modes of intervention.

However, missing this critical dimension of cultural studies, one would necessarily miss the impact of the cultural studies project in either a theoretical or a practical sense. Freud's misrecognition of just this dimension of the subject in his dream makes his narrative the symptom of that misreading and of his own resistance to the semiotic subject at the heart of *The Interpretation of Dreams*. Fish's resistance to this dimension of cultural studies, likewise, makes his anticultural studies narrative a symptom of his cultural and political conservatism. It is this dimension of the subjective critique, however, that enlivens the cultural studies project. Engaged in this resituating, many cultural critics believe that intellectual and political possibilities remain "open," undecided, and—at least for the present moment—accessible to intervention by those whose interests are not confined by traditional disciplinary boundaries.[4]

Notes

1. For further reading on this movement, see Kellner. For more recent work, see Johnson; Hall, "Rediscovery."
2. For introductory discussions of the "subject" in contemporary discourse, see Derrida, "Structure"; Foucault; Silverman.
3. For the political dimension of the "subject," see Spivak, "Subaltern"; Franco; Aronowitz. See also Miller and, particularly, Deleuze and Guattari, Guattari.
4. I would like to thank Richard Barney, Susan Green, Michael Morrison, and Ronald Schleifer for their comments on an earlier draft of this essay.

Works Cited

Aronowitz, Stanley. "The Production of Scientific Knowledge: Science, Ideology, and Marxism." Nelson and Grossberg. 519-37.

Deleuze, Gilles, and Félix Guattari. *Anti-Oedipus*. Trans. Robert Hurley, Mark Seem, and Helen R. Lane. Minneapolis: U of Minnesota P, 1983.

Derrida, Jacques. "Structure, Sign, and Play in the Discourse of the Human Sciences." Richard A. Macksey and Eugenio Donato, eds. *The Structuralist Controversy*. Baltimore: Johns Hopkins UP, 1972. 247-72.

———. "The Principle of Reason: The University in the Eyes of Its Pupils." Trans. Catherine Porter and Edward P. Morris. *diacritics* 13 (1983): 3-20.

Fish, Stanley. "Being Interdisciplinary Is So Very Hard to Do." *Profession* 89 (1989): 15-22.

Foucault, Michel. "What Is an Author?" Josué V. Harari, ed. *Textual Strategies*. Ithaca, NY: Cornell UP, 1979. 141-60.

Franco, Jean. "Beyond Ethnocentrism: Gender, Power, and the Third-World Intelligentsia." Nelson and Grossberg. 503-15.

Freire, Paulo. *Pedagogy of the Oppressed*. Trans. Myra Berman Ramos. 1968. New York: Continuum, 1982.

Freud, Sigmund. *The Interpretation of Dreams*. Trans. James Strachey. 1953. New York: Avon, 1965.

Gates, Henry Louis, Jr. "Whose Canon Is It, Anyway?" *New York Times* (26 February 1989), sec. 7: 1.

Guattari, Félix. *Molecular Revolution: Psychiatry and Politics*. Trans. Rosemary Sheed. Middlesex: Penguin, 1984.

Giroux, Henry, David Shumway, Paul Smith, and James Sosnoski. "The Need for Cultural Studies: Resisting Intellectual and Oppositional Public Spheres." *Dalhousie Review* 64.2 (Summer 1984): 472-86.

Hall, Stuart. "Cultural Studies: Two Paradigms." *Media, Culture and Society* 2 (1980): 57-72.

———. "The Rediscovery of 'Ideology': Return of the Repressed in Media Studies." Michael Gurevitch, Tony Bennett, James Curran, and Janet Woollacott, eds. *Culture, Society and the Media*. New York: Methuen, 1982. 56-90.

Hayman, Ronald. *Leavis*. London: Heinemann, 1976.

Johnson, Richard. "What Is Cultural Studies, Anyway?" *Social Text* 16 (Winter 1986-87): 38-80.

Kellner, Douglas. "A Bibliographical Note on Ideological Cultural Studies." *Praxis* (1981): 84-88.

Lacan, Jacques. *The Four Fundamental Concepts of Psycho-Analysis*. Trans. Alan Sheridan. New York: Norton, 1978.

———. *Le seminaire: Le moi dans la theorie de Freud et dans la technique de la psychanalyse*. Paris: Seuil, 1978.

Mehlman, Jeffrey. "Trimethylamin: Notes on Freud's Specimen Dream." Young. 177-88.

Merod, Jim. *The Political Responsibility of the Critic*. Ithaca, NY: Cornell UP, 1987.

Miller, J. Hillis. "The Search for Grounds in Literary Study." Robert Con Davis and Ronald Schleifer, eds. *Rhetoric and Form: Deconstruction at Yale*. Norman: U of Oklahoma P, 1984. 19-36.

Nelson, Cary, and Lawrence Grossberg, eds. *Marxism and the Interpretation of Culture*. Urbana: U of Illinois P, 1988.

Shor, Ira. *Culture Wars: School and Society in the Conservative Restoration, 1969-1984*. Boston: Routledge, 1986.

Silverman, Kaja. *The Subject of Semiotics*. Ithaca, NY: Cornell UP, 1987.

Spivak, Gayatri Chakravorty. *In Other Worlds: Essays in Cultural Politics*. New York: Methuen, 1987.

———. "Can the Subaltern Speak?" Nelson and Grossberg. 271-313.

Williams, Raymond. *The Long Revolution*. New York: Columbia UP, 1961.

Young, Robert. Headnote to Mehlman's "Trimethylamin." Young, ed. *Untying the Text: A Post-Structuralist Reader*. Boston: Routledge, 1981. 177-78.

Suzanne Clark is an associate professor of English at the University of Oregon. She has published articles on literacy, rhetoric, critical theory, and modernist literature in a number of collections and journals, including *Genre*, *College English*, and *The American Scholar*. Her book, *Sentimental Modernism: Women Writers and the Revolution of the Word*, was published in 1991.

Robert Con Davis teaches American literature and critical theory at the University of Oklahoma. Among his many publications on topics relating to contemporary criticism and psychoanalysis are *Lacan and Narration: The Psychoanalytical Difference in Narrative Theory* (1984), *Contemporary Literary Criticism* (second edition 1989), *Literary Criticism and Theory: The Greeks to the Present* (with Laurie Finke, 1989), and *Culture and Cognition: The Boundaries of Literary and Scientific Inquiry* (with Ronald Schleifer and Nancy Mergler, 1992).

Linda Shaw Finlay, chair of the department of philosophy at Ithaca College, is interested in epistemology and the philosophy and politics of education. Her publications include an essay on Paulo Freire in *Freire for the Classroom: A Sourcebook for Liberatory Teaching*, edited by Ira Shor.

Barbara Foley, associate professor of English at Rutgers University at Newark, is the author of *Telling the Truth: The Theory and Practice of the Documentary Novel* (Cornell University Press, 1986). She is currently at work on a study provisionally titled *Radical Representations: American Proletarian Criticism and Fiction*.

Henry A. Giroux teaches at Pennsylvania State University and is the author of numerous books and articles. His most recent books include *Education under Siege* (with Stanley Aronowitz); *Teachers as Intellectuals*; *Schooling and the Struggle for Public Life*; *Popular Culture, Schooling, and Everyday Life* (edited with Roger Simon); *Critical Pedagogy: The State and the Struggle for Culture* (edited with Peter McLaren); *Postmodern Education* (with Stanley Aronowitz); *Postmodernism, Feminism, and Cultural Politics*; and *Border Crossings: Cultural Workers and the Politics of Education*.

Paul F. Griffin is coordinator of liberal arts at Johns Hopkins University's Peabody Institute. He works principally on the relationship between ethics and culture, and has published essays treating this theme in William Blake, William Kennedy, fiction of the

1950s, and contemporary cinema in *CEA Critic*, *Midwest Quarterly*, *San Jose Studies*, and *Cimarron Review*. He is currently at work on a study of the representation of the family as a moral force in popular culture.

Jerry McGuire is managing editor of *College Literature*. His most recent work on the psychocultural structuration of cinematic space has appeared in *Yearbook for the Interdisciplinary Studies of the Fine Arts* and *Studies in Psychoanalytic Theory*. His book of poems, *The Flagpole Dance* (1990), was published by Lynx House Press.

Robert Miklitsch is working on a book on Marxism, culture criticism, and postmodernism. He currently teaches in the English Department at Ohio University.

Donald Morton writes on contemporary critical theory, pedagogy, and institutional practices. With Mas'ud Zavarzadeh he is coeditor of a collection of theoretical essays, *Texts for Change: Theory/Pedagogy/Politics* (1991) and *Theory, (Post) Modernity, Opposition* (1991). He teaches in the English Department at Syracuse University.

Kostas Myrsiades, professor of comparative literature and English at West Chester University, is editor of *College Literature*. He is the author of eight books and numerous articles of criticism and translations of modern Greek folklore and poetry.

Linda S. Myrsiades, assistant professor of English at West Chester University, is associate editor of *College Literature*. Her publications include many articles on Greek theater and two books coauthored with Kostas Myrsiades, *The Karagiozis Heroic Performance in Greek Shadow Theater* (New England University Press, 1988) and *Karagiozis: Culture and Comedy in Greek Puppet Theater* (Kentucky University Press, 1992).

Michael Payne is John P. Crozer Professor of English at Bucknell University and coeditor of the twelve-volume *Bucknell Lectures in Literary Theory* (Blackwell), which began publication in 1990. His recent writings include papers on *The Tempest*, the Book of Revelation, Jacques Derrida and Martin Heidegger, and John Milton and Samuel Johnson.

Nathaniel Smith is assistant to the vice president for educational services at Franklin and Marshall College. A member of *College Literature*'s advisory board, he has written or edited books on courtly literature, Catalan studies, and the style and language of the troubadours.

Paul Smith teaches cultural studies in the English Department, Carnegie Mellon University. He is the author of *Discerning the Subject* (University of Minnesota Press, 1988).

Mas'ud Zavarzadeh, who teaches in the English Department of Syracuse University, writes on the political economy of (post)modern theory. His most recent book is *Seeing Films Politically* (1991).

INDEX

academe, viii, 45, 75, 94, 98-99, 137-38, 145, 161, 165, 167-68, 189-90; critiques, 188; and politics, 144-48
Adams, Henry, 141
Adorno, Theodor, 9, 113
aesthetics: and oppositionality, 139-44; and politics, 139-44
"Against Marcion," 175
Agassiz, Louis, 127, 130
agency. *See* subject; subjectivity
Aguero, Kathleen: *A Gift of Tongues: Critical Challenges in Contemporary American Poetry* (ed.), 159
Alcoff, Linda, 30, 34
alienation, 80, 167
Allen, Paula Gunn, 158-59, 164
Althusser, Louis, 89, 125, 127, 129, 143
Anderson, P., 9
anti-Semitism, 142
Anubis, 180
Anyjidoho, Kofi, 162
Arac, Jonathan, 139
"Arbeit Macht Frei," 55
Aristotle, 142, 196
Arnold, Matthew, 189
Aronowitz, Stanley, 6, 11, 40, 85, 125, 146
Atkins, Douglas: *Writing and Reading Differently: Deconstruction and the Teaching of Composition and Literature,* 121
Auden, W. H., 155
Auerbach, Erich, 97
Auschwitz, viii-ix, 1
authority, 16, 61, 121-22, 134, 146; instructional, 122; patriarchal, 198; personal, 83; phallic, 97; and the signifier, 197; teacher's, 71, 105, 122, 125, 131
Awoonor, Kofi, 159, 162

Baker, Houston, 161
Bakunin, Mikhail, 6
Balzac, Honore de, 57
Barker, Frances: *Literature, Politics and Theory: Essays from the Essex Conferences, 1976-84,* 99
Barr, James, 185-86
Barthes, Roland, 7, 80
Bartholomae, David, 121, 125-26, 128
Bartky, Sandra Lee, 35
Batsleer, Janet: *Rewriting English: Cultural Politics of Gender and Class,* 99
Baudrillard, J., 6
Benjamin, Walter, 42, 102
Bennett, Tony, 144
Bennett, William, 138
Berman, Marshall, 7, 9
Bertoff, Anne E., 76, 79, 86
Bettenson, Henry, 175
Bhabha, Homi, 123, 132-35
Bible, 173, 176, 182, 185-86; 1611 authorized version, 186
Birke, L., 31
Bizzell, Patricia, 121, 126
Black Panther, 110-12
Black Panther party platform, 110-12; "What We Want, What We Believe," 109
Blake, William, 179, 181; *Milton,* 181
Bloom, Allan, 138
Bloom, Harold, 181
Bolshevism, 3
Booth, Wayne, 60-61
Boyd, John, 180
boundaries, 5-6, 18, 21, 34, 40, 121, 188; centers, 21; of discourse, 121; margins, 21, 147, 190; politics of, 147
Bourdieu, Pierre, 65, 70
Bové, Paul: *Intellectuals in Power: A Geneaology of Critical Humanism,* 97
Brecht, Bertolt, 102, 105-6, 109, 112
Brooks, Cleanth, 138, 144
Brown, Cynthia, 74
Bruce-Novoa, Juan, 159, 161, 164
Bruchac, Allen, 161
Bruchac, Joseph, 161, 166
Bruffee, Kenneth, 126

Calinescu, Matei, 6
Campenhausen, Hans von, 175

canon, 66, 68, 74, 84-85, 91, 94, 98, 144, 172-86; busting, xi, 137-39, 142-43, 147; canonicity, 153-68; canonized texts, 75; multicultural, 75; multiplicity, 185; New Testament, 173, 176; noncanonical, 172; opening of, 146, 154, 160; and poetics, 153-164; race, class, and gender, 155; repressing thought, 157
capital, ix; cultural, 65-66, 71-72; educational, 65
capitalism, 11
Carby, Hazel, 98
Carlyle, Thomas, 182
Castro, Michael, 166
Chaucer, 153
Cherryholmes, C., 40
Chesnutt, Charles Waddell, 180; *The Marrow Tree,* 139
Childs, Brevard, 185-86
Chomsky, Noam, 105
Chopin, Kate: *The Awakening,* 140
Christian, B., 9
Christianity, 174, 183, 185
Clark, Suzanne, x
class: relations with gender and race, 13, 17-18, 25, 28-29, 34, 39, 43, 45-46, 65, 90, 93, 122, 128-29, 135, 139-40, 145; sensitive, 113; struggle, 146
Clifford, J., 21
Codex Sinaiticus, 173
Coleridge, Samuel T.: "Rime of the Ancient Mariner," 96
College Literature, vii
Collins, Billy, 153
Collins, J., 153
colonization, 121-22, 131, 133-34
The Color Purple, (Walker) 133
Comley, Nancy R.: *Text Book: An Introduction to Literary Languages,* 96
Con Davis, Robert, xi-xii
Connor, S., 20
Conrad, Joseph, 62
conscientization, 79, 81, 87 n. 9. *See also* Freire, Paolo
consensus, 11, 15
constructions: of reality, 77; of viewpoint, 198-99
contradiction, 143-44
Cooper, Anna Julia, 182-83, 185; *A Voice from the South,* 181-82
Crawford, John, 158
Crimp, D., 21
Critical Inquiry, 97
Cromwell, Oliver, 180
cultural studies, xi, 67-68, 91, 116, 188-91, 198-201; constituted by knowledge and power, 199; as mediating position, 199; as oppositional criticism, 190; programs, 191; and the subject, 198-201
culture, 21, 41, 133; anarchy, ix; and colonization, 121; context, 68; cultural capital, 65-66, 71-72; cultural competence, 110-11; cultural literacy, 69, 85, 109-12, 122, 133; in cultural studies, 198; deprived, 3; diversity, 165; dominant, 21, 78, 81; Eurocentric, 6, 19, 21, 25, 45; knowledge, 200; mass, 113; patriarchal, 19; pedagogy, 41; politics, 18, 40-41, 113; popular, 18, 21-22; print, 113-14; production of, 19-20, 33-34, 44, 72; radical politics, 4-5, 112; repression, 157; shared, 81; structuralist, 198; struggle over, 40, 189; technology and, 113-14; territoriality, 6; values, 68-69; visual, 113-14
curriculum, 41, 66, 68, 89-90, 94; academic, 81; Carnegie Mellon, 90-92, 130; culturally determined, 85; Duke, 90-92, 130, 145; and literature, 83; race, gender, and class, 145; reform, x, 75; Stanford, 145; Syracuse, 92, 130; traditional, 92-93

Dauenhauer, Richard, 159
Davis, Rebecca Harding: *Life in the Iron Mills,* 139
deconstruction, 96, 121, 137, 173
Debray, Regis, 143
de Jean, Joan, 96
de Lauretis, Teresa, 29-30, 34, 198
de Man, Paul, 92, 96, 142, 189
democracy, 1-3, 35-37, 39, 44, 46; critical, 38; failure of, 3; radical, 4; and schools, 4; struggle, 45
Denham, Robert D., 167
Derrida, Jacques, 23, 92, 95-96, 110, 132, 134, 142-43, 173; and canon formation, 184, 186; and deconstruction, 183-84; and différance, 184; feminism, 183; *Of Grammatology,* 172, 183; ideology, 183; and Milton, 183; and otherness, 185; "The Principle of Reason: The University in the Eyes of its Pupils," 199; *Qui a peur de la philosophie?,* 95; racism, 183; and theory, 183
Devi, Mahasweta: "The Breast Giver," 70
Dewey, John, 38
Diamond, I., 30

Dickens, Charles, 57
difference, 20-21, 25, 27, 33, 35, 39, 122, 127-29; constructions of, 39; and teaching, 164-68. *See also* postmodernism
Dirty Dancing, 115
discipline, 121-35
discourse, 4, 14, 16, 45, 78; of education, 7, 126-29; ethical, 39; literary, 143; modernist, 1; of possibility, 125; postmodern, 14; of power, 147; relativist, 31; of resistance, 125; shared, 5; textual authority, 40; totalizing, 7
domination, 20
Douglass, Frederick: *Narrative of the Life of an American Slave,* 139
Dove, Rita, 154
Du Bois, W. E. B.: *The Souls of Black Folk,* 139
Dukakis, Michael, 124
dystopia, 42

Eagleton, Terry, 9, 24, 44
Eastern Europe, 2-4, 36, 107
Ebert, Teresa, 24
Eco, Umberto, 92
education, vii-viii, 65, 90; educator, 76; liberal, 90; reform, 74-78, 80; as social reproduction, 105; transformative, 79. *See also* pedagogy; teaching
Elbow, Peter, 125
Eliot, George, 182
Eliot, T. S., 52, 147, 155, 179, 181
Emerson, Ralph Waldo, 139-40, 143
Empedocles, 159
empiricism, 124, 127
empowerment, 167-68
Empson, William, 181
Engels, F., 104, 107
Enlightenment, 1, 3, 8, 16, 36; defects of, 12; and politics, 190; and reason, 41
entitlement, 167-68
Enzensburger, Hans, 113
epistemology, 74; constuctionist, 76, 82, 84, 87 n. 4; reform, 75; traditional, 76
Epistles, 175-76
equality, 33, 39
essentialism, 24-25, 27, 35, 41
ethnocentrism, 25, 185

Faulkner, William, 141, 144; *Absalom, Absalom!,* 145; "Dry September," 55, 58-59; "A Rose for Emily," 60
Fauset, Jessie Redman: *Plum Bun,* 39
Felman, Shoshana, 96, 126, 131-32, 135
feminism, 25, 28, 35, 126, 130; and agency, 32-35; and difference, 32-35; and ideology, 128; negative politics, 30; and politics, 28-35; radical, 35, 148 n. 2; relation with postmodernism, 27, 31; and resistant readers, 124; theory, 24, 137; totalizing, 25. *See also* gender
Fetterley, Judith, 124
Finlay, Linda Shaw, x
Finnegan, Ruth, 159
Fish, Stanley, 83-84, 91, 190, 201; "Being Interdisciplinary Is So Very Hard to Do," 188
Fitzgerald, F. Scott, 135; *The Great Gatsby,* 129
Fitzpatrick, Peter, vii
Flax, Jane, 31-32
Foley, Barbara, xi
Foster, H., 21
Foucault, Michel, 35, 45, 79, 92, 97, 104, 106, 128, 189, 199
Frankfurt school, 9, 114
Franklin, Benjamin, 178
Fraser, Nancy, 12, 15-16, 25, 42
freedom, vii, 3-4, 8
Freire, Paolo, x, 74-86, 125; change, 76; *Cultural Action for Freedom,* 76; educational reform, 75-76, 80; empowerment, 83; epistemology, 76-77, 80-82, 84; illiteracy, 78-80; intersubjectivity, 77, 83; knowledge, 76-77; literacy, 74-75; literacy and criticism, 78-82; literacy and literature, 82-86; literacy programs, 76, 125; *Literacy: Reading the Word and the World,* 84; *Pedagogy of the Oppressed,* 74, 76, 80, 82, 200; *Pedagogy in Progress,* 82; *The Politics of Education,* 81, 85, reflexivity, 75. *See also* conscientization
Freud, Sigmund, xi, 52, 180, 191-197; dream analysis, 191-95; *The Interpretation of Dreams,* 191-94; and the Irma text, 191-97, 199; repression of the body, 196; and semiotics, 193-94; the subject, 193, 200; tenants of interpretation, 192-93
Frye, Northrup, 167; *Anatomy of Criticism,* 167
Fuller, Margaret, 141
Furter, Pierre, 80
Fynsk, Christopher: "A Decelebration of Philosophy," 95

Gabriel, Susan: *Gender in the Classroom,* 95
Gallop, Jane, 96
Gates, Henry Louis, Jr., 182, 188, 190; "Canon Confidential: A Sam Slade Caper," 172

Geertz, Clifford, 74-76
gender, 27; constructions of, 24, 28-30, 34; relations, 29; relations with class and race, 13, 17-18, 25, 28-29, 34, 39, 43, 45-46, 65, 90, 93, 122, 128-29, 135, 139-40, 145. *See also* feminism
Gibson, William, 102
Giddens, A., 37
Gilbert, Sandra: *The Awakening* (ed.), 140
Gilman, Charlotte Perkins: "The Yellow Wallpaper," 138
Giroux, Henry A., viii-ix, xii, 22, 38, 40, 78, 80, 85, 109-10, 113-16, 125, 189; "The Need for Cultural Studies," 189; *Schooling and the Struggle for Public Life,* 114; *Teachers as Intellectuals,* 112
gnosticism, Valentinian, 174
Goodman, Ellen, 134
Gospels: John, 176, 185; Luke, 175; Mark, 176; Matthew, 176, 185
Graff, Gerald, 110
grammatology, applied, 96
Gramsci, Antonio, 46, 102, 196
Greimas, A. J., 196
GREPH (Group for Educational Research in Philosophy), 94-95
Griffin, Paul F., ix
GRIP (Group for Research into the Institutionalization and Professionalization of Literary Studies), 94
Grossberg, L., 24
Groz, E. A., 5
Grumet, M., 41
Grusin, Richard A., 141
Guattari, Félix, 146

Habermas, Jürgen, 5, 9-12, 15, 76
Hall, Stuart, 188, 198, 201
Hallberg, Robert von: *Canons,* 97
Hammer, R., 19
Hancock, John, 178
Handwerk, Gary, 61
Hannam, Mark, 2
Haraway, Donna, 27, 31
Harding, S., 31
Harrington, Michael: *Socialism,* 107
Harris, Marie: *A Gift of Tongues: Critical Challenges in Contemporary American Poetry* (ed.), 159
Hartsock, N., 9
Harvey, David, 52
Hassan, Ihab, 52
Havel, Vaclav, 36
Hayman, Ronald, 189
Hebdige, Dick, 13, 21-22
Hegel, G. W. F., 16, 106, 115, 184, 196
Heidegger, Martin, 184
Hemingway, Ernest, 135; "A Clean Well-Lighted Place," 55, 57-58; *The Old Man and the Sea,* 129-30
Henricksen, Bruce: *Reorientations: Critical Theories and Pedagogies,* 95
hermeneutics. *See* interpretation
Herz, Neil, 96
Heyen, William: *The Generation of 2000: Contemporary American Poets,* 154
Hicks, Emily, 18
Hill, Christopher, 179
Hirsch, E. D., Jr., 38, 69, 85, 109-11, 115, 124; *Cultural Literacy,* 109
history, 3-4, 17, 25, 36; and construction, 18, 34, 41; historically situated, 82; historicize, 69; reading, 40
Holocaust, 55
Homer, 180
Horus, 180
Howard, Richard: *Alone with America,* 153
Huizinga, John, 159
Hutcheon, L., 14
Hutchinson, Thomas, 178
Huyssen, A., 12

ideology, 24, 41, 107; bourgeois, 147; capitalist, 125; change, 27; functions, 90; and individualism, 126; and language, 144; misrecognition of, 200; and modernism, 26; negating dominant, 143; positions, 7; Western, 190
illiteracy, 78-80, 83
interdisciplinarity, 188
interlection. *See* interruption
interpretation, 60-62, 78-79, 81, 83-84, 86; biblical, 177; and construction, 196; Freudian, 191-98; hermeneutic, 68; New Critical, 139
interruption, ix, 70-71
intersubjectivity, 75, 77, 83
Invasion U.S.A., 114
Irenaeus, 174, 177; *Contra Haereses,* 174
Irigaray, Luce, 92
irony, 52-62; ethical, 61; stable, 60-61
Isis, 180

Jagger, A. M., 31
James, Henry, 141-42; "Turn of the Screw," 139

Jameson, Fredric, 167, 196
Jesus Christ, 174, 180
Johnson, Barbara: "The Pedagogical Imperative: Teaching as a Literary Genre," 96
Johnson, Joseph, 179
Johnson, Michael: *Writing and Reading Differently: Deconstruction and the Teaching of Composition and Literature,* 121
Johnson, Richard, 188
Johnson, Samuel, 181
Joyce, James, 57; "Counterparts," 55-57; *Dubliners,* 56
Judaism, 174

Kampf, Louis, 104
Kant, Emmanuel, 199
Kaplan, C., 32
Kaplan, E. A., 27, 32-33
Karcher, Carolyn, 139
Kearney, Richard, 22
Keller, E. F., 31
Kellner, D., 10
King, Martin Luther, Jr., 116; "Black Power," 115
knowledge, 40-41, 75, 80, 121; act of, 191; changing, 77; conceptions of, 76; construction, 75, 78, 125-26; cultural, 200; empiricist, 76; literate, 111-12; marketing, 166; production of, 18, 30, 38, 40, 44, 93-94; social use, 189; and students, 81; teleological, 76; value-free, 78; Western, 188
Kuhn, Thomas, 75

Lacan, Jacques, xi, 92, 126, 131-32, 191, 194-98; authority, 197-99; dream as text, 196; experience as uninterpretable, 197; and gender politics, 197; interpretation as subjective activity, 195, 198; and the Irma text, 195-197; on language, 197; model of the subject, 195, 197; Schema L, 196-98; *The Self in Freudian Theory,* 194
Laclau, E., 2, 8, 14, 16, 22-23, 40
language, 27, 76-77, 81-82; genetic code, 23; in language, 61; linguistic medium, 23; multiplicity, 144; possibility, 30, 39, 41-42; system of signs, 23; utopian, 42
Lash, S., 18
Lather, P., 32
Lauter, Paul, 104, 153, 158
Lee, Spike: *Do the Right Thing,* 115-16
Leninism, 3
Leavis, F. R., 189; *Nor Shall My Sword,* 189; *Revaluations,* 99
Levine, Sherrie, 22
Lévi-Strauss, Claude, 161, 185, 195; *Tristes Tropiques,* 184
liberalism, 8
Lipsitz, G., 19
literacy, x, 124-25; cultural, x, 69, 109-12, 122, 133; making, 74-86; multiple, 85; political, 109-10; reading and writing, 75; speech, 75; and understanding, 78
literary studies, 68
literature, 66, 72, 102-3; and class, 103; as commodity, 66-67; culture-producing, 83, 104; as ideology, 69; literary, 83; literary texts, 67; making, 74-86
Lucretius, 159
Lyotard, Jean-François, 2, 5, 15-16, 18, 96

Macaulay, T. B., 159
McCarthy, Thomas, 12
Macedo, D.: *Literacy: Reading the Word and the World,* 84
McGuire, Jerry, xi
Macherey, Pierre, 144
McHugh, Patrick, 167
MacIntyre, Alasdair: *After Virtue,* 52
McLaren, Peter, 19, 84
McRobbie, A., 32
Malcolm X, 116; *Autobiography of Malcolm X,* 115-16
Malraux, André, 74
Malson, M., 26, 33
Marcion, 185; *Antitheses,* 174
Marcus, G., 21
Marcuse, Herbert, 145
margins, 20-21, 37. *See also* boundaries
Marx, Karl, 16, 69, 93, 104, 106-8, 111, 196; *The Communist Manifesto,* 106-7
Marxism, 3, 26, 65-66, 111, 114, 125, 128, 137, 141, 145-47, 155, 163, 167
Mehlman, Jeffrey, 194
Melville, Herman, 139; "Benito Cereno," 139
Merod, James, 105, 188, 190
Merrill, Robert, 8
Michnik, A., 36
Miklitsch, Robert, ix-x
Milton, 172-73, 175-83; and African-American literature, 185, 177-83; and Anna Julia Cooper, 181-83; *Areopagitica,* 177, 181; British Homer, 179; canonical position, 180; "First Propulsion," 177, 183; and Ishmael Reed, 180-83; "On the Morning of Christ's

Nativity," 180-81; as an other, 185; *Paradise Lost,* 182; and Phillis Wheatley, 177-83; poetics, 178; reading the Bible, 177; responses to, 183; *A Treatise of Civil Power in Ecclesiastical Causes,* 177
Minh-ha, T. T., 18, 21
Missing, 114
MLA (Modern Language Association): *Profession,* 95
modernism, 1; aesthetic, 6-7; and culture, 18; defense of, 11; emancipatory project, 9; failure of, 8, 25; and ideology, 26; political, 8-9; vs. postmodernism, 12; as a term, 5
Morgan, Thaïs: *Reorientations: Critical Theories and Pedagogies,* 95
Morris, Meaghan, 27
Morton, Donald, x; *Theory/Pedagogy/Politics: Texts for Change,* 95
Moscow on the Hudson, 114
Mouffe, Chantal, 1-2, 8, 23

Nabokov, V., 138; *Lolita,* 53; *Pale Fire,* 53
naming, 78-80, 82
narrative, 18, 30-31, 35; local, 17; master, 1-4, 15, 17, 20, 31, 40; metanarrative, 19, 25, 27, 31, 167; multiple, 19, 39-40; totalizing, 19, 40; utopian, 168
NCTE (National Council of Teachers of English): *Practicing Theory in Introductory College Literature Courses,* 95
Nelson, Cary, 154-57, 160, 166; *Repression and Recovery: Modern American Poetry and the Politics of Cultural Memory,* 95, 154-55
New Testament, 173, 176-77, 185; Acts, 176; canon, 173, 176-77; Epistles, 175-76; Galatians, 176
New York Times Book Review, 172
Newman, C., 5-6
Newton, Isaac, 179
Nicholson, Linda, 15-16, 25, 32
Nietzsche, F., 52-53, 103, 107
nihilism, 57-58
Norton Anthology of Modern Poetry, 154-56

objectivism, 77-78
objectivity, 62
Ohmann, Richard, 109
Olatunji, Olatunda, 161
Old Testament: Law, 175; Prophets, 175
oppositional, 4, 6-7, 26, 28, 137-48; and aesthetics, 139-44; criticism, 188; ideology, 149 n. 3; and politics, 139-44; psychoanalytic, 196; scholars, 145
Oreskes, M., 36-37
Orpheus, 177
Orwell, George, 104, 108; *Animal Farm,* 53, 106-8; *Nineteen Eighty-Four,* 53
Osiris, 181
other, 3, 20-22, 124, 181, 185, 190, 196, 199
Owens, Craig, 19

Palmer, Parker, 62
Parker, Andrew, 142
patriarchy, 1, 13, 26, 28, 31, 142, 198; discourse, 29
Paul, Epistles, 175
Paul, Sherman, 157
Paulson, William: *The Noise of Culture,* 103-4
Payne, Michael, xi
pedagogy, viii-x, 102-16, 132; canonical, 69, 71; critical, 5, 37, 39-40, 42-43, 45, 89-99; and difference, 127-29; method, 76, 82; new, 97; political, x, 104-8, 110, 132; and politics, 38, 104, 108-16; postmodern, 46, 122, 129; poststructuralist, 121; practice, 44; radical, x, 2, 37, 45, 93-94; relations with power, 39; situation of, 70; and theory, 137; traditional, 93. *See also* education; teaching
Peller, Gary, 16
Penley, Constance, 42
poetics, 153-68; of canonicity, 153-64; class, race, and gender, 156-57, 166, 168; cultural, 161; ethnopoetics, 155, 158-60, 164; fragmentary, 164; marginal, 155; minority, 155, 167-68; modernist, 156, 160; Native American, 158; new canon, 165; and politics, 142, 168; tribal, 155
poetry, 153-68; academic, 160, 167-68; anthologies of, 153-54, 156; and anthropology, 158, 161; and the canon, 153-60; and cultural work, 156; diversity of, 158-59, 166; minorities and, 166; noncanonical, 156; rap, 162-64; tribal, 164; workshop, 167
politics, viii, 2, 22, 37, 92, 99; and academe, 144-49; and aesthetics, 139-44; cultural, 20, 24-25, 40, 112; and democracy, 36, 45; and difference, 4-5, 15, 19; emancipatory, 14, 38; and feminism, 28-35; function of, 90; and literacy, 109-10, 115; and oppositionality, 139-44; and poetics, 142; of possibility, 30; and postmodernism, 27; practices, 145; radical, 45; and rationality, 128; relations, 94; and resistance, 146; and

struggle, 35; and teaching, 64-72, 102-16; of voice, 43-44
Pope, Alexander, 177-78, 186
Popkewitz, T., 41
Porter, Carolyn, 139-40; *Seeing and Being: The Plight of the Participant Observer in Emerson, James, Adams, Faulkner,* 141
Poster, M., 1, 18
postmodernism, 14, 22; boundaries, 14; challenge of, 18; as a condition, 15; critical theory, 89-99; as critique, 15, 20; curriculum, 93; diffuse influence of, 13; discourse of, 9, 14; as negation, 17; as neoconservative, 12; pedagogy of, 27, 35-44, 93; politics of, 13, 16, 27; as possibility, 13; relation with modernism, 9-13; as a revolt against reason, 10; site of ideological struggle, 13
poststructuralists, 89, 96-97, 99, 126, 137
Pound, Ezra, 127, 142, 155
power, vii, xi, 15, 17, 20, 30, 121; construction of, 30; language of, 35; relation with discourse, 10, 13, 22; relation with students, 126; relations, 34, 43, 123; struggle for, 24, 26-27
Propp, Vladimir, 193
Proust, Marcel, 53
psychoanalysis, 193-96, 198
Pynchon, Thomas, 172

Quasha, George, 153
Quinby, L., 30

race, 146; construction of, 116; relation with class and gender, 13, 17-18, 25, 28-29, 34, 39, 43, 45-46, 65, 90, 93, 122, 128-29, 135, 139-40, 145
Radway, Janice, 188
Rambo, 114
rationality, 6-7, 10-11, 23
reading, 83, 90-91, 94, 112, 128
Reagan, Ronald, 107
reason, 10, 15-17, 25, 30-31
Red Dawn, 114
Reed, Ishmael, 180-81, 183, 185-86; *Mumbo Jumbo,* 180
reflexivity, 31, 81; collective, 11; self, 23, 39, 102, 163
Reising, Russell, 139
reproduction: cultural, 104; social, 64-65, 123
resistance, ix-x, 6, 20, 22, 29, 35, 70-71, 121-35; and discourse, 125; productive, 123; reader, 124; and relationship, 129-35; student, 124, 126; teachers, 125, 132; to theory, 122
rhetoric, 137, 153
Richards, I. A., 97
Rocky IV, 115
Rodriguez, Fred: *Education in a Multicultural Society,* 165
Rorty, Richard, 9, 14, 52-62, 75-77, 85
Rosaldo, Renato, 21
Roth, R., 20
Rothenberg, Diane, 155-56; ethnopoetics, 155, 158, 166; *Symposium of the Whole: A Range of Discourse toward an Ethnopoetic,* 159
Rothenberg, Jerome, 155-56, 158; *Alcheringa,* 159; ethnopoetics, 155, 158, 166; *Symposium of the Whole: A Range of Discourse toward an Ethnopoetic,* 159
Rousseau, Jean-Jacques, 185; *Essay on the Origins of Language,* 184
Ryan, K., 11

Said, Edward, 20, 132, 190
Salvador, 114
Saussure, Ferdinand de, 92, 148, 185; *Course in General Linguistics,* 184
Scholes, Robert, 126-28, 130; *Text Book: An Introduction to Literary Languages,* 96; *Textual Power: Literary Theory and the Teaching of English,* 121
Schomburg Library of Nineteenth-Century Black Women Writers, 172
Schroeder, Pat, 134
Scott, Joan Wallach, 33
Scriptures, Hebrew, 173-74
Sculley, James, 22
semiotics: and psychology, 193-94
sexism. *See* feminism; gender
Shakespeare, William: *Hamlet,* 133
Shapiro, S., 39
Shelley, Mary, 179, 181; *Frankenstein, or, The Modern Prometheus,* 179
Shelley, Percy B., 155
Shor, Ira, 125; *Culture Wars: School and Society in the Conservative Restoration, 1969-1984,* 189
Showalter, E., 29
Shumway, David: "The Need for Cultural Studies," 189
Siegel, James, 96
signifier, 14, 23
Silverman, Kaja, 198
Simon, R., 22, 39, 116
Smith, Nathaniel, x

Smith, Paul, ix, 189
Snyder, Gary, 161
Sosnoski, James: "The Need for Cultural Studies," 189
South Atlantic Quarterly: "The Politics of Liberal Education," 95
Spivak, Gayatri Chakravorty, ix, 18, 21, 70, 188, 190, 198, 201; *In Other Worlds: Essays in Cultural Politics,* 190
Stevens, Wallace, 155
structuralists, 89
subaltern, 70
subject, x, 89-90, 125, 191; agency, 35, 40, 70, 80; centered, 7; construction of, 40, 190, 198-99; critique of, 188; decentered, 27; and Freud, 193, 200; and Lacan, 195, 197; negation of, 23; political, 2-3; positions, 34, 39, 41, 44, 114, 127; students, 81, 122
subjective (understanding), 62, 199
subjectivism, 77
subjectivity, viii, 29, 70; construction of, 28, 35, 39; and cultural studies, 200; essentializing, 126; identity, 24; and Lacan, 195, 198; multiple, 24; patriarchal, 25; postmodern, 34
subversion, 137-48
suffering, 54-56
Sundquist, Eric J., 139
Swift, Jonathan: *Gulliver's Travels,* 200

Tafolla, Carmen, 164
Taylor, A. J. P., 106-7
Taylorism, 111
teaching, vii, 99; authority, 71, 105, 125, 129, 131; classroom, 62; and difference, 164-68; and discourse, 122; as an institution, 67; and literature, 67, 75, 84; material context of, 106; narrative, x; as a political act, xi, 64-72, 102-16; politically responsible, 69-72; power relations in, 126; presentation, 80-81; and social reproduction, 65, 128; subject-position in, 105, 108, 127-28; teacher-student relation, 65, 81, 104, 106, 122, 126, 132; teachers, 43, 86 n. 1, 109. *See also* education; pedagogy
Tedlock, Dennis: *Alcheringa,* 159
Terence, 178
Tertullian, 175, 177
thinking: critical, 75, 125-26; historically situated, 82
Thomas, Dylan, 153
Thompson, Denys, 166; *The Uses of Poetry,* 159, 162
Thompson, E. P., 36
Thoreau, H. D.: *Walden,* 1
thought: postmodern, 54
Timothy, 175
Touraine, Alain, 70
Turner, Victor, 159, 161
Twain, Mark: *Adventures of Huckleberry Finn,* 139
Tyler, S., 21

Ulmer, Gregory, 96, 121; *Applied Grammatology: Post(e)-Pedagogy from Jacques Derrida to Joseph Beuys,* 96, 121; *Teletheory: Grammatology in the Age of Video,* 96
Under Fire, 114
Ungar, Steven, 96
Untermeyer, Louis: *Lives of the Poets: The Story of One Thousand Years of English and American Poetry,* 153
Urry, J., 18
utopia, 42

Virgil, 178

Waggner, George: *Red Nightmare,* 107
Wakoski, Diane, 154-57, 160, 168
Waller, Gary, 92
Warren, M., 19
Webb, Jack: *Dragnet,* 107
Weiler, Kathleen, 124-25; *Women Teaching for Change,* 124
Weinberger, Eliot, 157
Welch, S. D., 31
West, Cornel, 189, 201; "The Paradox of the Afro-American Rebellion," 115
Wetherby, 21
Wheatley, John, 177
Wheatley, Phillis, 177, 179, 181, 183, 185; "To Maecenas," 177
White Night, 114
Whitman, Walt, 157
Widdowson, Peter: *Rereading English,* 99
Wiesel, Elie: *Night,* 55
Wilding, Michael, 139
Williams, Raymond, 113, 198; *Marxism and Literature,* 103; *Preface to Film,* 114; *Television: Technology and Cultural Form,* 114
Williams, William Carlos, 155
Willis, Paul: *Learning to Labor: How Working-Class Kids Get Working-Class Jobs,* 122
Wilson, Harriet: *Our Nig,* 139

Wollstonecraft, Mary, 179, 181; *The Female Reader,* 179, 182
Women's Review of Books, 95
Worth, C. J., 94
Wright, Richard: *Uncle Tom's Children,* 145
writing, 124-26; and pedagogy, 125, 130

Yale French Studies: "The Pedagogical Imperative: Teaching as a Literary Genre," 96
Yeats, W. B., 52
Young, Robert, 196

Zavarzadeh, Mas'ud: *Theory/Pedagogy/Politics: Texts for Change,* 95
Zolberg, Zora, 158